The Gnostic

A Journal of Gnosticism,
Western Esotericism and Spirituality

Issue 6

Copyright Page and Acknowledgments

The Gnostic 6, 2015.

© Bardic Press 2015 All articles and illustrations are © copyright their respective creators, and are used with permission excepting short extracts that qualify as fair use.

All rights reserved. No part of this publication may be reproduced without the permission of the relevant copyright holder.

Opinions expressed are those of the contributors and not necessarily those of the publisher.

Editor: Andrew Phillip Smith

Published by Bardic Press
71 Kenilworth Park
Dublin 6W
Ireland.

ISBN: 978-1-906834-16-6

Thanks to the contributors and all others who have made this possible, including but not limited to: Tessa Finn, Stevan Davies, Gary Lachman, Andrea Frank, Sean Martin, Bill Darlison, Jeffrey Kupperman, Steve Dee, Ken Henson, Alex Rivera, Scott Stanley Smith, Inner Traditions,

The Gnostic

A Journal of Gnosticism,
Western Esotericism and Spirituality

Issue 6

Andrea Frank, Stevan Davies, Gary Lachman, Sean Martin, Bill Darlison, Jeffrey Kupperman, Tobias Churton, Steve Dee, Ken Henson, Alex Rivera, Scott Stanley Smith, Sarane Alexandrian et al

Edited by Andrew Phillip Smith

Bardic Press
Dublin 2015

Contents

From the Mouth of the Demiurge
6

Interview with Z'ev ben Shimon Halevi
Andrew Phillip Smith
7

Wills's Cigarettes
Andrew Phillip Smith
15

James Therrien: a Eulogy
Robert Wood
17

Black Mirror drawings
Ken Henson
19, 20, 61, 120, 164, 172

Moses the Stargazer
Bill Darlison
21

Better Than Soaking
Sean Martin
31

Archons, Archons Everywhere!
Jeremy Puma
43

An Interview with Gary Lachman
Andrew Phillip Smith
47

Spirit Possession, Pentecost and the foundation of Christianity
Stevan Davies
56

Andrea in the Country of the Cannibals
Andrea frank
62

Journeying With the Gnostics: Confessions of a Teenage Evangelical
Steve Dee
88

After Simon, the Deluge
Tobias Churton
93

Marsilio Ficino and Alchemy as Material Theurgy
Jeffrey S. Kupperman
99

The Crucifixion of Christ-j242
Andrew Phillip Smith
103

Is There Life After Death?
Scott Stanley Smith
112

How to Make Love With an Invisible Creature
Sarane Alexandrian
121

An Interview With Gerard Russell
Andrew Phillip Smith
130

The Gods of Imagination
Alex Rivera
136

Fragments from the Secret Book of John: An Illuminated Retelling
Richard A Dengel
152

We Are the Immovable Race
Jeremy Puma
165

Meeting With Rasputin
Elizaveta de Stjernvall
167

The Magic Aphorisms of Eugenius
Thomas Vaughan
171

Into the Bridal Chamber: Sin
Andrew Phillip Smith
173

Mysticism
William James
177

Book Reviews
Andrew Phillip Smith
196

Biographies
207

Food for Thought
210

Editorial

From the Mouth of the Demiurge

Here we are at the final regular issue of *The Gnostic*, in as much as *The Gnostic* has ever been regular either in the sense of conforming or in coming out according to a predictable pattern of time. I've said that before and been wrong, so I may always find myself saying it again. But this really is probably the last issue. After all, the most recent issue, number 5, was published back in 2011, four years ago. But I do intend to publish a special one-off themed issue which will look like *The Gnostic*, share many themes with *The Gnostic*, and may even be subtitled *The Gnostic 7*.

This has always been a quirky sort of publication, centred on Gnosticism but incorporating many of my own specific interests. By the second issue a clear format had developed and I have had no desire to break away from it since. But that does mean that it has been difficult to change what *The Gnostic* is in essence. It all makes sense somehow, if only to me. New contributors have often been bewildered by the article lengths (anything from 500 to 12,000 words), on the cultural level of writing, varying from from comic strips and extended blog posts to academic articles, and by my reluctance to impose either a single citation style or even to decide on UK or USA spelling standards. Let the writer use whatever she is happiest with, is my reply.

My next book *Lost Teachings of the Cathars*, will be published November 2015 in conjunction with *Secret History of the Gnostics*, and working on the research for *John the Baptist and the Last Gnostics*, my book on the Mandaeans, I find myself more interested in traditions other than the Gnostic. Gnosis and Gnosticism will always have a part in my spiritual outlook.

Bribes, sweeteners, backhanders and baksheesh, blackmail payments, old newspaper clippings, museum-level antiquities, kitsch trinkets, maps of pre-sand Egypt, 200-year-old bottles of Château Latour, 300-year-old bottles of Tokay, Gnostic gems and amulets, ancient Coptic spell books, title deeds to 10 acre farms, fake IDs, comments, critiques or proposed contributions are, as always, welcome. Please email them to andrew@bardic-press.com or post them to:-

Andrew Phillip Smith/The Gnostic

71 Kenilworth Park

Dublin 6W

Ireland.

The more mundane virtual message can also be posted to our Facebook page https://www.facebook.com/TheGnostic

Although I usually reach a stage in producung each issue when I hate *The Gnostic*, myself, and all the firstborn of Egypt, I'm pleased with what I've achieved with *The Gnostic*, a large part of which has consisted of the people who have been generous enough to contribute for the love of it.

After the special issue of *The Gnostic* I may consider a new publication, if I can find a collaborator. Applications considered!

If you find a typo, keep it to yourself.

Andrew Phillip smith

An Interview with Z'ev ben Shimon Halevi

APS: You're best known as a kabbalist, as a writer on the Kabbalah. Is that how you would describe yourself?

ZBSH: I should think that's a pretty fair definition, yes.

APS: But you have broader esoteric interests too.

ZBSH: Yes, well let me kick it off. My background: I come from a semi-orthodox Jewish background, partly Sephardic; that's Spanish Jews who left Spain in 1492, went to Turkey, from Turkey to southern Russia, and then my grandfather in 1900 was on his way to New York and stopped in London and was told his ticket didn't go any further so I finished up being an Englishman. My mother's side were Ashkenazi—that's Yiddish-speaking as against Ladino—came from Lithuania or Poland and also finished up in London. I was born in 1933, in the year that Hitler came to power, lived through the war as a boy and then went to art school, did my National service in hospitals and then went to the Royal Academy and then worked in the theatre. And all that time I wanted to be a writer. But my earliest memory was I wanted to be an archaeologist, and what happened was that I became an archaeologist in finding out what Kabbalah was really about, what the essence of it was about. That's how I started writing about Kabbalah in modern terms.

APS: When did you really start to get involved in Kabbalah?

ZBSH: It started really when I was about 22, 23, 24. Some of my friends were into Ouspensky-Gurdjieff and I joined an Ouspensky school about the age of 23, 24. I studied with them for 12 years. That gave me an esoteric background without the ritualist side, the tribal side. I was dragged to a synagogue when I was young. My Hebrew wasn't very good, but I wanted to know what was at the heart of it. So for twelve years I studied with the Ouspensky-Gurdjieff people and then we had a study group on Kabbalah led by an occultist and what he put out, because he was also an Ouspensky-Gurdjieff man, was the essence of it. And of course we saw the Tree. Once the Tree was there, we then started as a group to study it and out of this came what was called the Jacob's Ladder. Which was in the kabbalistic tradition but was lost and was rediscovered. And my job, that I was given, was to update it in terms of modern psychology and science, along with the traditional history of Kabbalah. That was the essence of it.

APS: So that set you on your writing path. I know one of your books was *Psychology and Kabbalah*.

ZBSH: They came naturally together, because we live in this age and what's happened in the history of Kabbalah is at first it was biblical and then with the influx of Hellenic philosophy it became metaphysical. In Europe anyway it then became slightly occult, but that never really hit the Jewish community. That continued until the twentieth century when we suddenly realised that just like it had to update its metaphysics in the middle ages, today it has to update its psychology. That was the job I was given, which was to write a number of books to put it in contemporary terms. Since then they've gone into fifteen different languages so there must be something in it.

APS: I find that very interesting because I have a background in Gurdjieff-Ouspensky work as well. Which school was it?

ZBSH: It was an Ouspensky school in London called the School of Economic Science and then what was called the Study Society. Out of that came this small kabbalistic study group and then my instructions were to go out on my own and eventually we founded the Kabbalah Society which we called the Toledano tradition. The reason for that was that Toledo in the middle ages was a meeting place between Jews, Muslims and Christians who were particularly interested in metaphysics and philosophy. So you had the amalgam of that Hellenic view and the traditional biblical view. Out of that came what was called Kabbalah in about 1200-1300. Ever since then it's been unfolding in Renaissance Italy and in France and of course Masons go back to Kabbalah, there's a lot of kabbalistic stuff there.

APS: I've noticed in your books you sometimes use Gurdjieff's Law of Octaves or the Law of Triads in connection with the Tree of Life.

ZBSH: That's the Ouspensky-Gurdjieff. In its basic reality you have the three pillars, which are simply for the yin, yang and the dao, or raja, sattvas, tamas in the Hindu tradition. There's all the same, just a different culture.

APS: And you see these as objective?

ZBSH: Yes, they are as objective as the laws of science. They're even more objective, because science has energy and matter, but we would add the addition of consciousness, in this case divine consciousness right down the central pillar, unfolding in four stages, four great worlds, which other traditions would call the terrestrial and the astral and so forth. They have various names but there are four great worlds and there are in fact four octaves which interconnect and interleave with each other, which is what what we call the great Tree, which kabbalists call sometimes the 50 gates, sometimes the 49 gates. And lots of things we could mention in Jewish esoterica are never explained but once you have the key of the Tree and the Jacob's Ladder the whole thing makes sense.

APS: How do you feel about the Kabbalah's Jewish origin?

ZBSH: It's much older. Traditionally it goes back to Abraham who was initiated by Melchizedek, who was said to have had neither father nor mother, and which meant he was a supernatural being. Then there are traditions that he goes back to Enoch, which means "an initiate", who was the first fully realised human being. And Abraham was given the teaching, the bread and the wine, that means the teaching, the theory and the practice, and that emerged through the middle east, taking a bit from Persia, for instance the Messiah is a Persian idea, it's not a Jewish idea. Lots of bits and pieces, but then they fused them together. And of course it's embedded in the bible, which is really a family history, a tribal history, but the teaching is there. You get a thing like the Menorah, the seven-branched candlestick. That's the origin of the Tree. There's the central column, two wings, 22 decorations representing the 22 letters: it's all there. The rabbis have forgotten about it, but there you are.

APS: You've said that you are modernising the Kabbalah.

ZBSH: Yes, I'm bringing it up to date, as they did in the middle ages. At that time Greek philosophy was all the rage among the intelligentsia. One has to realise that most Jews could read and write, which was very unusual in the medieval periods. You had to be able to read and write at the age of 13 and went to school.

APS: Yes, that was unusual.

ZBSH: That's why the Jews got on very well because they were urban people. They became the tradespeople along the trades routes, the intelligentsia, the doctors, the astrologers. They were part of general civilization. Not all of them, but the intelligentsia of the Jewish community.

APS: You were mentioning in Spain about having Jews, Christians and Muslims all interacting at the same time ...

ZBSH: They got on very well, particularly in Toledo in the medieval period. People would come from all over Europe and from North Africa. It was like the Oxford or Cambridge or Dublin university of its time. People came there, that's where the action was.

APS: And in the South of France in the medieval period.

ZBSH: That's right. That might be of interest because I've explored these places. I've walked down the streets where the old Juderias were. I was walking down one particular place where a man called Isaac the Blind lived, who was a very famous kabbalist. I thought, "I wonder which house was his," and I thought, "That's the one." And when the local archaeologist came to see he said, yes, that's the one. So I got it right.

And I have a memory of Toledo. When I was about 10 or 11 during the war I was looking at a children's encyclopedia and I came across a picture of Toledo and I thought, "I must go there, I must go there." When I was about 19 or 20 I hitch-hiked to Spain with a friend and when I walked through the streets of Toledo I felt, "I know this place, I know this place," So my Spanish inheritance had returned to me and these experiences make you realise there's a lot more to life than ordinary history.

APS: And to what would you attribute those experiences? Past lives?

ZBSH: Oh yes. Reincarnation is called *gilgulim*, the wheels, or transmigration.

APS: You mentioned Ouspensky. Recurrence, in which the same life is repeated, was Ouspensky's big idea. How do you treat that?

ZBSH: Well, the impression I get is he got it half-right. He had lived before, but to live the same life doesn't make any sense. That way you're going nowhere. But if there's a progression of lives—different families,, different cultures—that makes sense. We all move through history. It would be very boring to live the same old life over and over again.

APS: Well, yes! It can be a bit defeating as an idea, recurrence. How were your efforts to modernise Kabbalah received in various quarters?

ZBSH: That's a very interesting story, particularly among Israeli scholars. There was a great resistance among the rabbis. I'm not kosher. On the other hand I gather people read my books in Israel and in various Jewish communities, like in the States, secretly, but they hide them away. And the reason they say is that at long last it makes sense. Because like all esoteric traditions they turn into a kind of religious mumbo jumbo. But to get something which has the clarity of the Tree, where you can relate it to psychology, and say, "Yes, that's the right pillar, and that's the left pillar, I can see how it works," how the psychopathology works in the Tree of Life diagram, for example. The Jungian and Freudian sit beautifully on it. I've written several books on the kabbalistic psychology.

APS: How would you link Jung's ideas particularly with the Kabbalah?

ZBSH: His key is the archetypes. The medieval

and ancient worlds had archetypes, like the planetary archetypes, but he took it to a much more personal level. Like we have the archetype of the warrior, Mars. Well that can be the very aggressive man, it can be the Amazon, it can be the sharp business man, it can be the bully in the playground, it can be the hero. So all these archetypes which are based on the martial archetype, or Gevurah in terms of Kabbalah. Discipline, you see. It's the sephirah of discipline, of control. There are shadow sides as there are light sides to each of these. That's a whole study in itself.

APS: What do you make of the recent, or in the last few years, trend of interest in Kabbalah, or some sort of strain of Kabbalah?

ZBSH: Well, it's a fashion. There was a time in the nineteenth century when it was very fashionable, and you've got the Theosophical Society, they picked up bits and pieces, as they did from all over the place. In renaissance Italy it was all the rage amongst the intelligentsia. At one point it was in France and Spain, and in England of course it was there. There were secret Jews in London in the Elizabethan period. And the Masons, Freemasonry is based on Solomon's Temple which is pure Kabbalah. The structure of the building. One of my close friends put the ground plan of Chartres Cathedral on the Tree and where you get Yesod, which is the place of the ego, is the maze, where you are lost wandering round and round. And you go up the central column towards where the choir is, which is the emotional triad of Gevurah, Chesed and Tiphareth, and you get up to the place of Daath, which is the high altar, and it all fits beautifully. So they knew a thing or two. But then the city of Chartres had a scholarly Jewish community when the cathedral was being built.

APS: Very interesting.

ZBSH: There were times when Christian scholars and Jewish scholars got on very well. At Oxford, for example, there were Jews at Oxford in the medieval period and they obviously taught them Hebrew apart from letting out rooms to them. The Jews used to travel between Oxford and London. A few went up to Cambridge, but there was the synagogue in Oxford. In fact, the Bodleian was built on a Jewish burial ground. All sorts of interesting stories.

APS: How central a role do you think Hebrew should have in the study of Kabbalah?

ZBSH: If you're very nationalistic, rather like the Brits were 100 years ago, the sun never sets on our flag. Some Jews are very tribal. Some Jews are internationals, and some Jews are beyond even that. What I try to do is to say, look, this is the basic metaphysics and the symbolism. Hebrew is the language which carries it, there's no doubt about that. A lot of Hebrew words are very appropriate. But if you take away the language, you've got the essence of the teaching of the Torah, of the teaching. But the Rabbis disagree with this and say, well, you've got to have references. You've got to have authenticity. And when you point out that that's what's called the written tradition, the authentic as in "author," as against the oral tradition, they can't quite grasp what the oral tradition is, not realising it goes from person to person or it's an inside process, with, if you like, your inner teacher. For example, I was sitting in my study once, and a particular kabbalistic writer came up, and I suddenly got this picture of a harbour facing south with a citadel with peculiar trees. Anyway, I looked up where this author was born and it was in Malaga, which is where Ibn Gebirol, a great Neoplatonist Jew, a kabbalist, was born. I actually stood at the place looking south on the harbour with modern ships. I was given that glimpse, that vision, and that is the oral tradition.

APS: What kind of practices would you recommend?

ZBSH: Just be present. The eternal now. Just be ever-watchful. There are two states called the gatlut and katnut states which is the greater and lesser states, and the greater state is obviously when you're alert. When you're in Tiphareth, when you're in the self as against the ego, which is the lesser state. Which means you're preoccupied with what's going on at the moment.

Whereas if you're in the self you have access to all the worlds. Once I was on the Isle of Skye and I was was sitting down overlooking the loch and I suddenly saw the mountains under the ice. 12-15,000 years ago! I suddenly saw this flash. They were as tall as the Alps at one point but they'd been ground down. You suddenly get these flashes. These cosmic glimpses. Different time, different space. For example, you get three people looking at the sea. One is the farmer and he says, "Aahh, that's pretty good ground for growing corn." And then there's the engineer and he says, "There's coal under there." Then there's the artist who says, "Yes, I could make a very good impressionist picture of this." Three people looking at the same landscape but seeing different realities.

APS: Mentioning artists again, you said you studied at the Royal Academy and then you were involved in drama. How have you been able to bring that into your esoteric work?

ZBSH: Well, I wasn't interested in drama myself. The reason was I went to the Royal Academy because I was interested in being a painter. But during my National service I was in a hospital and I started to sketch but was put on duty with somebody who was about to die. I sat and observed and I saw him slip away. I suddenly realised, as his face turned to stone, that he was now part of history. So I wrote this down in my sketch book. And I continued that practice till one of my student friends said, "You're much more of a writer than an artist. They were right. But because I think in a visual way and often talk to people from Oxford and Cambridge and say, "Well you see ideas, I see pattern and symbols,"

which is very much the artistic view, the poetic view. That led eventually towards writing. Like most young fellows who want to write the great English novel, or the great Irish novel, I never had any luck with that. When I left the Academy I had to find a job so I went to work at a theatre workshop where we made things out of papier maché for the Royal Ballet and for various west end shows and when I left there, because I wanted to be a writer. I saved up £1000 and one of my teachers said, "Write about what you know." So I thought, "What do I know? I know about prop making, how you make theatrical props." So I did a book with drawings on one side and text on the other and it was published straight away. All my novels were turned down. All 13 of them. This one shot straight through. I thought, when it comes to Kabbalah, it's the same principle. The essence is to entertain and inform. The entertainment is the pictures.

APS: I can hear from the way you describe things that you have a strong visual sense.

ZBSH: Well that's the artistic training. When I talk to people from Cambridge or Oxford we talk a different language. That's where I have problems with the scholars, because they'll read a text and they'll say, "So-and-so was born in such a place" and they used so-and-so and they wrote this and they wrote that." I said, "But you're looking at the text and can't you see the Tree? Can't you see what they're really talking about?" Which is why I've always had this hostility from scholars. In fact, I was talking to an Israeli scholar. He said, "We scholars make a living out of lunatics like you." I replied to him, "Yes, it's true, but you're like sports writers who write about every angle of the game but you've never actually been on the pitch." He was furious. He was a very good scholar, but he wasn't a kabbalist.

APS: I've come across you appearing in other people's works occasionally. For instance Richard Smoley or Joyce Collin-Smith, that's where I probably first came across you.

ZBSH: Well, she was a student of mine at one point. Have you read my autobiography?

APS: I didn't know you'd written an autobiography.

ZBSH: It's called *The Path of the Kabbalist*. You'll find a lot of what I'm talking about in there.

APS: I have a few of your books, but not that one. What about people who have made a particular impact on you. Teachers, students, fellow travellers and friends, whoever?

ZBSH: Many, many, too many to talk about. Some of whom are still alive, some who are dead. People from all over the world. From Brazil, Mexico, New Zealand. These books have gone everywhere. I'm absolutely astounded. But apparently there's a need for them. Since the 1970s there's been this deep need to turn away from formal religion and formal philosophy to something which is truly esoteric. It's got to be in a language which is comprehensible, which I try to write in basic English.

APS: How do you see the world developing, in terms of esoteric ideas? It's also very hard to predict the future in terms of what's happening externally in many ways.

ZBSH: Well, we live in a very interesting period. I lived through the war, when that kind of thing went down the drain. In the nineteenth century you had the Theosophical Society and other ones. Then came a period of great cynicism after the First World War, but you had Gurdjieff and Ouspensky then. And then after the Second World War, in the sixties you've got this generation, many of whom had fought in the war and then come back, because they lost their youth, and then they wanted to have fun. But some of them thought there must be more to life than just having fun. That's when the esoteric movement began to move, and it enlarged enormously all over the world, and it began to fade. And what we've got now is the essence of that particular generation. I'm the generation prior to that generation. How old are you?

APS: 49.

ZBSH: Well, you know that sixties generation.

APS: Yes, I was born in 1966.

ZBSH: Whereas the kids of the 70s, they're more interested in business, in getting on. We say one in 100 is interested in this work. When you've got a population of 60 million, that adds up to a lot of people. I come across them in every walk of life, all over the world. They've read my books and they say, your books have actually changed my view of life. In one case someone came up holding one of my books and said, you've saved my life, I was going mad. When I saw the diagrams I thought, there is sense in existence, there is a purpose. That's wonderful for a writer to have.

APS: And how old are you now?

ZBSH: I'm 82. I've only got 18 years before I'm 100. My health is pretty good, because I walk a lot. I used to cycle a lot. I will work in the morning. I have proper office hours. I might go out in the afternoon. Or I might work for three days and then take the car to the countryside, walk in the woods where I was a boy, and I walk and walk and walk, and it's paid off.

APS: Yes, walking's good. Your age must give you quite a perspective on the world.

ZBSH: As you get older you start to see the scale of history, but you also see your contemporaries. For example when I was at college there were the brilliant kids, and they really were very talented, and some of them were very famous for two or three years. For example, there was one painter there who was wonderful and had a meticulous style, and he was really in fashion for five years, but then he went out of fashion. So there was that popular side, but then there were the serious painters, who were painting away no matter what happened because they loved painting. They were Van Goghs. And they're still painting. And you see people who succeeded and who failed, and you can see why they succeeded and why they failed, and it's to do with the love of what you're doing. Not love of fame or money but love of what you're doing. One in a hundred. A lot of them dropped off, went into business, went into advertising, but everybody has free will, they have the choice. One man said to me, he was a very talented man, he said, "I failed because I was scared." I said, "Scared of what?" He said, "Scared of going out into the world." What he didn't want to say was he was scared of being found out. He wasn't quite as clever as he thought he was. He was a big fish in a little pond. And it was very sad because he was a very talented man, very intelligent. On the other hand you get the plodders who work for forty, fifty years and they suddenly produce some masterwork. It's the only thing they do but life is worthwhile. I'm a tortoise. I'm not a hare, I'm a tortoise.

APS: What are you working on these days?

ZBSH: I'm just finishing a book which may be the last book I do, I'm not sure, called *Kabbalistic Contemplations and Meditations*. Same formula, pictures on one side, text on the other. And it's the essence of all the other books. So if someone's sitting in a bath or on a plane or in a train or in their back garden, they've got that one image and then there's the explanation, the essential information or knowledge about it. That's at the beginning of the book, and then at the end of the book there are various exercises I've used over the years. For example, there's the house of the psyche, So you start off the journey going into a landscape, and what the landscape is, is how your life is at the moment. It might be a desert, it might be a storm, it might be very fertile. And you arrive at a house which is your house, which you've built all your life. It might be an old-fashioned house, it might be a castle, it might be a hut, it describes symbolically where you are at the moment. When you enter the house each of the rooms is part of the Tree. So you go down into the basement of Malkuth and you have a look at the boiler, which might tell you something about the condition of your heart, or the kitchen, or what your diet is. You might go to your secretary's office, that's Hod, to see how efficient you are. And you slowly climb up the Tree to the top of the house, to the attic which is where your sanctuary is. And there you mediate. And you come down the Tree again and you take note, for example, whether the house is empty, what the atmosphere is, or if it's full of personalities. If you take the planetary point of view, you've got your Mars and you've got your Venus. You might have a soldier there, and a rather good-looking bird, you might have a rather jovial-looking man, a grandma and the crazy grandpa, these are all archetypes. And doing that exercise over a period of half an hour is very revealing. For example, you go into the garden which tells you something about your general health. And then there's the pet you keep, and in one case it might be a cat. In one case it was a snake. It was interesting. I did this exercise, and one guy said, "Yes, I have this big snake," and all the girls looked at each other, because of course it's a classic phallic symbol. He really gave away the game. He didn't realise that. On the other hand you might get someone who had an ailing dog, or something like that. So your animal soul is expressed. That is part of the latter part of the book. It will come out either later this year or next year.

APS: Who will be the publisher?

ZBSH: The Kabbalah Society. The reason for that is ordinary publishers are very choosy what goes into fashion and goes out of fashion. So we decided, a group of us, that we would finance, because we're a charitable trust, books that would always be in print. As a graphic designer, which I was trained as, I can design it and write it, and other people can edit it. My wife has done most of the editing, for example, and it goes out into the world. We've just had one of them published in Russian, which is marvellous, which is the language of my grandfather. Very nice to see that. I think we've got four in Hebrew. So there's quite a lot going on.

APS: And what is Kabbalah Society?

ZBSH: It's a very loose organisation, a charity. We don't have any properties. It's volunteer people. We've got a volunteer secretary and a volunteer accountant. And they just take care of the finance. I used to run summer schools. They give me a grant once a year, which keeps the wolf from the door. They organise trips abroad, things like that. We took a group of, say, thirty people to Spain to look at the kabbalistic cities. I might be invited to Budapest. The Kabbalah Society in Budapest, people who study my books, are part of that orbit and would invite me there and I would give a weekend course in Budapest. It's been going for nearly forty years.

APS: The Old Synagogue in Budapest is worth seeing.

ZBSH: It's fabulous. Without Kabbalah I wouldn't have gone to half of these places. I've tracked down where the kabbalists were, all over Spain, going to the actual cities where these people lived. I've been to Israel many times, sat in the synagogues where they did their work.

APS: What's your view of death? What happens to us when we die? What are the possibilities?

ZBSH: We take our clothes off, the clothes of the body, and we go to another reality. In the same way we put on our clothes when we come into the body. There's far more to life after death. I have a memory just before I was born of three characters saying to me, "It would be a bit boring in paradise," one of them said, but, no, no, earth is where the action is. It's where we can participate in the evolution of humanity. It's where I write the books. You can actually change people's lives. It's amazing the stories I've heard. What more could a writer ask for?

APS: I think that's a great way to end. "Earth is where the action is."

Andrew Phillip Smith

Wills's Cigarettes

While searching online for material on the Gnostics I came across an Abraxas Ring cigarette card on eBay. I discovered that this was one of a set of 50 Lucky Charm cards given away in Wills's Cigarettes in 1923. The cigarettes themselves were Wills's No. 1, made by W.D. & H. O. Wills of Bristol and London.

Each card consists of an "amulet" of some sort or other. The illustrations are quite appealing with their clean style and gentle colouring. Each of the objects comes from the collection of the British Museum. It might be interesting to know if any of these are currently on display. The last time I went to the British Museum they had a nice display of various small religious artefacts through the ages. "The Hand", #19, associated with the god Sabazios, may have been the same one that I saw in an exhibition of magical items that included some of John Dee's artefacts.

The cards were "issued by the Imperial Tobacco Co. of Great Britain and Ireland". Framing these amulets as "lucky charms" made them understandable to the working people who would have been the main consumers of these cigarettes. Lucky charms were still quite popular in Britain when I was young (I've no idea if they are now). Typical examples are St Christopher Medallions, pixies and all sorts of small metal objects that look like they could double as Monopoly pieces.

WILLS'S CIGARETTES.

THE TAU CROSS.

It is admittedly odd to see in #24 a swastika in a British setting with no mention of Hitler but the ancient symbol had not yet been co-opted by the Nazis. In addition to the Abraxas ring there are other cards that are, rightly or wrongly, associated with Gnosticism. "The Greek Vowels", #22, gives a typical vowel sequence such as might be found in certain Nag Hammadi texts, or elsewhere in the Hellenistic Egyptian world. The Ankh, #15, is wholly Egyptian of course, but does occur in the Nag Hammadi Library. I chose the serpent for the back cover due to its Gnostic or Ophite associations.

The "Gnostic Talisman", #38, is a Greco-Egyptian talisman. The back of the card tells us, "The religion of the Gnostics was a strange intermingling of of pagan and Christian ideas. It was a system of complicated symbolism made purposely obscure and mysterious." The most unusual for me were the Magic Nails, #36, inscribed with Greek letters and once again described as "Gnostic amulets".

Imagine the thrill of finding one of these in your cigarettes as you chain-smoked your 80 cigarettes a day, drawing the smoke of unfiltered high-tar tobacco into your lungs. Even 50 ancient amulets might be too few to ward off the resulting lung cancer, bronchitis and emphysemia!

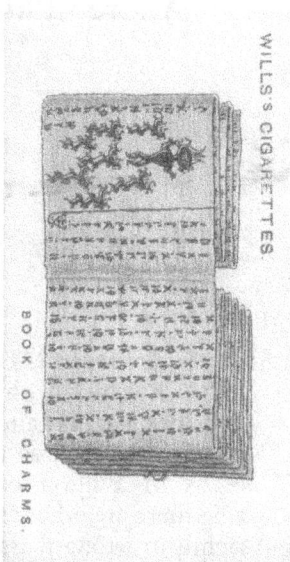

Robert Wood

James Therrien: a Eulogy

James Therrien (Soulgazer) was born, February 8, 1954 and passed away December 15, 2014. He was pastor at the Alpah & Omega Christian Gnostic Church. He was a good man who deeply influenced my life, and that is all I will say because all I will do is fail. At the bottom of the moving eulogy given by Robert Wood during a service, there is an audio interview of James for Aeon Byte Gnostic Radio (begins at

this short and to the point. Though I did not know him for long, he impacted my life and so many others. He started Alpha & Omega: Christian Gnostic Church in 2001 a welcoming haven for those who were rejected everywhere else. It was 2009 when I first met him. I was trying to find myself. I was going through the motions of living, not knowing where to look. I was not expecting much and thought this was

approximately minute 20).

Today we are gathered here to honor the memory of James Therrien, also known by the online handle of "Soulgazer". I could easily write a book on all the lessons I learned based on the guidance he gave me but I will try to keep

just going to be a footnote and the last church I ever attended. I never thought I'd be where I am today.

He told me he didn't think he would ever become a pastor either. He quickly became like a father to me. And that's the strange thing about life: when you think you know everything and have everything figured out, some surprise comes and tells you "That's not how it is". He was a man who did not like baggage and had the courage to say things even if it was difficult. He had a love for life. He had an understanding of how precious each moment in our life is like no other person I ever knew. He knew how to point out those little things that make life special and what was just garbage that kept us from seeing it. He had a faith, a confidence, about living an authentic life that I hope that everyone is willing to emulate.

Even after his first stroke in 2011 and he felt he was unable to continue running his church; he still kept his confidence and did not give in to fear. He had such a sense of peace that just made you want to stick around him. Let me assure you he was a man, a human, but he emulated his inner Christ and showed what that really meant by example. He showed that "living by faith" was not about being ignorant of the world but having confidence that everything will work out how it's supposed to and that we do impact the people we encounter in our lives.

Though he has left this world and continued on where ever he has been called to go, and the wisdom he had has parted from us, the source resides in each of us. We all have a piece of James within each of us. While we are saddened by losing our good friend, he is no longer suffering and has been called home. I know he died without regrets, and it was evident in the life he lived. He made the most of each moment he was here. Each of our times here is short, and one day we will be called home with our brother James. Our monkey suits will break down and we won't be able to do the things we once were able to do today. Are we living a life where we are honest with the choices we make for better or worse? Or are we letting constructed fears dictate what we do? We have the same light within us that James did, and it is our choice to let it shine or keep it covered. I know that I will let my light shine and will emulate the man who was like a father to me.

Today is the winter solstice, and so the shortest day of the year. Even though it marks the beginning of winter, we must recognize that the days can only get longer from this point on. Though we mourn and grieve now, as we continue in our lives we will celebrate what light and wisdom James has shown to each of us.

Friendofsophia, a relatively new member of Alpha & Omega Christian Gnostic Church had this to say about James. "I first heard of James from his Aeon Byte interview. It led me to seek out his writings, online forum, and church. His writings and his spoken words have impacted me in a major way. His courage to start something because he saw the need for it is inspiring. He was able to simplify the most profound concepts without losing much in the translation. He had a way about him that one could just know that he wasn't full of shit, and at the same time be able to recognize a genuine sense of love for the reader or listener. He was always one to point out the "frosted" and "wheat" side of everything as well as to remind us all that he can only point to the door, that we must walk through ourselves with his simple yet profound: "your mileage may vary."

Many more words were spoken by others but this is what I have recorded. Dear heavenly Father-Mother, we know that you have called James back home and that one day you will call each of us. Grant us the understanding of how precious our lives are and help us to make peace with anything that we feel ashamed of in our lives. We know that within you is a love that surpasses all understanding and have long forgiven us even if we have chosen not to forgive ourselves. Grant us the faith and courage to face the fears in our lives that want to dominate and control how we live for we know that in faith there is freedom from fear. Allow us to recognize that your Christ is not a being that is far from us nor a corpse that requires praise but the perfect image of God that resides with us, that we give birth to when choose to allow truth and love in our lives. Amen.

Ken Henson

Black Mirror Drawings

I make drawings while looking into a black mirror as a part of my spiritual practice. For centuries, magic mirrors have been used as tools for scrying. Gazing into the mirror helps the medium achieve a trance state, and the mirror's surface acts as a portal through which visions may be seen. Unlike my other drawings and paintings, these images are not guided by aesthetic decisions. They are simply artifacts left in the wake of ritual. Contemplating these drawings enhances my memory of the time I spend in meditation. Some of the drawings document my reflection, which becomes distorted and otherly in the visionary state, while other drawings are notations of different scenes that appear in the mirror.

There are magicians from the past who are famous for their use of magic mirrors. In their collaborative efforts to commune with angels, the Renaissance magicians John Dee and Edward Kelley used a finely polished black obsidian mirror, now in the collection of the British Museum. Paschal Beverly Randolph, who was more a product of the spiritualist mediumship popular in the 19th century, used a "magnetic mirror" as a tool for clairvoyance. My personal path is directly influenced by a strain of the mystical and magical currents indigenous to my Midwestern Cincinnati, OH. Specifically, I research a small circle of physicians and chemists affiliated with the Eclectic and Homeopathic medicine movements of the 19th and early 20th centuries. These individuals truly were eclectic, drawing from an assortment of traditions: Paracelsian and Neoplatonic philosophies, Theosophy, mystic Freemasonry, Spiritualism, Swedenborgianism, Native American spiritualities, and the teachings of the Hermetic Brotherhood of Luxor, an organization that focused on the art of practical magic, including the use of magic mirrors.

The home base for my research is The Lloyd Library and Museum, which was founded by John Uri Lloyd, one of the most influential members of the Eclectic Medicine movement. Today, Lloyd is recognized in esoteric circles for his occult novel *Etidorhpa* (Aphrodite backwards), an allegory about initiation into the Western Mysteries. *Etidorhpa* was notably illustrated by Lloyd's dear friend John Augustus Knapp, who would later become the illustrator of many of Manly P. Hall's works, including his magnum opus *The Secret Teachings of All Ages*. The Lloyd Library, best known as a botanical, pharmaceutical, and scientific library, is also full of antique books on magic and alchemy. In the archives there are a series of letters written to Lloyd, dated 1899-1900, from L. M. Taylor, the publisher of a periodical out of Washington D.C. titled "The Occult Mirror". Apparently this journal was dedicated to anecdotal stories surrounding one particularly large mirror that attracted a community of scryers. I can't say with certainty that Lloyd had his own magic mirror, or that he was a member of the Hermetic Brotherhood of Luxor, but we do know that a member of his close circle, Dr. Jirah Dewey Buck (who founded the first American branch of the Theosophical Society) was a member of the H.B. of L.

Bill Darlison

Moses the Stargazer

When William Drummond, Member of Parliament, diplomat, linguist and amateur bible scholar, published Oedipus Judaicus: Allegory in the Old Testament in 1811, he considered the contents so explosive that he restricted the book's distribution to a handful of chosen friends. Through his analysis of the original Hebrew, Drummond had come to the heretical conclusion that the stories in the Jewish scriptures, particularly those stories which, when interpreted literally, paint a less than favourable picture of God, are astronomical allegories and have little or no historical content.

Drummond's caution was probably wise. His contemporary, Rev. Robert Taylor (1784-1844), shared many of his astro-theological notions but lacked his prudence, openly preaching his 'blasphemous' ideas in London and Dublin, and earning himself a prison term for his audacity.

Drummond's book concentrates principally on the Book of Joshua, which describes the indiscriminate slaughter of the indigenous peoples of the land of Canaan by the invading Israelites. It is probably the most-bloodthirsty book in the whole Bible, and it leaves all but the most partisan reader with a sense of outrage at the injustice and the barbarity perpetrated at the supposed command of God; and the astronomical absurdity of Joshua commanding the sun to stand still leaves the reader marvelling at the scientific illiteracy of the ancients. But, says Drummond, there's no history in the Book of Joshua, and it is certainly not a product of primitive science. On the contrary, the science of astronomy is its main concern. It is, he says, an attempt to demonstrate the superiority of a new astronomical system over an older, less accurate one, and the cities conquered by Joshua are calendrical elements which need to be changed in order to make them more reliable. For example, Joshua's first conquest, the city of Jericho – which is preceded by sending in two 'spies' - is an allegory of the necessary destruction of a misleading lunar calendar, and not about the annihilation of an earthly city. Jericho (יריחו) is indeed derived from the Hebrew word for moon (ירח – pronounced *yaraiak*).

> The word Jericho either means the Moon in her several quarters, or the lunar month divided into weeks. The Hebrews compassed the city seven times. Does this not allude to the seven days of the week, or to one of the moon's quarters? It seems to me that the abolition of the lunar month of 28 days, by the addition of two days, is typified by the destruction of Jericho.

Similarly with the nonsensical reference to the stationary sun a little later in the text:

> Sun, stand thou still upon Gibeon, and thou, Moon, in the valley of Aijalon.

This, too, says Drummond, is concerned with the calendar, and refers to the discrepancy between the astronomical year of 365 ¼ days and the 'sacred' year of 365 days. Since, every fourth year, a day was intercalated, this was tantamount to the sun 'standing still'. This happens in Gibeon, a name which is generally taken to mean something like 'high hill', but which comes from a Semitic root meaning 'concave' and so could mean 'the concave vault of the sky above.' Aijalon comes from the Hebrew word for 'ram' and so refers to the zodiacal sign of Aries, the sign which marks the beginning of the solar year.

Even today, two hundred years after Drummond and Taylor, conventionally religious people may baulk at such an approach to 'holy scripture', and even the more sceptical among us may wonder why the ancient Hebrews chose to couch their scientific treatises in such fanciful narratives. Drummond himself offers no definitive answers, but he suggests that the oriental mind is more given to figurative expression than its occidental counterpart, and he offers a note of caution we would all do well to heed:

> I must expect to be condemned by the matter-of-fact people, who are persuaded that the Eastern prophets, who wrote three or four thousand years ago, composed their works upon the same model, and with the same regard to facts, as may be seen always attended to in the praiseworthy pages of the Annual Register, and of the London Gazette.

The Exodus

There's no doubt that the story of the Exodus which we find in the second book of the Hebrew Bible is, like the story of Joshua, a difficult one to accept at face value. The burning bush, the ten plagues, and the parting of the sea, while simply demonstrating the awesome power of an interventionist God to the fundamentalist Jewish or Christian believer, present untold problems for those of a more sceptical disposition. But the story has certainly captured the imagination of believer and non-believer alike, and numerous attempts have been made to explain these strange occurrences. In the 1960s, Erich von Daniken suggested that aliens were involved, and that the burning bush was a spaceship; maverick Russian-born science writer, Immanuel Velikovsky (1895-1979) proposed that the planet Venus, ejected from Jupiter about 1500 BCE (or so he thought) was captured by the Earth's gravitational pull causing world-wide calamities, of which the biblical plagues and the parting of the waters were just a few. Some liberal historians and biblical scholars suggest that the principal events of the Exodus were real enough, but that they have been exaggerated in the telling and retelling over centuries. The recent Ridley Scott film, Exodus, gives a naturalistic explanation of the whole story: Moses bangs his head before encountering the burning bush and so is probably hallucinating, and the plagues and the parting of the waters are just ordinary biological or meteorological phenomena which require no divine intervention by way of explanation.

The main problem for one who would like to believe that the story has a historical foundation is that there is precious little (if any) archaeological evidence to support it. The British archaeologist, John Rohmer, says that the Sinai Peninsula, where the escaped Israelites supposedly spent forty years, yields evidence of encampments by individual people millennia ago, but evidence that 600,000 men, along with their women and children – probably 2 million in total – wandered there for forty years, cannot be found.

> Although its climate has preserved the tiniest traces of ancient Bedouin encampments and the sparse 5000-year-old villages of mine workers there is not a single trace of Moses or the Israelites; and they would have been by far the largest body of ancient people ever to have lived in this great wilderness. Neither is there any evidence that Sinai and its little natural springs could ever have supported

such a multitude.

There's another problem. The God who is the central character of the story is portrayed as an appalling, capricious, bloodthirsty, partisan tyrant. He hardens Pharaoh's heart and then punishes him and his people for stubbornness; he kills all the first-born children of the Egyptians, and he drowns the whole Egyptian army. These are hardly the actions of the loving God Jewish and Christian people have been taught to believe in. What's more, the creator of the universe is so anthropomorphised that he speaks with Moses 'face to face', eats with him, shows him his 'hind parts', changes his mind, gets angry, demands sacrifice, encourages the Children of Israel to trick their Egyptian neighbours, and acts so much like an petulant, autocratic bully that no amount of special pleading on the part of believers can make us warm to him.

So, what's going on here? Is the story just a fanciful piece of jingoistic propaganda demonstrating the special favour God has shown to the Jews, or could there be another explanation which does not require us to believe the incredible or to postulate the improbable?

I think there is. The 'passover' is not God passing over the blood-smeared houses of the children of Israel while he smites the Egyptians; the pass-over is the movement of the equinoctial sun from the zodiacal constellation Taurus into the constellation Aries. This story, like the story of Joshua, is not historical, it is astronomical, perhaps even astrological, describing an astronomical phenomenon called the precession of the equinoxes.

THE PRECESSION OF THE EQUINOXES

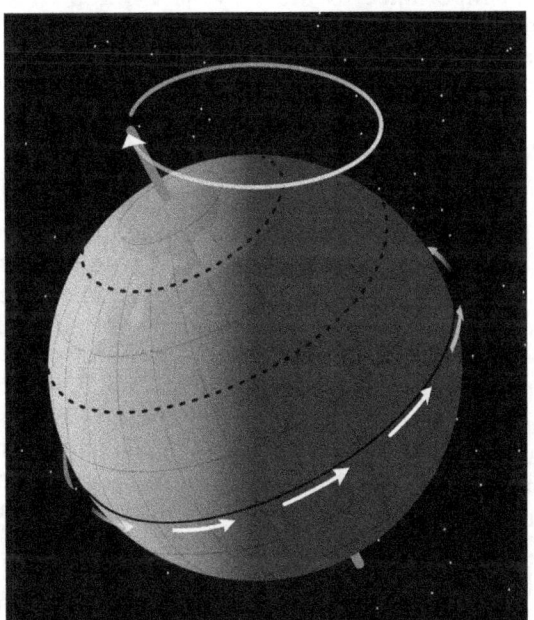

In addition to its obvious diurnal and annual cycles, the earth has a third cycle produced by its axial wobble. This means that the sun's position at the spring equinox changes ever so slightly from year to year with reference to the fixed stars. The sun appears to move backwards ('precesses') along the zodiac, the whole cycle taking some 25,920 years, with the sun spending a little over 2,000 years in each of the zodiacal signs. To move just one degree takes 72 years, which probably accounts for the importance this number has in both the Jewish and Christian scriptures.

It is generally supposed that the Greek astronomer Hipparchus (190-120 BCE) discovered this phenomenon, and although he may be credited with the first scientific description of it, there can be no doubt that it was known about well before his time. In fact, Santillana and von Dechend, in their book Hamlet's Mill, which deals with the mythological influence precession has had on our thinking and on our literature, say that the ancient peoples must have had towering geniuses just as we do and, given the fact that they had ample time and opportunity for systematic and careful observation of the skies they must have been aware of precession. They quote the Italian Church dignitary, Domenico Testa, who defended the idea that the universe was created about 4,000 BCE on the grounds that, had the ancient civilisations had millennia in which to observe the stars, 'even the very sweepers of their observatories would have known about precession'.

Indeed, the ancients did know about precession. And some Jewish genius chose to write about it as a brilliant fictional narrative rather than as a dry scientific treatise. Unfortunately, he didn't foresee the trouble that his imaginative efforts would cause down the centuries when his manuscript fell into the hands of the literalists.

Awareness of astronomical phenomena such as precession was of vital importance to the ancients, who sowed and planted according to the sun, moon and stars, and for whom an accurate calendar was a matter of life or death. But there's also another possible reason why the precession of the equinoctial sun from one constellation to another was considered to be important: our ancestors sensed that the such a pass-over signalled a change in the spiritual consciousness of the human race, and that the sun's 25,920 year journey round the zodiac symbolised the twelve phases through which we collectively progress as a species. As the sun moves into each of the constellations, the dominant imagery of spiritual consciousness changes, but not without a monumental struggle between the movement for change and the forces of reaction. The 'Chosen People' are the ones who are prepared to make the transition, who are prepared to cross over to the other side. Indeed, the word 'Hebrew' comes from the Hebrew verb *lehavor*, (לעבר) which means 'to cross over'. In the name 'Abraham', we can see the same root. Abraham, who moved from his homeland to the land that God would show him and found the ram caught in the thicket, is considered to be the first Hebrew. But all who are prepared to 'cross over' when the time is appropriate are his descendants. The name Moses, too, seems to mean 'one who is drawn out', or 'one who draws out', giving the sense, once again, of movement from one phase to another.

When the sun moved from Taurus to Aries, about 2000 BCE, the Bull gave way to the Ram; 2000 years later, when the equinox moved into Pisces, the Fish began to dominate, and early Christianity adopted the Fish as its dominant symbol, as Jesus inaugurated a 'new pass-over'. Now, we stand on the verge of yet another 'pass-over' as the equinoctial sun moves into Aquarius, the Man Carrying a Jar of Water, and who can deny that great changes in our understanding of ourselves and our place in the universe are taking place on an unprecedented scale and that the forces of resistance are arming themselves for battle?

FROM TAURUS TO ARIES

The spring equinox took place in the constellation Taurus from about 4,000 BCE to 2,000 BCE., and, whether by conscious design of the priestly caste or by the unconscious assimilation of genuine cosmic 'influences', this was undoubtedly a time when cow and bull cults began to dominate human consciousness. In Egypt we find the ceremonies centred around the bull, Apis; in India, Hinduism begins, and the cow becomes sacred; the Minotaur, half-man, half-bull, becomes the sacred emblem of Crete. In this period, too, we see the beginnings of the bull cult which was eventually to become Mithraism, a religion which seriously vied for supremacy with Christianity, and in which bathing in the blood of a sacrificed bull was at the centre of its ritual and its symbolism.

Taurus is said to be an Earth sign, and its astrological symbol is ♉ representing the head and horns of the bull. Physiologically it is said to be associated with the throat and neck.

Vera Reid, in her book *Towards Aquarius*, sums up the astrological characteristics of Taurus:

> This sign has affinity with the soil, money and material possessions. Its chief characteristics are endurance, persistence, conservation, latent strength, love of comfort, good food and security, coupled with practical artistic ability.

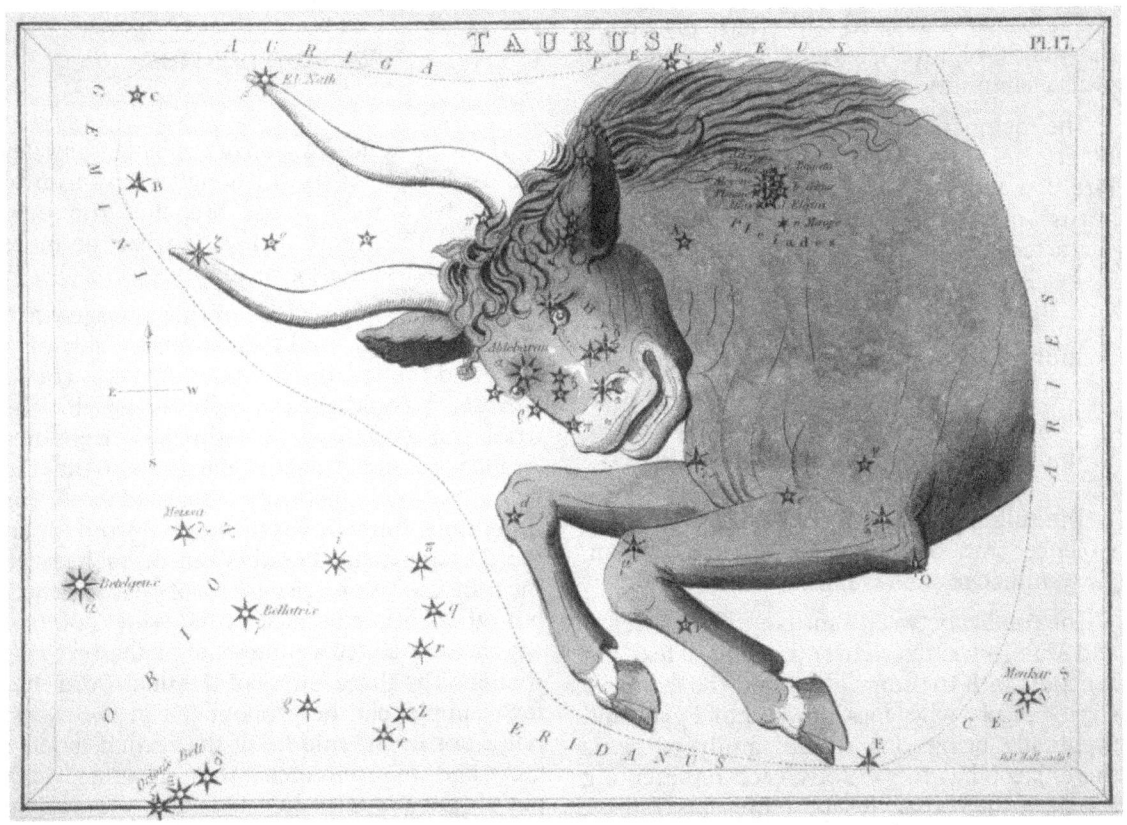

Taurus, Aldebaran and the Pleiades

As depicted in Urania's Mirror, a set of constellation cards published in London c. 1825

(Wikipedia)

'Endurance and persistence' taken to extremes, give stubbornness – exactly the trait we find in Pharaoh, who is constantly said to be 'stiff-necked'. We might also add that Taurus is considered to be the sign of the builder and it is interesting to note that the pyramids of Egypt are thought to have been built during the Age of Taurus. Significant, too, that the work undertaken by the Israelites in Egypt was building work.

The planet associated with Taurus is Venus, the planet of love, pleasure, sensuality, ease, peace, femininity, community and fertility.

The equinoctial sun entered Aries about 2000 BCE. Aries is the Ram. It is considered to be a Fire sign and its symbol is ♈, representing the horns of the ram. Its astrological characteristics are:

> ....ideality, truth, prophetic vision, individualism, energy and courage – qualities which imply leadership and that pioneer spirit which goes forward undaunted against overwhelming odds.

The ruling planet of Aries is Mars, planet of violence, war, bloodshed, adventure, honour, glory, initiative and revenge.

The conflict between Taurus and Aries, Venus and Mars, is written all over the biblical text, but it begins with the story of Joseph, the favourite son of Jacob, who goes down into Egypt and eventually brings his whole family to settle there. Jacob has twelve sons, each representing a sign of the zodiac. Joseph represents Taurus. His name comes from the Hebrew root יסף (*yasaf*) which means 'to add, or increase' (very Taurean qualities) and we first meet him in the Book of Genesis, dressed in his 'coat of many colours' (or, maybe just a long tunic). Whatever its precise nature, the text seems to imply that it was hardly a garment suited to hard work, and that Joseph was pampered and workshy. This is one reason (another is his insufferable boasting about his dreams) why his brothers eventually try to get rid of him.

A Dot Means a Lot

In Genesis 49, Jacob blesses his sons, indicating their astrological characteristics. The first part of the blessing he gives to Joseph looks like this in the Hebrew:

בֵּן פֹּרָת יוֹסֵף בֵּן פֹּרָת עֲלֵי־עָיִן
בָּנוֹת צָעֲדָה עֲלֵי־שׁוּר׃

The King James Version of the Bible translates it thus: 'Joseph is a fruitful bough, even a fruitful bough by a well; whose branches run over the wall.' This, more or less, is what the more modern translations give, too.

But the first two words of this passage - פרת בן (*ben parat*) - could easily mean 'son of a cow', and the last three - צעדה עלי שור – (*tsada alay shor*) could mean 'walk on a bull'. The word בנות (*banot*), which the KJV translates 'branches' usually means 'daughters'. And the word עין (*ayn*) poetically translated 'well' (or sometimes 'fountain') is the normal word for an eye. Discrepancies like this can occur because the translator is exercising a bit of poetic licence, but others occur because of the vowel points – which were added centuries after the text was written. The three letters of the final word שור, for example, can be pronounced in two ways: put a dot in the middle of the second letter - שׁוּר – and we pronounce it *shur*, meaning 'wall'; put the dot above the second letter - שׁוֹר - and we pronounce it *shor*, meaning 'bull'. It all depends upon where you put the dot.

Drummond redistributes the dots and translates the whole of this verse:

> A son of a cow is Joseph, a son of a cow beside the eye (the star Aldebaran, called 'The Eye of the Bull'): the Pleiades (called 'The Daughters' by the Chaldeans) walk upon the back of the bull.

The poetic, fanciful, and almost meaningless conventional translation hides – whether deliberately or accidentally - the obvious Taurus elements which a more literal translation would yield.

Dots are significant in another important word in the Exodus story. The sea which the Israelites cross is written יַם־סוּף (*yam suf*), and this, thanks to the Septuagint Greek version and the King James English version, is generally translated Red Sea, even though the word 'red' appears nowhere in the Hebrew text. Modern translations call it, more accurately, the Sea of Reeds but nobody seems to know precisely where it was. However, change the dot in סֻף (suf) and we get סוֹף 'sof', which means not 'red' or 'reeds', but 'end'. The Israelites cross the 'sea of the end' which has no geographical location at all, but symbolizes the end of one cycle and the beginning of another; the end of slavery and the beginning of freedom; the end of Taurus and the beginning of Aries.

of the Children of Israel, Pharaoh orders the death of all their new-born males, but Moses is hidden in the bulrushes by his sister, is adopted by Pharaoh's daughter and eventually has to flee Egypt to escape punishment for a crime. He goes to the land of Midian where he meets the seven daughters of Jethro, one of whom, Zipporah, he marries. This looks like an inconsequential biographical detail, but it could well be a reference to the Pleiades, the beautiful group of seven stars in the constellation Taurus, which have been known as 'The Seven Sisters' or 'The Seven Daughters' throughout the world and throughout the ages. Some cultures have seen them as birds, and have referred to them as 'The Hen with her Chickens'. The name Zipporah comes from the Hebrew word for bird.

Chapter 3, one of the most famous and most important chapters in the entire Bible, describes Moses's encounter with the Burning Bush. Moses is looking after his father-in-law's flocks when he comes to Horeb, the 'mountain of God', and the Angel of the LORD speaks to him out of a bush 'which was burning but which was not consumed by the fire.' Numerous attempts, as one might imagine, have been made to identify the kind of bush which Moses saw, and numerous attempts have been made to explain the strange phenomenon of a bush which was

Moses and the Burning Bush
Painting from St. Isaac's Cathedral, St. Petersburg

THE BURNING BUSH

The first two chapters of Exodus recount the death of Joseph and the birth and early life of Moses. Disturbed by the growth in numbers

burning but not being burned up. Cambridge physicist, Colin Humphreys, claims that it was a natural gas source which had become ignited and which was blazing away with no diminution of the flame. But, of course, there is no need to go to such lengths.

The burning bush is the sun, the one source of flame which never dies.

And the bush speaks to Moses, telling him to take the shoes from his feet because he is standing on holy ground. (Joshua receives a similar instruction from the angel of the LORD just before the attack on Jericho). Rev. Robert Taylor sees this as an instruction to the reader as much as to Moses or to Joshua: you are entering strange territory here; this is different from your normal, everyday, prosaic understanding of things. Take off your workaday shoes, switch off your mundane mind, and approach these words with reverence and a bit of imagination.

God tells Moses that he must go to Pharaoh and tell him to let the Children of Israel leave Egypt. 'Who shall I say sent me?' asks Moses. Then comes one of the most profound, enigmatic, misunderstood, and mistranslated statements in the whole Bible. In Hebrew it reads:

אֶהְיֶה אֲשֶׁר אֶהְיֶה

(*ehyeh asher ehyeh*). This is not, as some translations have it, 'I am that I am'. There is no present tense, or present participle of the verb 'to be' in Hebrew. The tense is future. Translated literally, it means 'I shall be what I shall be', and it implies that God too is 'on the move', or that a new understanding of deity is imminent. It will involve a movement away from the Earthy things of Taurus into the Fiery things of Aries.

MOSES' STAFF

In Chapter 4 of Exodus, God tells Moses to convince the Egyptians of his divine mission by throwing down his staff in front of Pharaoh. When he does this, the staff turns into a snake, but, unfortunately, Pharaoh's wise men can do the same. Their staffs turn into snakes too. But Moses's snake eats them up.

Once again, only a little imagination is required to understand this story. The snake with its tail in its mouth – the ouroboros - is a timeless symbol of the zodiac, the eternal cycle of the sun in the sky. The wise men of Egypt have their own, faulty, understanding of the cyclical nature of things, but that of Moses is superior to theirs. Moses knows that the sun, the great symbol of deity, is moving on, stimulating a corresponding development in religious understanding and expression. The Egyptians want things to stay the same. Egypt (called in Hebrew מִצְרַיִם *mitzrayim*, 'narrow straits') is a place of constriction, conservatism, and refusal to change.

Pharaoh is the most stubborn Egyptian of all. Pharaoh (פַּרְעֹה) is an Egyptian word, but it remarkably similar to the Hebrew word for 'bull' (פַּר - *par*) and for 'cow' (פָּרָה - *parah*). Pharaoh is the personification of Taurus, of the stubbornness – 'stiffneckedness' the text calls it, recalling the Taurean connection with throat and neck - which persists even in the face of repeated demonstrations that change is necessary; and the ten plagues are a dramatic account of the catastrophic effects of such stubbornness. The final plague, the one which convinces Pharaoh to let the people go, is the death of the first-born. This signifies the destruction of the whole Taurean system; it has outlived its usefulness and can be passed on no longer. A new beginning is required.

THE PASSOVER MEAL

Before they set off on their journey out of Egypt, the Children of Israel have to prepare a meal. It will be eaten on the 14th day of the first month, i.e. the full moon after the spring equinox, emphasizing the astronomical origin of the festival. The ingredients of the meal and the instructions for its consumption reflect Aries. The lamb, taken from the sheep or the goats, is to be roasted in the fire (it is not to be boiled in water) and they are to eat it with bitter herbs (not the 'comfort food' associated with Taurus). The bread is to be unleavened; this, too, signifies a new beginning. It was customary to use bread from the previous batch to leaven the current one, so the elimination of the yeast symbolises a complete break from the past. The meal is to be eaten 'in haste', with loins girded and feet shod. Aries demands alertness, vigilance, action, self-mortification, and courage.

FROM SHUR TO ELIM

There is another indication that the whole story concerns the movement from Taurus to Aries. At the end of Chapter 15, we read:

> 22And Moses led Israel from the Sea of the End and they went out into the wilderness of Shor (The Place of the Ox); they travelled three days in the wilderness but did not find water... ...27And they

The Golden Calf
(Nicholas Poussain)

went to Elim (The Place of the Rams) where there were twelve springs of water and seventy date palms, and they camped there by the water.

Once again, a dot means a lot (see above). Shur, which is the way the text is normally pointed (i.e. 'vowelled') , means 'wall'; but the three letters which make up the word could easily be rendered Shor, which means 'ox' or 'bull'. There is neither doubt nor ambiguity about the association of the word *elim* with rams. Translators always consider Shur (or Shor) and Elim as places on the journey, even though no two seem to agree on where these places might have been. But the names tell us clearly that we are not concerned with terrestrial cities; the wilderness of Shor, the place of the Ox (Taurus) was arid, but Elim, the place of the Rams (Aries) had twelve springs of water and seventy date palms, and was a much more life-enhancing place.

THE GOLDEN CALF

But not everyone is happy. The people complain about lack of water and lack of food; they long for the 'flesh-pots' of Egypt, where their bellies were full even though they were slaves. When Moses goes up the mountain to receive the commandments from God, the people rebel and persuade Aaron to fashion a god for them. And what does he do? He makes a golden calf, an image of the previous dispensation, an image they were familiar with, a comforting image they can bow down to and worship. Here we see backsliding, fear of the unknown, a longing for the past which chains these people and, if truth be told, which chains all people.

CONCLUSION

The more I read this paradigmatic biblical story, the more I am impressed by the levels of meaning it contains. The astronomy/astrology is just one of the numerous dimensions of a saga which has inspired oppressed people for millennia. And the story has relevance to the religious and spiritual conflicts which are evident in the modern world. In the words of Bob Dylan, 'The times they are a-changing'. As we stand on the verge of a new Age, as the equinox passes from Pisces into Aquarius, we can ponder our own reluctance to embrace the spiritual challenges of the future. We can go out in faith, like Moses, prepared to jettison all those attitudes – such as scriptural literalism, obsession with religious 'history', tribalism - which enslave us still, or we can languish in pharaoh-like obtuseness and suffer the consequences of our intransigence.

One final point: some things we must not jettison. When Moses leaves Egypt he takes the bones of Joseph, the 'bones' of Taurus, with him. The message is simple and obvious: the past is not to be completely abandoned. The imagery of the former age may be outdated and its principles in need of revision, but anything of value that it has taught us must be carried forward into the future.

Sean Martin

Better Than Soaking
Landscape, Place and the Body in the Work of David Lindsay
(or, David Lindsay and the Perils of Walking)

I **BETTER THAN SOAKING**

David Lindsay liked to walk, going for long tramps over the South Downs, Dartmoor, or the highlands of Scotland. A writer steeped in Norse myth and lore,[1] Lindsay's ideal conditions for a walk were winter, mist and rain which, as his biographer Bernard Sellin noted, were 'a convenient substitute for distant Scandinavia'.[2] On these meandering rambles he would, I imagine, collect his thoughts, mull over what he had been writing that day, or put as much distance as possible between himself and the latest rejection letter on his desk. Lindsay's literary career was sandwiched between the two world wars, and he never enjoyed the success he felt he deserved. His first novel, *A Voyage to Arcturus*, was published in 1920 to uncomprehending reviews and minimal sales; over half the print run was remaindered. Neither his sales nor his reviews improved particularly and, when the Second World War broke out, he seems to have given up writing altogether. He left his final novel, *The Witch*, nearly complete, but never returned to it. He died in July 1945, some eight weeks after the end of the war in Europe. Ironically, a revival of interest in Lindsay's work began the following year, when Gollancz reissued *Arcturus*. Lindsay's career was marked by nothing if not bad luck and bad timing.

Lindsay's protagonists reflect in varying degrees their author's frustrations, visions and temperament. All share the conviction, or have it revealed to them, that the world is 'a vast shadow house of earth and sky'[3], 'rotten

---

1 See Julian D'Arcy, *Scottish Skalds and Sagamen: Old Norse Influence on Modern Scottish Literature* (East Linton: Tuckwell Press, 1996). Chapter 8, 134-53, is on Lindsay.

2 Bernard Sellin, *The Life and Works of David Lindsay*, 36.

3 *The Violet Apple and The Witch*, 367.

with illusion from top to bottom; not a sound piece anywhere, but all springs, glasses, and traps throughout'.[4] I can picture Lindsay grimly entertaining such thoughts while caught in a storm on the Downs, or taking shelter under a quoit on Dartmoor. Walking is the path to knowledge, *solvitur ambulando*, as the Latin phrase has it - 'it is solved by walking'.

But variations on that motto could apply, too: 'it is banished or exorcised by walking', if we imagine disheartening correspondence from the publishers John Long and Jonathan Cape on Lindsay's desk, with whom he was negotiating, circa 1923-4. (Lindsay was never able to take up an offer from Cape which could have been the kind of shot in the arm his writing career needed - due to being contractually tied to John Long, who published *Sphinx* in 1923, but then had the temerity to reject Lindsay's next novel, *The Violet Apple*. Lindsay was ultimately left without contracts with either publisher.[5])

Walks in Lindsay's works - whether traversing the unknown geography of another planet, tramping across the stormy, windswept landscapes of this, or merely negotiating a flight of stairs in an apparently ordinary house - have the role of opening up the protagonist's mind, of offering them a challenge. Landscapes and seemingly mundane houses possess something of the 'Delphic ambiguity which torments our daily lives',[6] as Loren Eiseley put it, an ambiguity - or doubleness - that Lindsay expresses in all his books. Nature is revealed red in metaphysical tooth and claw. It is often not a pleasant experience; in some cases it leads directly, or indirectly, to the characters' deaths. As Bernard Sellin notes, 'there are few enough pleasant reveries in Lindsay's work. It is not Nature's role to soothe, but rather to awaken man to a meditation on the meaning of his own life'.[7] Sellin reminds us that nature is Lindsay's books is not a backdrop against which the action unfolds, but is 'a reflection of another world that is more genuine than the tangible world, Nature thus lends itself to become the substitute for ultimate reality.'[8]

Although he spent a decade living near the sea in Cornwall, Lindsay was not a coastal person, being drawn inland instead to the mountains and hills. Perhaps the only significant description of the sea in his work occurs early on in *A Voyage to Arcturus*. The characters Maskull and Nightspore are due to leave for the star Arcturus from Starkness Observatory in northeast Scotland. While waiting for Krag, who will act as their guide, they kill time by demolishing a bottle of Scotch, before Nightspore decides a walk is in order. 'Walking is better than soaking', he tells Maskull, and suggests they go and visit the nearby cliffs known as the Gap of Sorgie. 'What's that?', Maskull asks, and Nightspore replies cryptically, 'A showplace.'[9]

The Gap of Sorgie is not so much a view, as an absence.[10] Maskull and Nightspore inch out along a shelf of rock in the cliffs, until they are able to look down into the ocean waters below

---

4 *Sketch Notes for a New System of Philosophy*, note 534.

5 See Bernard Sellin, *The Life and Works of David Lindsay*, 30-31.

6 Loren Eiseley, Introduction to *A Voyage to Arcturus* (Ballantine, 1972), x.

7 Bernard Sellin, *The Life and Works of David Lindsay*, 70.

8 Bernard Sellin, *The Life and Works of David Lindsay*, 71. On the role of nature in Lindsay, see 60-72.

9 *A Voyage to Arcturus*, 33-34. Page numbers quoted are for the Allison & Busby edition, except where noted.

10 D'Arcy 141 notes that 'sorge', the probable origin of 'Sorgie', means 'sorrow' in German. As Lindsay could read German, D'Arcy speculates that Lindsay must have been aware of this. Perhaps it is the sorrow that we are stranded in a false world, and that our true home is elsewhere. See the quotation from Visiak, below, about his night-time walk with Lindsay.

them: 'The shelf did not extend for above a quarter of a mile, but its passage was somewhat unnerving; there was a sheer drop to the sea, four hundred feet below. In a few places, they had to sidle along without placing one foot before another. The sound of the breakers came up to them in a low, threatening roar.' They lie down flat on the rock when it 'broadened out into a fair-sized platform'. Below them is the Gap of Sorgie: 'Nothing was to be seen; the gloom had deepened, and the sea was nearly invisible. But, while he [Maskull] was ineffectually gazing, he heard what sounded like the beating of a drum on the narrow strip of shore below. It was very faint, but quite distinct. The beats were in four-four time, with the third beat slightly accented. He now continued to hear the noise all the time he was lying there. The beats were in no way drowned by the far louder sound of the surf, but seemed somehow to belong to a different world...'[11] Maskull questions Nightspore about the meaning of the drum taps, and what it would imply if he hears them again. 'It bears its own message,' Nightspore replies. 'Only try to hear it more and more distinctly... Now it's growing dark, and we must get back.'[12]

Of course, Maskull does hear the drum taps again, almost as soon as they arrive on Tormance, the planet orbiting Arcturus on which most of the novel's action takes place. He spends most of the rest of the book following the drum taps, which lead him through a variety of wildly differing landscapes, from the mountainous Ifdawn Marest to the suffocatingly lush river valley Matterplay. In each place, Maskull meets people who represent a philosophical principle (pleasure, austerity, will, etc), which is then shown to be false. As Colin Manlove points out, *A Voyage to Arcturus* is 'radically subversive', because, as readers, we have 'the ground so continually and brutally taken from beneath our feet, just as in literal terms the planet's geography frequently betrays Maskull',[13] such as in the frequent landslides of the Ifdawn Marest.

Maskull also grows new sensory organs as the situation demands. The woman Joiwind, the first character Maskull meets on the new planet, gives him a blood transfusion to enable him to survive on Tormance (and, in a sense, complementing the blood-letting Krag performed at Starkness). All of these physical transformations are aids to Maskull's awakening. At the end of the novel, Maskull has a vision in which the drumbeats are shown to be the beating of his own heart.[14] He has, in effect, been following a knowledge that has been inside him all along. As another woman, Tydomin, tells Maskull at one point, 'Perhaps the explanation is... in your body.'[15]

Maskull is fortunate in that, on Tormance, his lengthy walks in pursuit of the drum beats are aided by a modified body. On earth, the body is shown to be an obstacle to progress, both literally and metaphorically. Climbing the tower at Starkness, Maskull immediately gets into difficulties: 'Hardly had he mounted half a dozen steps, however, before he was compelled to pause to gain breath. He seemed to be carrying not one Maskull, but three. As he proceeded, the sensation of crushing weight, so far from diminishing, grew worse and worse. It was nearly physically impossible to go on; his lungs could not take in enough oxygen, while his heart thumped like a ship's engine.'[16] He gets to a window and, realising he can't climb any higher, sits in the recess of the window. To his surprise, the window 'was not a window at all but a lens' through which he can see the binary star of Arcturus and the planet Tormance.[17] But Maskull will not be able to visit Tormance - and have his illusions stripped from him the way a skinner might flay a hide - unless he can climb to

11 *A Voyage to Arcturus*, 35.

12 *A Voyage to Arcturus*, 36.

13 Manlove, 166.

14 *A Voyage to Arcturus*, 276-77.

15 *A Voyage to Arcturus*, 130.

16 *A Voyage to Arcturus*, 36.

17 *A Voyage to Arcturus*, 37.

the top of the tower. The remedy for this is to be bled: like an old barber-surgeon, Krag opens a wound in Maskull's arm, alleviating the pressure he had felt in the tower, to acclimatise him to the gravity of the world to come. (A process completed by Joiwind's blood transfusion in the following chapter when they arrive on Tormance.)

But such bodily or sensory knowledge - an embodied gnosis, perhaps? - is denied the characters in the other books. In *Sphinx* (1923), the characters are resolutely trapped in their own bodies and the deceptions they practise; only Nicholas's machine for recording dreams can provide the new sensations and knowledge that the extra sense organs do on Tormance. In *The Violet Apple* (written 1924-6, pub. 1976), eating the two small apples provide the sensory, bodily gnosis that Lindsay wants to describe (or hint at). Like the Gap of Sorgie, Lindsayan gnosis is here also an absence, a 'thirty hours' chasm' in normal waking experience.[18] (It's a shame Aldous Huxley never read this novel, whose plot could be crudely summed up as two lovers-to-be both taking the same mind altering substance, and tripping their tits off.)

Just as the characters in *Sphinx* are trapped by their own bodies and normal perceptions, so are they frequently depicted as 'scrambling through the tangle'[19] of branches in the woods. The novel is set in Hampshire, near the New Forest, and the woodland setting, where the trees seem to imprison, combine with a heatwave to trap the characters in a sluggish, despondent state. (A very different use of a woodland setting, in *The Violet Apple*, will be discussed below.) It is Lindsay's novel of spiritual inertia, where glimpses of a true or transcendent reality are almost completely drowned out by triviality. A nighttime walk back to his house, after some time spent with Celia, the woman to whom he's grown close, causes Nicholas Cabot to slip into a philosophical frame of mind:

'Nicholas walked back by the road, as the short cut through the fields and spinney would be too dark. There was no moon, and the sky was already alight with liquid stars, which appeared larger and nearer than those seen in a town sky. His eyes were upturned for the greater part of the way home.'[20]

The lights of Mereway,[21] the house where he is staying, are on when he returns, a feeble counterpoint to the stars. Nicholas goes up to his room, and sits smoking by the open casement window. (An echo, perhaps of the casement window in the tower at Starkness Observatory.) The night is warm and still, and the darkness,

'solemnised his feelings… until he appeared to be the only living intelligence in the universe.

'Women, vanity, love, no longer occupied his mind. He reflected on his work, and wondered whether it were after all worth while! Those awful stars - all blazing suns - suggested by comparison the absolute insignificance and impermanence of the human race, and the consequent lunacy of the human quest for lasting fame, whether in art, science or any other sphere. The achievements of the greatest benefactor of terrestrial humanity could not by any possibility survive the decay or destruction of the earth itself, after which

---

18 The title of chapter 11 of *The Violet Apple*, the UK edition published by Sidgwick & Jackson. The US edition, published by Chicago Review Press, omits all chapter titles.

19 *Sphinx*, 43.

20 *Sphinx*, 169.

21 House names in Lindsay are a fairly good indicator of what you might expect to find inside. Needless to say, any house called 'Mereway' is bound to be a quagmire of petty concerns. See Sellin, ch. 2.

- in a few hundred thousands of years at the outside - the curtain would drop, and they would be as completely wiped out, forgotten, and without result as the chalk pictures of a pavement artist which might have existed twenty years ago!'[22]

Nicholas decides that, whether humanity dies out or migrates *en masse* to another planet, he must continue with his work; it is his only option.

'His own discoveries concerning sleep and death might eventually influence the moral laws and scientific forms of a population numbering, not millions, but billions, on the other side of the universe. His name would be lost, but the fruits of his audacity might survive! More wonderful still, his might be the creative idea which would succeed in bridging the twin-worlds of the living and the dead!'[23]

Sphinx contains one of the very few 'pleasant reveries' in Lindsay's work, when Nicholas goes for a walk in the woods to mull over the work he is doing on his dream machine, but then sees Evelyn and Maurice Ferreira 'scrambling through the tangle'. This is significant, as the dastardly Ferreira is effectively the villain of the piece, whose deceptions and manipulative behaviour form the novel's centre of gravity.

Evelyn uses Nicholas's machine on four occasions, and repeatedly dreams of being in the woods. She is not so much party to a transcendent reality, as she is seeing the true nature of her normal waking state:

'It was almost like being between walls, the trees were so thick, straight, branchless and tall. The intervening spaces were rendered impenetrable by the close tangle of underbrush... The ground was inches deep in loose, fine dust, which upon the slightest disturbance by her foot filled the air with its choking particles, having a peculiarly disgusting, acrid smell, like burnt rags. To a considerable distance above her head everything was in shadow, but above the tree-tops showed a pale blue sky, creating a singular impression of heat and discomfort. The whole atmosphere of her situation was one of perpetuity.'[24]

On another occasion, with 'the trees... closely-knit and impenetrable'[25] as ever, Evelyn sees another character, Lore Jensen, in a state of somnambulant distress. Ferreira is nearby, and Evelyn senses that Lore is in great danger. Ferreira is depicted as 'wearing ordinary clothes, but his face was the face of a *devil*.'[26] Ferreira's grin recalls the grin of Crystalman, the deceptive demiurge of *A Voyage to Arcturus*. Later, Evelyn senses that 'the quiet forest had an atmosphere as if an awful crime had been committed there. The acrid air felt polluted, so that it physically sickened her to breathe it... A leaden paralysis chained her to the spot.... the ideal world was ended, and reality had burst in to take possession.'[27]

In the final dream, Evelyn is able to break free of the imprisoning woods, and finds herself on a mysterious beach. The place has all the grandeur and otherworldliness of the Gap of Sorgie, but also a tangible magic: 'She had never known anything so mysterious and sacred;'[28] 'She was seeing all things through her heart.'[29] Despite

---

22 *Sphinx*, 170.

23 *Sphinx*, 170.

24 *Sphinx*, 148-9.

25 *Sphinx*, 186.

26 *Sphinx*, 187.

27 *Sphinx*, 212.

28 *Sphinx*, 274.

29 *Sphinx*, 275.

this, 'She was alone and bereaved there.'[30] The 'lonely savage, melancholy reality' clashes with the 'peculiar music' she is not so much hearing as breathing (finally being free of the acrid dust of the woods). She keeps 'pulling at the chains of her body'[31] as if she wishes to escape once and for all to the better place that she senses. Later (this is by far the longest dream in the book), Nicholas and Lore are there, on horseback, about to leave Evelyn to her fate - she must return to waking reality:

> 'The rhythm of the music became so pronounced that it seemed like the throb of a mighty engine, yet the theme was sad and majestic beyond description. The two horses bounded forward, unurged, into the surf. Nicholas looked straight ahead, but Lore turned back, to wave once more...'[32]

II Living Houses, Deceptive Houses

The tower at Starkness is one of several paradoxical buildings that await the perambulating Lindsayan protagonist. They are more than they appear to be, combining the near with the far, the inside and the outside, present and past, or this world and some other. (These combinations are like dreams, and are akin to the paradox that Maskull is, in some respects, walking towards himself.) Like any good paradox in a spiritual quest - for that is what Lindsay's books are, as are the journeys the characters take within them - they are dangerous paradoxes. Describing *A Voyage to Arcturus* as 'in reality, a long earth journey,'[33] Loren Eiseley notes that it is not 'a superficial tale of odd beings with odd organs on a planet remote from our own. This is not a common story of adventure. Rather, it is a story of the most dangerous journey in the world, the journey into the self and beyond the self.'[34]

In *The Haunted Woman* (1922), the upper rooms of Ulf's Tower are said to have been carried off by trolls,[35] and anyone who can access the tower's East Room, via a mysterious staircase that appears seemingly of its own volition, will have a vision of another reality, as much as Maskull did through the lens-like window at Starkness. This is what happens to Isbel Loment, the novel's protagonist, and Henry Judge, the older man she forms a relationship with, and with whom she enters the East Room. The world they see is the true one, in which they can perceive their true selves also.

Isbel's final meeting with Judge takes place in the grounds of Runhill Court. We see the scene from Isbel's point of view: approaching the house, she sees a woman walking, whom Isbel takes to be Mrs Richborough, a fusspot of an old dowager. But Isbel tells herself it can't be the older woman, as she died unexpectedly the previous night. Isbel follows the figure into the mist-shrouded parkland surrounding the house. She loses the older woman, but then suddenly finds that Mrs Richborough is standing next to her in the fog. Mrs Richborough confirms to Isbel that she is dead, and appears to have been walking with her eyes closed. Mrs Richborough vanishes, leaving Isbel shaking from head to foot.

Isbel becomes aware of a rhythmic, heavy pulsing (the drum beats from *A Voyage to Arcturus* in a new guise?), and then encounters Judge, who is in an equally unsettled frame of mind. He demands to know if Isbel has been into the East Room that day, and Isbel tells him that she hasn't. Judge then admits that he has been into the East Room, and has climbed out

---

30 *Sphinx*, 275.

31 *Sphinx*, 275.

32 *Sphinx*, 283.

33 Eiseley, vii.

34 Eiseley, viii.

35 *The Haunted Woman*, 40.

of the window into the grounds. For Judge, the day is bright and spring-like, seeing none of the autumnal fog that Isbel sees. Ishbel follows Judge into the fog, and finds herself on a sunny hillside. Runhill Court has vanished from sight, although Judge tells Isbel that, as far as he is concerned, they are still inside the house. Ahead of them is a musician dressed in archaic clothes. They have seen the man before, on earlier visits to the East Room, but have never seen his face. Until now. Isbel has the feeling that the musician is the centre point of the landscape, the figure around whom everything moves. The musician turns to face Judge. Isbel is too far away to see the man's features, but sees Judge instantly collapse and die. The sunlight disappears, and the cold, clammy fog returns.

In *The Witch* (published 1976), Morion House, the home of Urda Noett, *The Witch* of the title, is similarly between worlds. The protagonist, Ragnar Pole, feels himself drawn towards a meeting with Urda at her house, when she will give him a vision of heaven. Faustine Gaspary, a woman who likewise feels herself drawn to Ragnar, feels that such a vision should not be for the living to experience. (The face of the musician in *The Haunted Woman* is in some way similar, or the vision from the tower at the end of Arcturus.) Faustine has also dreamt of Morion House, and the sense of foreboding about the place is increased by Ragnar's brother Waldo, who also attempts to meet Urda at the house, but is refused entry. In the garden, Waldo sees a strange, very thin man, waiting by a tree. Waldo senses that the man represents death, specifically Ragnar's. When Waldo goes out into the garden, the man has gone, leaving in his place a fissure of darkness in the shape of a man. (The Gap of Sorgie in human form?)

Ragnar and Faustine, undeterred, call at Morion House in order for Ragnar to receive some kind of gnostic initiation from Urda. She is 'not at home' according to Mrs Toller, but 'I think she is out walking'[36]. Faustine feels that she should not enter the house, and Ragnar goes in alone. Mrs Toller remarks, 'It is a pity that Faustine Gaspary will not consent to see something of my house. It is not one of those old houses, and dead houses, her spirit abhors… It is a very living house… It is a deceptive house.'[37] (Mrs Toller's words could also be very apt descriptions of the body, the senses and the ego.)

Ragnar finds himself descending a gloomy staircase that soon becomes 'the terraced falling path of a hillside. The carpet had changed to rough, bare ground, that felt to his feet like rock and earth… He heard the noise of the trees softly bending under the wind. Certainly, he was not in a house, but out of doors again…'[38] Echoing the 'impossible' meeting between Judge and Isbel, Ragnar meets Faustine again 'outside', and the rest of the novel details the walk undertaken by Ragnar and Faustine towards Urda's real house, which is up on the Downs ahead of them. The world seems to fall away as spiritual truths envelop Ragnar the way the mist did to Isbel at Runhill Court. He becomes aware at one point that the tall, thin man Waldo had seen is pursuing them. Faustine manages to tell the man to go away, as it is not the right time for him to apprehend Ragnar. Urda is somehow controlling the landscape, but unlike the musician in *The Haunted Woman*, a confrontation with her does not imply physical death, but a rebirth. The novel ends with Ragnar on the threshold of Urda's house.

---

36 *The Violet Apple and The Witch*, 342.

37 *The Violet Apple and The Witch*, 343.
38 *The Violet Apple and The Witch*, 343.

The Gnostic

III A Quality in the Place

Devil's Tor (1932) was the last novel Lindsay published in his lifetime. It got the best reviews of his career, gaining the attention of J. B. Priestley, L. P. Hartley and Rebecca West, whose review of the book was perhaps the most sympathetic Lindsay received for any of his novels.[39] Sadly these did nothing to boost Lindsay's sales or income. (Unbeknownst to Lindsay, during the 30s, his work came to the attention of a small group of writers based in Oxford who called themselves The Inklings. Among their number were J.R.R. Tolkien and the figure who perhaps is Lindsay's most important early fan, C. S. Lewis.)

The opening of *Devil's Tor* describes a walk by Ingrid Fleming and Hugh Drapier across Dartmoor to see the tor of the title. They get caught in a fearful storm - 'neither day nor night, but a sort of ghastly dusk'[40] - and Ingrid admits she can feel 'uncanny presences' as they approach *Devil's Tor*, but what they are, she's not sure. 'Maybe our inadequate modern occult faculties no more than represent some atrophied sixth sense, then [in the deep past of prehistory] rich and splendid.'[41] Drapier agrees, telling Ingrid that 'I've spent too much of my life amongst mountains not to be well acquainted with their weird influence. It's one of the multitude of things a townsman remains ignorant of.'[42] I think we can be fairly certain both characters are expressing Lindsay's own views on, and experiences of, landscape.

Drapier 'had in mind how prolonged lingerings in solitary high places were wont to conjure up the phantom voices and sudden irrational panics. A nervous [for that is what Drapier mistakenly believes Ingrid to be] young girl would be peculiarly sensitive to the combination of loneliness, silence, wild Nature, skies, and altitude. Of course she would dream. The frame and content of her dreaming signified nothing. Only, she seemed to have a preference for this particular height for her rambles, and was that chance, or did it express a quality in the place? He was quite curious to see the Tor. She might even possess the second-sight, which was an authentic psychic gift. In the Scotch Highlands it still survived while in the black-wintered, troll-ridden Norway of old it must have been so common as to almost pass notice. The whole family regarded Ingrid as the typical Norse Colborne.'[43]

The storm worsens, with 'a solid wall of rain, descending vertically from the sky':

'They ceased talking to regard the entire sky in front of them being lit by a wavering blue glow, the effect of lightning above the low intervening clouds. The squall stopped as suddenly as it had come, and all the air was still, when a prolonged bass growl of thunder filled the silence like a solemn, supernatural voice. When they had heard it out, Ingrid commented soberly:
'That's the grandest music, after all.'
'Yes, it speaks straight to the soul' [Drapier said].'[44]

Lightning strikes *Devil's Tor* revealing a tomb, into which they descend, getting the plot underway. But not before Ingrid has experienced a typically Lindsayan moment. She has a vision, seeing for a split second a woman:

'During the rest of the evening and night she could never decide upon the character

---

39 See J. B. Pick, 'A sketch of Lindsay's life as man and writer', in *The Strange Genius of David Lindsay*, 24-26.

40 *Devil's Tor*, 21.

41 *Devil's Tor*, 12.

42 *Devil's Tor*, 12.

43 *Devil's Tor*, 12. Colborne is Ingrid's mother's maiden name.

44 *Devil's Tor*, 21.

of that vision. It had come and gone with the swiftness of thought. Yet only its speed and its nature had been unreal, otherwise it had transcended everything that she understood by reality. Whether it were some intuition of hers taking visceral shape, or absolute hallucination, or a hill-haunting, as a house might be haunted, or a personal apparition manifesting itself to her for a purpose, or a transformation by her faculties of some queer efflux from the Tor - she could not come to any peace or settlement about it.

'Looking towards that cavity where the monument had stood, she thought she had seen - no, she had seen - a woman, or, to be more exact, the upper half of a woman, of marvellous height, since her unseen lower limbs must have stood in some depression still deeper than the excavated bed, and her head was yet but little lower than Ingrid's own. She conceived that it had been a sudden rift in the white wreaths of fog which had opened and closed again that track of vision for her as far as the hollow, exhibiting the woman erect in its depth, facing her. And she had been clothed in dark-coloured clinging antique draperies, of no recognisable fashion,[45] but the wonder had been her flesh - and her beauty altogether - the full beauty of a beautiful woman expressed in supernatural terms, which made something totally different of it. Her face, neck and arms along had been bare, but the colour of these had resembled snow illuminated by moonlight, instead of the muddiness of human flesh. That face's beauty had been neither young nor old, living nor dead, but was set apart from all comparisons. It had been wise and tranquilly terrible, like a celestial's.

'Then, before Ingrid's amazement had had time to turn to the bristling horror that is the body's blind, ungovernable defence against all that comes suddenly upon it from an alien world, the phantom had been blotted from her sight by the thickening of the mists once more.'[46]

At such moments, the landscape reveals itself not to be a 'vast shadow house of earth and sky' but a *haugr*, an Old Norse word meaning 'hill, fell, burial mound or entrance to the world of the departed'.[47] Just as the mysterious staircase appears 'where it listeth' in *The Haunted Woman*, inviting the seeker to ascend to the East Room of Ulf's Tower and confront the true nature of themselves and the world; and just as Nicholas, with his dream machine in *Sphinx*, hopes to 'bridg[e] the twin-worlds of the living and the dead', so do the landscapes in *Devil's Tor* and *The Witch* become fairy hills, suddenly amid the rains, revealing the true world beyond. (I use the directional advisedly. It is above, beyond, behind, immanent, transcendent.)

Such revelatory walks were the stuff of Lindsay's own life, too. As his friend E. H. Visiak recalled:

... we were out for a walk, one night, in the countryside. Suddenly I was brought to a stand, arrested by the very strange aspect of the moon. It was at the full, bright, white, yet having a transparent, vacuous appearance, as if it itself was an orifice in space.

---

45 Old clothes signify the supernatural - the musician in *The Haunted Woman* wears them, as do Nicholas and Lore in the dream at the end of *Sphinx*.

46 *Devil's Tor*, 28-29.

47 Quoted in Robert Macfarlane, *Landmarks*, 177.

'Oh, just look at that moon!' I exclaimed. He was already looking up at it. 'White,' he murmured. 'White, empty.' His face looked wild and tragic, and he cried with startling emphasis, 'I ought never to have been born in this world!' I was amazed, but I said mechanically, 'In what world, then, ought you to have been born?' 'In *no* world!'

He went on urgently as if he were under a stress, a great urgent desire to express himself, to make me understand. I cannot recall his actual words, but they were spasmodic, disjointed, intensely passionate endeavours to express a yearning, an ideal, an antithesis, the unearthly, unimaginable contrast to normal experience, sense, sensation; the absolute negation of mundane conditions: an unthinkable and, to me, appalling state of arctic or extra-arctic abstraction. To himself, it was something pure, essential, ineffable - the Muspel, or 'Divine Light' of his *Arcturus* in its positive aspect, as inexpressible. I suppose, it would correspond to the Buddhistic *Nirvana*, with the great paradox, 'It is not this, and it is not that.'[48]

During the period in which Lindsay was trying to get a contract with Jonathan Cape, he was writing *The Violet Apple*. The book is set - significantly - at Easter. At the end of the book, protagonist Anthony Kerr, a playwright, goes for a walk in the woods. His life, and engagement to Grace Lytham, seem to be in tatters. This is in no small part due to his friendship with another woman, Haidee Croyland, a freer spirit than Grace, who pre-empts Anthony in eating the small apples supposedly from the Garden of Eden that provide them both with visions of another, transcendent, reality. Walking toward the woods, Anthony experiences 'bodily lightness'[49] and a feeling that 'everything combined to free his mind from... heavy sluggishness'.[50] Although his pride has been dented by 'the sudden mysterious failure of his artistic ideals and metaphysical flashes of insight [that eating the apple brought]'.[51] He is feeling well, and at something like peace. He vows 'to build up my life anew.'[52]

When Anthony reaches the trees, however, he recognises the landscape, although he has never been there before. It is the landscape of a watercolour 'in the style of Corot'[53] that hangs on the wall of Anthony's London flat. (A landscape known, significantly, as Wych Hill.) As in the painting, a quirk of the trees' branches forms a cross shape. Rather, it is not the branches that form the cross, but delineate the space around it. The cross is actually formed by the sky beyond. Like the Gap of Sorgie and the man in the garden at Urda's house, the ultimate reality is hinted at by an absence in this. Anthony realises 'that the sign should be a living sign for him - no mere dry historical memento of what had taken place in Palestine two thousand years ago, but something which existed at this very moment as a force, a surety, a prediction.'[54] The wind gets up, and 'it seemed to him that this sweet-smelling spring hurricane was trying to blow everything deathly and sepulchral out of him'.[55]

Haidee is in the copse, almost as if she had been waiting for him (although she claims she has not been). She too has experienced a feeling of lightness and renewed perception, when gazing at wild daffodils or 'a piece of gleaming

48 E. H. Visiak, 'Lindsay as I knew him,' in *The Strange Genius of David Lindsay*, 100-101.

49 *The Violet Apple*, 242.

50 *The Violet Apple*, 243.

51 *The Violet Apple*, 243.

52 *The Violet Apple*, 244.

53 *The Violet Apple*, 15.

54 *The Violet Apple*, 246.

55 *The Violet Apple*, 246.

polished copper'.[56] False or superficial beauty has 'nothing solid' about it, as 'it has no body'.[57] She too has seen the cross formed by the trees and feels that the moment is auspicious.

Resurrection, Lindsay seems to be saying, has to take place in this world of illusions, in the here and now. The sublime true reality, *the other*, can be glimpsed only, and that is perhaps enough. Anthony's and Haidee's previously thwarted relationship can now flower, and they leave the wood, vowing to get married and vowing to each other that they can 'continue to move *towards* the other, in full confidence that we shall never attain the full perfection in the body - though, let us trust, in another world.'[58]

*

This essay is dedicated with affection and gratitude to J.B. Pick (1921-2015), writer, critic, poet and Lindsay scholar extraordinaire.

'This is the hidden wood
Where all the lost birds sing.'

******

sean@891filmhouse.com

Bibliography

Julian D'Arcy, *Scottish Skalds and Sagamen: Old Norse Influence on Modern Scottish Literature* (1996). East Linton: Tuckwell Press.

Aldous Huxley, with a Foreword by J. G. Ballard, *The Doors of Perception and Heaven and Hell* (1994). London: Flamingo.

David Lindsay, *A Voyage to Arcturus* (1920). London: Ballantine, 1972, with an Introduction by Loren Eiseley; London: Allison & Busby, 1986.

, *The Haunted Woman* (1922). Edinburgh: Canongate, 1987.

, *Sphinx* (1923). New York: Carroll & Graf, 1988.

, *Devil's Tor* (1932). London: Putnam.

, *The Violet Apple and The Witch* (1976). Chicago: Chicago Review Press.

, *The Violet Apple* (1978). London: Sidgwick & Jackson.

, *Sketch Notes for a New System of Philosophy* (2015). Edited, with an Introduction, by David Power. Cleethorpes: EDP Projects.

Robert Macfarlane (2015). *Landmarks*. London: Penguin.

Colin Manlove (1994). *Scottish Fantasy Literature: A Critical Survey*. Edinburgh: Canongate.

Bernard Sellin (1981). *The Life and Works of David Lindsay*. trans. Kenneth Gunnell. Cambridge: Cambridge University Press, 2006.

J. B. Pick, E. H. Visiak and Colin Wilson (1970). *The Strange Genius of David Lindsay*. London: John Baker.

---

56 *The Violet Apple*, 247. Aldous Huxley makes pertinent comments about seeing the 'is-ness' of things in The Doors of Perception, while in Heaven and Hell, he describes the importance of shiny and luminous objects in visionary experience. See Huxley (1994), passim.

57 *The Violet Apple*, 248.

58 *The Violet Apple*, 251.

Jeremy Puma

Archons, Archons Everywhere!

Everybody loves the Archons. There's something almost romantic about having a metaphysical "Legion of Doom" on whom we can blame the idiocies of existence in the World of Manifestation. Although their ontological status remains a subject for debate (short answer: Maybe they're real, maybe not?), what I'd like to discuss now is their behavior– how we can investigate where they're found, how they act, and what it means to live in a world governed by a crowd of Cosmic Goons.

First off, let's start by recognizing that the idea of a singular, evil Demiurge has caused more annoying confusion within modern Gnostic thought than any other concept found in the myth. Is the Demiurge the same thing as Jehovah? Is Yaldabaoth identical to the various creators in the Hebrew Bible? This question leads to some serious ugliness, and I'd like to table discussion of the Demiurge for the moment. You see, we're more likely to deal with Archonic questions than those related to the Demiurge. After all, everybody knows that the real problems here in the World are always caused by some kind of committee.

And, that's what I think will be the most useful way to think of the Archons, for the most part– not as dark and sinister forces dry-washing their tentacles with glee while directing black-robed worshipers to nefarious deeds (although they could certainly act that way if they wanted to). Instead, it's best to think of the Archons as old white guys in Armani suits, sitting around boardrooms and coming up with ways the status quo can be made more 'efficient.' They're not Evil Tyrants; they're Career Bureaucrats.

As I've tried to underscore many times, the Archons aren't actual humans (and don't get me started on the "Archons are Extraterrestrial Aliens!" stuff). Instead, they're manifestations of universal qualities with a particular commonality– the commonality of creating limitations. What does this mean? Well, I've discussed elsewhere, traditionally the Archons were the rulers of Fate. This is why they were assigned to the planets and the zodiac, and why astrology was such a no-no within certain Gnostic circles. In classical, Sethian Gnostic thought, when you're ruled by the Archons, you're subject to the distinctions they've created between the qualities represented by, say, "Venus," and the qualities represented by "Jupiter," and the forces that manifest when those planets move through the signs of the zodiac. When, however, you've achieved gnosis, horoscopes don't work for you any longer. Or, rather, you use horoscopes to determine what not to do, not what will happen to you.

Thing is, this quality of creating limitations and distinctions then transfers to the movement of the heavenly spheres, which in turn becomes how we begin to measure time. When was the first Saturday? What is the measurement of the equinox based upon? These limitations aren't always bad; sometimes they're quite useful, if not downright essential. However, once created as firm distinctions, they become problematic when used by the Archons to maintain the status quo.\

This is the Archonic modus operandi:

1. Create a compartmentalization of some kind. It may be useful at first, like measuring the

seasons so we can plant and harvest. It may be arbitrary, like separating people by skin color or declaring national borders.

2. Impel that distinction, as a system, at all costs (Archons also represent impelled systems). Even if that distinction ends up killing lots of people, it's the distinction that's important, not the people. We see this a lot in bigotry and nationalism, lynchings and border wars.

3. If a new distinction becomes necessary, maneuver manifestations within the cosmos so that the outline looks different, but the contents remain the same. We're seeing this right now in the co-option of the "green" movement by the corporate world. The contents have changed ("Our Eggs Are Now Organic!") but the outlines remain the same ("You Have to Buy Eggs from Us/Trust Us!").

Again, I want to emphasize that many of these distinctions are useful. The Archons aren't evil, they just want to stay in power, and the best way to do that is by making sure everything stays the same.

So, how best to defeat these Powers? Thankfully, we're not totally helpless; we've got the Aeonic Powers on our side as models for aspiration. And, perhaps the most important tool in our toolbox, we've got Reason and Wisdom, which are activated by the simple act of asking questions. I'm not talking about just asking questions about little things, I'm talking about asking difficult questions and taking them as far as you can go. As an example, here are some of the ways we might consider asking questions that get us behind the machinations of the Archons and their plots:

1) Instead of asking, "are eggs good for me?", we ask, "Where do these eggs come from?"

2) Instead of asking, "am I happy with my job?", we ask, "what is wrong with the Protestant Work Ethic?"

3) Instead of asking, "why are we at war with this country?", we ask, "why are there countries?"

4) Instead of asking, "which of these corporations is the better one?", we ask, "what foundational problems do these corporations cause?"

5) Instead of asking, "why are orthodox/fundamentalists/other races so repressive/bad/different," we ask, "why are we so concerned about finding fault in others?"

This is what Jesus means in the Gospel of Thomas when he says, "Let him who seeks continue seeking until he finds. When he finds, he will become troubled. When he becomes troubled, he will be astonished, and he will rule over the All."

Notice that not all of these questions have answers; the fact is, we're stuck in the World of Limitations and are subject to those Limitations. Most of us have to interact with Archonic limitations in order just to get by. You've likely got to buy eggs, and clothes, and go to work to make money. There is no total escape from the Archons; this isn't a problem to eliminate, it's a problem to manage. However, instead of accepting these limitations as de facto aspects of life, we can change our attitudes towards them.

There are certainly practical benefits to doing so. I mentioned above that some limitations of time are based on planting seasons. Most religious festivals tend to mark these limitations and calendrical events, a process epitomized by (for example) the neopagan "Wheel of the Year." A lot of these seasonal/harvest festivals survived into traditional religious calendars as well (where would Lent be without Easter, and where would Easter be without the "renewal" of springtime?). However, this kind of celebration is directly related to the Archonic processes I mentioned above, which we can delineate as follows:

1) Humans realize that they can determine when best to plant/harvest/hunt based on the movement of the Sun, Moon and Planets. They create myths to help explain these things.

2) Humans codify these myths into a calendar system.

3) This calendar system determines mythical sociocultural rituals.

4) Most humans are no longer involved

in planting/harvesting, but mythical sociocultural rituals are maintained (status quo). Meaning shifts; there is a disconnect between survival/food necessities and myth. Outline remains the same but contents are different.

Now what do we have? We have impelled sociocultural cycles based on outmoded mythic limitations that have nothing to say any longer about planting and growing seasons for 9 out of 10 humans. And, since the climate is changing, the timing of planting and growing seasons will also be changing. If we want to get around the Archons, we should ask ourselves some questions. These questions are, do we want to be dependent upon outdated measurements for planting or growing? Do we want to depend upon systems employing these outdated measurements when they try to address these survival needs? Or, should we ask ourselves what we can do for ourselves to help be sure our needs are met sufficiently?

To put it another way: your myth tells you X, but your environment tells you Y. The Archons sell you things based on their understanding of X; how can you minimize your participation with X and maximize your participation with Y? Obviously, there are no easy answers, but the logical conclusion is that dependence upon traditional mythical tales AND dependence upon the modern systems based upon them will result in deficiency.

We need to reconfigure our myths in order to move forward successfully, and we may need to reconfigure our systems of measurement of planting/harvesting in order to survive a changing climate. To continue the metaphor, as the climate changes, your USDA Plant Hardiness Zone might be changing. As droughts increase in some areas and winter becomes harsher in other places, new patterns might be emerging that have nothing to do with the old calendars and the Archonic systems upon which they're based. And yet, the Archons, bureaucrats that they are, will insist upon trying to maintain the status quo and making change both difficult and procedural. Why go to a farmer's market when you can buy your organic greens from a company? Why grow your own greens, cheaply and according to your observations of your local environment, when you can have expensive greens out of season? Oh, you can have a garden, but you need to fill out the proper forms and be sure you're zoned correctly.

Listen: one of the best ways to understand how the Archons operate is to do a Google search for "Urban Garden Permit."

Keep in mind, this is the example as I've applied it, but the same Archonic methodology can be found in pretty much any walk of life. Whether literal or psychological, what we're doing is creating a language that will help us understand the processes inherent in the world of manifestations. In order to do so, and to find out where we can start asking some questions, we need to rewrite some stories.

So, let's identify some of the Archons and, recognizing that they work in committees and share duties, reconfigure our myth. Let's take some of the classical Gnostic figures and, based on their traditional planetary designations, determine what kind of worldly organizations they might be involved in.

In order to keep things simple, let's begin with the seven planetary Archons mentioned in the Secret Book of John. I've come up with a few specific examples of organizations that are ruled by each Archon, but just a handful you can use as examples and guidelines. Again, they work in committees- a company producing a new war game for your iPhone is influenced by Eloaios (Mercury, communications and technology) and Sabaoth (Mars, war and sports).

I also still want to underline that just because something is Archonic, doesn't mean it's BAD. I REALLY want readers to understand this. There are good people in all of these organizations, and these companies prduce things that can be incredibly helpful. It's the impelled limitations and systems represented by these companies that are Archonic, not the people who work for them or the products they produce. Regardless, this will help "put the face to the name," as it were, and may help us decide what questions we can start asking:

ATHOTH: THE MOON

As ruler of the Moon, Athoth rules organizations involved in religion, spirituality and occultism, health and psychology. Some of these organizations are, but are not limited to, restrictive religious communities and fundamentalist sects like ISIS, Scientology or the Taliban; pharmaceutical companies like Eli Lilly and Pfizer; insurance companies like Blue Cross, Kaiser Permanente, etc.

ELOAIOS: MERCURY

As ruler of Merucry, Eloaios rules organizations involved in communications, technology and transportation. Some of these organizations are, but are not limited to, Google, Comcast, AT&T, Facebook, Apple, Microsoft, etc. as well as Automotive Companies, Airlines, Cruise Lines, etc.

ASTAPHAIOS: VENUS

As ruler of Venus, Astaphaios rules organizations involved in agriculture and food production. Some of these organizations are, but are not limited to, Monsanto, Whole Foods, Kroger, factory farms and food producers, etc. as well as soft drink companies and conglomerates like ConAgra, General Mills, etc.

YAO: THE SUN

As ruler of the Sun, Yao rules organizations involved in energy, utilities and power (including, ironically, water), as well as entertainment. Some of these organizations are, but are not limited to, local utility companies, Exxon Mobil, BP, Chevron, Conoco-Philips, etc., and also Disney, Time Warner, 20th Century Fox, Universal Music Group, Sony, etc.

SABAOTH: MARS

As ruler of Mars, Sabaoth rules organizations involved in the military/defense, and professional sports. Some of these organizations are, but are not limited to, the Armed Services (any of them), Blackwater/mercenary organizations, Local militias, the NRA, as well as the NFL, the International Olympics Committee, etc.

ADONIN: JUPITER

As ruler of Jupiter, Adonin rules organizations involved in government. Some of these organizations are, but are not limited to, the House of Representatives, the Senate, the Supreme Court, the Executive Branch and its various Departments (you get the idea). Also, House and Condo Associations, City and Town Committees, school boards, etc.

SABBATAIOS: SATURN

As ruler of Saturn, Sabbataios rules organizations involved in finance and monetary concerns, as well as industrial manufacture. Some of these organizations are, but are not limited to, the International Monetary Fund, Bank of America, J.P. Morgan Chase, etc. as well as Dow, Dupont, Steel companies, machine manufacturers, etc.

This is obviously a limited and cursory overview, but should at least give the curious a place to start. Also, given that these seven Rulers also influence the forces associated with zodiacal signs, the curious researcher could divide their attributions even further. Indeed, using this as a guide, it's theoretically possible to sit down and come up with a grimoire of Archons and the companies and organizations they influence. This is, however, a project for a later time.

Andrew Phillip Smith

An Interview With Gary Lachman

APS: How would you describe your subject and your approach to it?

GL: My subject?

APS: In the broadest sense.

GL: I guess the essential thing most of my books revolve around is the evolution of consciousness, to be so bold, and I have one book called *A Secret History of Consciousness*, which is a more dramatic way to say it. But more or less I'm interested in looking at the value of different thinkers, the values of philosophers and spiritual seekers that have explored and examined and speculated on consciousness. They are generally dismissed by mainstream hard science or philosophy of mind schools, but there is a long history of what we can call alternative— but actually it's not really alternative, it's only more recent reductionist-materialist science of consciousness is really alternative; its a much more recent development. So the secret history of consciousness goes back quite a way. It's mostly about trying to link up and join up a variety of different thinkers and philosophers and writers and spiritual figures who have explored this other mode of consciousness, this more spiritual consciousness, and trying to find similarities between the different approaches and takes on it.

APS: Interesting, that wasn't quite the answer I was expecting, but I like your reply that it's about consciousness. How did that become your main focus?

GL: Well, when I say that, it covers a lot of ground, because I've written books about the occult, but when you say the occult that brings up certain connotations, and you also have to spend time explaining that you're not that. So I'm not a Satanist and I'm not into UFOs, and so on and so on. I have written quite a lot about that but that's mostly because many people involved in that have explored these other areas of consciousness from a magical, let's say, point of view. They come up with similar sorts of discoveries as someone from the philosophical or the artistic perspective does. I see no difference between these different approaches. Were you expecting me to say I write about the occult? Talking about Aleister Crowley, an occult figure, the most interesting thing I find about him is this period relatively early in his career when he's pursuing this kind of higher consciousness, he calls it "genius on tap" or something like that, induced genius, which he means as a kind of more intense, more powerful form of consciousness. This is relatively early in his career, but he's approaching this from a magical perspective, from studying different eastern techniques of meditation, yoga and that sort of thing as well.

APS: How would you, not necessarily give as a definition of consciousness, but how would you explain what the term consciousness means to you?

GL: Henri Bergson wrote something very simple that I wrote about in some of my books. I'm paraphrasing, but he said consciousness is something so immediate we don't really have a definition for it. Because once you start to look into it, its ramifications, its meanings, its different connections spread out and you lose an explicit definition of it. It's the difference between everyday consciousness, "I'm here, I'm a limited being, and there's this relatively stable, solid world outside me have to deal with, and I get through the day and my energy levels stay the same and every day is kind of the same, and it's relatively boring," but you have these moments sometimes where everything seems more vivid, everything seems more meaningful. You have a certain sense of a deeper significance, a strange kind of mystery happening in the background, and we call these sort of moments either poetic or aesthetic or mystical. So what's the relationship between the two, and what's happening? There's a very long culture in different parts of the world of using different varieties of plants to induce these states. There are cultures that use this more meditative approach to it. Sometimes they happen spontaneously, what Maslow called peak experiences. So I'm very interested in those, because they seem to me to bring a perception, not only a feeling but also a real perception, of a world that's much more interesting, and much more meaningful. And this is the everyday world that I'm encountering all the time, but suddenly I'm seeing it from this new more relational perspective. More of its living-ness, more of its actual being that I'm perceiving. And this is something that I think is tied in with our whole evolution, and I talk about an evolution of consciousness in quite a few of my books. One of the main ideas in the book I'm working on now is also a central idea in this kind of esoteric and mystical kind of culture, that at an earlier time, at a much earlier time in our history, human beings somehow walked closer to the gods; we had a more immediate and direct relationship to the spiritual. We had what one particular writer, Owen Barfield, called a more participatory relationship to the world. My relationship to the world now is between a very definite inner world that only I inhabit and this very definite outer world that is somehow alien and outside of me. But in these mystical poetical aesthetic states that separation breaks down. It becomes porous, and you have these experiences where you feel at one, where you feel that you're communicating with a tree or flower and so on, that sort of thing. So what's going on when that's happening? Many of these states are part of the occult and esoteric and magical, mystical, hermetic, tradition. In most of these traditions you do find a lot of exploration of those things that only relatively recently psychology is starting to look at.

APS: I won't spend too long on Crowley, but I remember you commenting in your biography that his life was a cautionary tale. That's something that comes over because you're writing not just about the ideas of all these people, but about their lives as well. How successful are all these psychic explorers at living what they're experimenting with?

GL: Different people have different lives. Someone like Aleister Crowley is a much more extravagant, wild, Dionysian guy compared to Rudolf Steiner, who's sobriety incarnate. He had a rather dull life—well, not really dull, but he is a much more sober, self-disciplined, controlled character. So they have different sorts of lives. Crowley, as I mention in the book I wrote about him, is a kind of cautionary tale because in one sense I have to congratulate him and thank him because he took a particular kind of approach to going beyond our immediate consciousness, our immediate experience of the world, and searching for some more intense way. He took a certain approach that we don't have to take any more, the road of excess, as William Blake says, "The road of excess leads to the palace of wisdom." Well, I'm not sure if it did in Crowley's case, but he certainly was on that road. If you know anything about him he was this remarkably versatile and talented, often brilliant, sometimes a genius character in the late nineteenth, turn of the century, into the forties of the last century. On top of being a poet he was a mountaineer and a master chess player, and a variety of other things as well. He was also a magician. He sort of pursued this antinomian path, which in many is kind of traditional in the western spiritual tradition, "antinomian" being beyond good and evil, beyond norms, breaking the taboos and breaking the laws, all that sort of thing, what people today call being transgressive. So Crowley was being very transgressive for his time, and he basically made a career of that. I think that one of the sad things is he also wasted some of his brilliance in this very habitual nose-thumbing to authority. But at the same time he did do remarkable things and he did modernise the whole approach to magic. He made it much more to do with the magician's own imagination and will and creative approach. But also Crowley had his own predilections, one of which was sex: sex and drugs. I did an earlier book, *Turn Off Your Mind*, which was about the 1960s, the occult revival of the 1960s. A variety of different occult ideas informed the pop culture of the 1960s, most notably in many ways in music culture. And Crowley s one of the figures that's on the cover of *Sgt Pepper's Lonely Hearts Club Band*, everybody knows that, so he was picked up at the same time. A lot of other people were as well. Madame Blavatsky for one: she was this wild Russian woman who started the Theosophical Society, in the late nineteenth century; C.G. Jung, the psychologist who was talking about the Age of Aquarius in the 1940s, writing books about flying saucers and things like that, he's also on the cover of *Sergeant Pepper's*. But when the sixties ended and we started to get a different kind of sensibility, that kind of mystical influence feeding into pop music and rock shifted a bit; it changed, people like Jung and Blavatsky and some of the others aren't really part of it any more, but Crowley stayed on. He was picked up by bands like Black Sabbath and heavy metal bands and so on and so on, and so the book is asking why? What is it that allowed him to become this idol in many ways, and the resurgence of interest in him as well, there seemed to be a few years back, whether it's still going on or not. Different rappers and people like Jay Z were getting into Crowley and so this franchise, this Crowley roccult and roll franchise is still going strong. One of the questions I pose in the book is, why is that? Why is that still going on? And obviously it has to do with this whole philosophy of success that makes you part of this rock or rap ethos, more so than in Crowley's life. I think that in many ways we should thank him for ploughing that route which sort of ended in a dead end. He ended up sadly a heroin addict. He had been one for many years, and died. All that kind of thing. So that was the moral aspect of that story, but there are other figures who don't come to such a disappointing end. Steiner, I'm not saying he was better than Crowley, but he started this movement called anthroposophy and now his influence has gone worldwide and its involved with the Waldorf schools and there's biodynamic farming and a variety of other initiatives at work in the world. So people's attractions change and peoples experience differs.

But it's a big universe.

APS: They're an interesting contrast the two of them, Steiner and Crowley.

GL: I'm not saying one is better than the other. Steiner himself was teetotal and celibate. Probably the most exciting thing happened in the early twenties when he was targeted by the early Nazi groups because he seemed to be in opposition. There's even a story of a gang going to one of his talks and having a shotgun and trying to shoot him. He had a bit of excitement but he wasn't a tearaway in the sense that

Crowley was.

APS: I've often felt with Steiner that when he applied himself to something practical he was a genius—there's the Waldorf schools, and you mentioned the biodynamics, and there are acting techniques that I've had a little involvement with, to do with voice production and so on. But when he didn't he was all over the place with his wild ideas.

GL: I think one of the sad things about Steiner is that the aspect of his work that he thought was the most important was that which was getting the least attention by the end of his life, and all the practical things were getting the most attention. He was very glad to have started the Waldorf schools and this school of architecture and all these other things, but he really felt that his most important contribution was this early philosophical work that he did, these epistemological books, a book of his called *Philosophy of Freedom*, but also work he did on Goethe, who influenced Steiner immensely. There's sort of a tragedy there as well. When I've written about Steiner that's the aspect I've concentrated on the most because that's the area I'm most interested in, which is Steiner's ideas about consciousness. He has a whole system, a whole way that he sees this notion of an evolution of consciousness, how consciousness itself, both in the individual and in the species, changes all the time. So this is something that I found very interesting about Steiner, that kind of idea.

APS: I don't know what kind of reception your biography of Crowley got, but I found it very sympathetic in general. Also, I particularly enjoyed your critique of the concept of Will in Thelema, being an essentially passive thing.

GL: It does seem like that to me. It does seem that it's more like the Dao. Again, it's not necessarily wrong, It's more the line of least resistance, to find your path. Crowley really just wanted to be left alone. He's a libertarian and it's interesting that one of the last writers that he got excited about was Ayn Rand. He read *The Fountainhead* and really liked it. That's a very interesting connection between two radically different public images, this crazy magician and this deeply conservative capitalist philosopher. He basically does want to be left alone and do what he wants and basically things go wrong when somebody else tries to get involved. "I'm following my will!" That's one thing I found a bit indulgent about it. You say I'm sympathetic, and in many ways I am, but I'm also very critical and if you take people seriously you have to give them your full intelligence. I'm just as critical about Crowley as many people I've written about, like Steiner and like Ouspensky, Blavatsky, Jung, Swedenborg. I do appreciate them personally, but at the same time you need to do them justice. Its the kind of thing they would do themselves, I think. The reception? Well, there's one-star reviews on Amazon and five-stars. I think the people who liked it liked it because it's fresh and new and it's not reverential. More about telling a story and looking at the ideas than looking at what he had for breakfast one morning or some other secret thing. So it's a critical biography. I'm taking his ideas and his life seriously in the context of other people like Jung or Gurdjieff or Steiner and so on. In many ways I think it's a shame and I think he was his own worst enemy. I think he had a lot of good ideas. I don't think Thelema was, and the *Book of the Law* thing was a problem, but this was his main thing. I like the scientific illuminism period of his when he was experimenting with drugs and meditation techniques and different sorts of ways of changing consciousness. Even at that point he's actually unsure about the use of drugs because he wants to know, as a good scientist does want to know, whether these experiences are objective or not. Whether these dimensions of reality, whatever you want to call them, whether the kind of consciousness that he's entering, have a real objective existence or whether they're just the affect of the drug. For a long while he hummed and hawed about it. Obviously he decides the drugs are okay, but it just shows that he actually did develop his ideas. He did have a scientific approach to these things, it's just that it's a shame that he had this stupid adolescent personality that got in his way most of the time. But this is also true of quite a few of these people. Alan Watts is like that too, as far as I could tell. There's something about the gurus of liberation that, looking back at them now, from the perspective of being interested in this stuff over forty years, I've been finding some of their methods and approaches questionable, put it that way.

APS: We can move on to Revolutionaries of the Soul. I particularly enjoyed discovering about figures I didn't know very much about. Owen Barfield and Jean Gebser are two of them, figures who get a bit lost in the margins. They're not quite in the world of esotericism and not quite in the world of respectable philosophy.

GL: Well, you're right. They're on this border. Barfield was in the Steiner world because he was an anthroposophist, but he was a writer in his own right. He was good friends with C.S. Lewis and Tolkien—he was part of this group who were called the Inklings who used to hang out at that pub in Oxford and talk about literature and so on, and he wrote a wonderful book in the 1920s called *History of English Words* and it investigates this notion of an evolution of consciousness, but looking at it through language, how the use of words or the meaning of words, the kinds of words and so on, how they reflect and embody different kinds of consciousness. It's a very brilliant book. He's a very interesting character. I had the very good fortune of actually meeting him when I first came to London in 1996. He was about 98. I think he died the next year or the year after. I went to visit him. He was living in East Grinsted, not far from Emerson College, which is a Steiner-based or anthroposophical-based adult education centre that's been there forever. He was wonderful. I spent an hour with him, talking. A couple of article on him including the piece in the book came from that interview with him.

Jean Gebser is another. He's a philosopher from the central-European, German tradition of Hegel and Heidegger and Spengel and all these cultured mandarins of the intellect. Barfield's fairly well represented in English-speaking countries because obviously he wrote in English but Gebser is not as well represented here. His major work, *The Ever-Present Origin*, was written in the forties, it was translated into English in the eighties, and I think that's just about all of his work that has been translated into English—there might be a few more pieces. But it's a remarkable study. He didn't use the term evolution he talked about different mutations of consciousness. He has ideas of different structures of consciousness.

The general narrative of most of these, if not practically all of them, is really this notion that at some earlier time our consciousness was much more participatory with the world around us. We didn't have this strict separation and were more connected to the source, the spiritual source. Gebser calls it "origin". But over time consciousness has moved away from that and become more concrete, more separate in our own period, which Gebser calls the "mental-rational structure" which began, he says, some time around 1250BC. Funnily enough there were other things happening around that time, so he might be right. There was the separation that characterises the mental-rational structure. We see the world outside as something outside, as something distinctly, inescapably outside, a screen that is hard and impermeable and not alive. Nature, we know is alive, and needs water and so on, but it's not alive in the way that we are, it doesn't have an inside. In this earlier kind of consciousness we were more aware of the inside but we were less... our inside and nature's inside were one inside, basically. We shared an inside but now we have our own. According to most schools of thought that separation was necessary to develop our own individual separate consciousness. It's an evolutionary benefit. Even though we still like the idea of group minds, separate egos have an evolutionary benefit. there's more potential for it. Mostly because it has to work harder in order to survive, and that increases creativity and novelty and so on. So there's good reasons why we've fallen out of paradise. At the same time all these things begin as advantages but as they develop completely towards their last stage they become something of a handicap and so that sense of separateness that characterised the modern structure of consciousness has gone as far as it can go, has exhausted its possibilities. He died in the early seventies but he believed we were on the brink of a change It's beginning to break down and he provides an enormous amount of evidence in the arts and science, from religion and philosophy, from sociology and so on and so on, that suggest that he's on to something. He did see this other structure emerging which he called the integral which in some way unites and integrates the previous structure—there've been three previous structures before the one we're on now, and the integral's the fifth. I won't go into detail about those. He's great, but he's not that well known. Ken Wilber's written about him a bit. I have. Georg Feurstein wrote a good book on Gebser. What I like about people like Barfield and Gebser is that, as you say, they're on the margins. They're not occultists, they're not spiritual teachers, they're thinkers,

they're philosophers, they're asking questions, they're applying their minds to questions of human existence. Their approach isn't based on matter, it is based on consciousness being primary, it's based on what we would call the spiritual, the non-material aspect of our existence being primary, rather than the current mainstream view which is the opposite. It sees some form of matter, some form of material kinds of things as primary, and it experiences the subjective in the world as some kind of epiphenomenon, something that doesn't have reality in itself, it's some kind of result given off by some other thing. This is relatively new. Some of the Greeks had ideas about that, Democritus and some people like that, but throughout most of western history that idea didn't hold and it started to take a real hold in the early 1600s. In the book I'm working on now I recognise that it has been about 400 years since the mental-rational structure has gone into the tail-end of its deficiency mode. This sounds incredibly abstract but basically it starts to go into its deficiency mode some time about the start of the Renaissance but things accelerate and you have around the beginning of 1600 the demise of the western esoteric tradition which had been around for millennia, going back to Pythagoras. Its most influential exponent was Plato and yet you have the demise of this tradition at this point and you have the rise of the kind of science that we look to today for the answers about life and all that. So it's been about 400 years and I think Gebser was right. I think you can see quite a few things that suggest this particular mode of being in the world is starting to break down. They're not all fantastic things but certainly within, say, science itself, the early twentieth century the early quantum theory and relativity the whole idea of matter goes out of the window. Atoms aren't these hard little billiard balls knocking against each other, they become these things we can't even talk about in our language. We refer to them through mathematical equations. Similarly in other aspects of western culture there's a similar process of unravelling going on. So I'm glad I was able to include him in that collection and his ideas have a central place in this book I'm working on now.

APS: And what's the name of the current book you're working on?

GL: My current book is called *The Secret Teachers of the Western World*. I've mentioned it a few times but I don't really want to talk about it because I'm still writing it. That's coming out later on this year, probably in the Fall. It's basically an overview of this kind of tradition. From people like Pythagoras up to relatively contemporary times.

APS: Then you have a book on Colin Wilson that you're working on?

GL: Yeah, then I'll be starting this book on Colin Wilson relatively soon after that. His books have influenced me a great deal. Probably one of the first books I read about any of these things is his book *The Occult*. It came out in 1971, I think I read it in 1975 and it's still a very, very good read. He's such a good writer, he makes all these things really interesting. And he has exciting ideas. For me I didn't have any interest in it until I read that book. I was interested in literature and philosophy. I read a lot of the eastern studies by Alan Watts and people like that. The occult per se I wasn't particularly interested in but Wilson talked about it in the context of literature and philosophy and science and history and he made it intellectually acceptable and also he had his own ideas about consciousness, because he linked the occult to this more intense form of consciousness that is basically the centre of all of his work. He has written about many different things, many different books, but they're all more or less focused on this question that I spoke about earlier. We have this everyday more or less average form of consciousness and then every now and then we have these moments when either something excites us or in some way we relax, something switches and suddenly things seem much more interesting and important and precious and special and we have this sense of "oh yes", a sense of remembering something that we new all along that was so obvious, how could you forget it? All of his work from his first book *The Outsider* which came out in 1956 to one of his last books called *Superconsciousness* which came out in 2008 is about this, basically. About being able to understand and induce these states at will. I can't go into great detail about it now but the essential thing is concentration, this focusing of the mind, and that is very different than what Crowley was doing. It's a different approach.

APS: Yes, I interviewed Colin Wilson around the time of *Superconsciousness*. We had a long essay about his Occult trilogy too. He's somebody who I read early on in my late teens, *The Outsider* and *The Occult* and so on, and then I thought of him after that as a bit of a dilettante and it's only in the last few years that I've read more of his output, and come back to him. He seems to be somebody who makes sense on his own terms. If you try to understand him in reference to the Gurdjieff Work or to the occult or whatever he doesn't quite make sense but if you look at his life on his own terms it does make sense.

GL: I've always found his ideas to make sense. All of his ideas on the occult and the mystical made sense to me because he talked about it in relation to consciousness. He relates it to the same concerns as books like *The Outsider*, these existential questions about meaning and this affirmation of consciousness, this yea-saying. I'm looking forward to doing the book because I've written about him, I've written articles and essays and his ideas come into my books but I'll have some space to stretch out as it were and really get to say why I think he's important. I think he was one of these people who had written too much—and for people like me that's not a problem because I enjoy reading him— but I can see that people coming to him and saying that he's written all these books, he writes about anything, they're different. There's books on the occult, there's books on crime, there's books on literature, on philosophy and so on, but there is an essential core idea linking them all together which has to do with questions of existentialism like freedom, the experience of freedom, which he links to consciousness and to the more expansive forms of consciousness that are associated with mystical and occult experiences. To someone like myself who's read all of his books and re-read quite a few of them I see him as an integrated whole and that's why I'm looking forward to doing the book, to be able to get that down. One of the things I like about doing these kinds of books on people like Jung or Colin Wilson or Steiner is that you get to say, "What do I get out of them?" and it's good to have the chance to do that because you can get done with them to some degree. I try to cover all the important stuff, but they're not biographies in the sense of trying to get as much information as possible. I basically want to get the ideas down and one way of doing that is writing it for somebody else to understand. In other words to communicate their life to make them clear to myself. They don't cover everything, so there's certain aspects of Jung that I focus on, certain aspects of Steiner and Swedenborg and so on. If you read all my books you would see that they're all connected.

APS: Yeah, that's something that I found interesting as well in *Revolutionaries of the Soul* is that several of these figures you've written articles about them, entire books about them and then they pop up again in something like Politics and the Occult. Do you find your understanding of these figures changing as you address them from different angles?

GL: Well, there's different aspects of their careers. With someone like Swedenborg I wrote an article—the one that's in *Revolutionaries of the Soul*—for *Fortean Times* and that focused on his scientific work. Only at the end do I mention the visitation by Jesus and Heaven and Hell. There's another article on Swedenborg that I wrote for an American magazine called *Gnosis* that was around in the nineties, edited by Richard Smoley and Jay Kinney, which focused on his trip to Heaven and Hell. So these characters are big enough to have different perspectives on. So in *Politics and the Occult* I looked at these people from the political angle, which doesn't come up in most of the other books. I did a book called *A Dark Muse* which is looking at this occult tradition

APS: Yes, I really enjoyed that one.

GL: and writers who were influenced by it in the last couple of centuries. One of the challenges of the book I'm working on now is that I'm addressing some of these people again, others I haven't before, that are new, but because it's a history you do have to cover people. So it's bringing up people and placing them in a different context. The other thing I always enjoy is tracing things back because by now I've been writing about this for quite some time but when I first started doing it a lot of the research was fresh and "this is interesting, him too" and you see these connections between people. That's one of the things that happened with me with Swedenborg. When I was doing *A Dark Muse* a lot of the writers I was looking at were influenced by Swedenborg so I thought I'd find out what he was about.

APS: With the current book you're meeting certain of these figures again following another thread through history. I have to say that in *Revolutionaries of the Soul* one figure I find difficult to find sympathetic is Julius Evola. How do you feel about him in general?

GL: Well, he's not one of my favourites. I don't share his political orientation. He's interesting. He's brilliant. He writes insightfully. He has peculiar twists on things and he sees things from a particular perspective that I don't share. This idea which I guess goes back to theosophical notions of human history, where he talks about a prehistoric solar race that lived in the North in Hyperborea and these were the Aryans, and they were the noble superior types and they somehow had to go down to the south and they mixed with these southern Lemurian types who were more feminine. In one sense I find it interesting because aside from the obvious racial stuff, which is so obvious that it doesn't bear talking about, it is interesting that he does portray them as this duality which is an idea that I have been looking at recently a lot. This polarity. He sees it on a very speculative historical or prehistorical basis. I don't care for his semi-fascistic politics, but again he is an intelligent writer. I think many of his critiques of western society are spot on. I don't care for many of the cures that he suggests. He's somebody that I think you need to read seriously, not just dismiss him as a loony. I'm repelled by this spiritual or esoteric racism in many ways that he portrays. I was glad to have an opportunity to write about him and I wrote about him a bit in Politics and the Occult as well. Out of this Traditionalist school that he's more or less associated with he's one of the more readable. I've always found him more readable than someone like René Guenon or Fritjof Schuon. What I like about Evola is he's more contemporary. He died in the 70s so in some of his later writings he's writings about the Beatniks, he's writing about the drug culture, about all that stuff that became the counterculture and became part of popular culture later on and there's a lot of acute social commentary coming from him. I think he's a very astringent, sharp thinker but I don't care for his basic background metaphysics and stuff like that. And he knows a lot. He knows a great deal and he seems to have read a lot. One thing is a book that he contributed to that's called *An Introduction to Magic*. It's an anthology of different articles in this magazine that he wrote in the twenties and there's some really interesting things. So it shows that stuff was going on elsewhere. Evola is around in the twenties and Crowley is around in the twenties so Crowleyean magic wasn't the only magic that was happening then and Evola's magic was different too. It's more Hermetic-based and it isn't based on kabbalah or Egyptian religion. So within the world of magic and the occult and all that he's an interesting flavour but not to be taken in large amounts.

APS: Maybe a bit like the Ezra Pound of the occult world.

GL: Yeah, more or less like that.

APS: I think we'd better wrap up.

GL: I hope you got something out of this.

APS: I enjoyed it, thanks Gary.

GL: My pleasure.

APS: I look forward to the current book.

GL: Yeah, I look forward to it myself!

Stevan Davies

Spirit Possession, Pentecost and the Foundation of Christianity

Pentecostal Christianity is a form of spirit possession, which is a common form of human experience. Spirit possession is found throughout the world from China to Africa to Brooklyn, New York, is practiced by many utterly different cultures and probably is a function of everybody's genetic potential. Whether it is manifested depends on cultural conditions. Spirit possession is an experience wherein one feels that one's primary ego or self has been set aside, turned off, or subordinated and a different ego or self has temporarily taken its place. The replacement ego often has poor control of one's physical being and so one lurches, stumbles, falls down, speaks incoherently. The experience gives pleasure, during and after, generates a feeling of importance, and is sui-generis and self-confirming. You know you had it because you had it, you were happy to have had it and your community agrees that you had it. For a while, anyway, your friends in the community regard you as a temporary incarnation of God. In most cultures the spirit experience is brief. The supernatural being comes into people and leaves again, but the Christian movement decided that the spirit came in and did not leave; its activity was sometimes manifested but mostly it remained quiescent.

Spirit possession may be understood as a function of one's internal psychological makeup and to arise from one's own unconscious mind. It can be classified as a dissociative psychological state. Or spirit possession may be understood to be an external supernatural being entering into one from the outside. Spirit possession is presumably cognate to demon possession in terms of psychological functioning, but the two experiences differ in major and obvious ways, with the spirit-defined experience being pleasurable, constructive and socially encouraged, the demon defined experience being displeasurable, damaging and socially condemned.

It would seem reasonable to agree with Luke (cf. Acts 2:1-33) that Christianity began when the associates of Jesus experienced possession by what they believed was the Holy Spirit. When Jesus' associates began to experience possession of a positive sort, they presumed that they were possessed by the same being Jesus had been possessed by, with whom Jesus was identified.[1] As did participants in the Azusa Street revival of 1906 in Los Angeles, the foundation of modern Pentecostalism, evidently many of the associates of Jesus found themselves able to induce the same experience in other people, some of whom also were able to induce the experience.[2] This led to an almost exponential expansion in membership.

The experience of spirit possession is theologically interpreted all over the world as being the experience of becoming a supernatural being. In Nigeria, Cuba, Belem and New York you become one of many Orisha deities. In

---

1 This leads to all sorts of conceptual complications, cf. e.g., Rom. 8 passim.

2 I have no idea how you bring about possession experiences in large numbers of other people who never have had the experience beforew, but thousands of active Pentecostal missionaries do know.

China you may become an ancestor. In Korea a supernatural General. In the Christian movement you might define the experience as that of the Holy Spirit of Jesus Christ the Son of God, but exactly whom you become at this point was not clearly defined. [3] Was it Christ (Gal. 2:20), or the Son of God (Gal. 4:6), or Jesus (Mark 13:6), or the Paraclete, or just a generic Holy Spirit, and how many of them were there (1 Cor. 12)? It doesn't matter for this argument; the fact is that Christianity became a pentecostal religion featuring the transmission of an experience both important and pleasurable believed to be the Holy Spirit. It doesn't even matter for this analysis whether there is such a thing as a Holy Spirit. The experience is real and measurable; it is testified-to by an eyewitness (Paul) who believes it to be fundamental to Christian communities, and Luke believes it to be the foundational event of the Christian movement. I think that Luke was right.

If Luke was right about this, there are interesting implications for historical Jesus questing. For one thing, Jesus becomes almost, but not quite, irrelevant to the foundation of Christianity. There was no necessity for the earliest Christians to pay significant attention to Jesus.

By analogy, in recent times the Pentecostal movement pays little or no attention to William Seymour, the minister responsible for the Azusa Street revival in 1906. They don't worship him, they don't study his teachings, they don't recite his life story, few Pentecostal Christians have ever heard of him. The founder of the movement[4] is not necessarily a focus of the movement.

By turning one's attention to the event of Pentecost and the spread of Spirit experience as the foundation of Christianity, one can see how the early members of the movement might not have had any particular interest in the life story of Jesus before his final week, and no interest in supposed sayings of his that later would be said to constitute his "teachings." The experience of the Holy Spirit dwelling within one is enjoyable, empowering, transmissible, self-affirming, and it is one on which solid and beneficial communities can be easily constructed.[5]

The Spirit experience can be used to confirm pneumatological, soteriological, Christological and theological theories and doctrines, as Paul knew quite well.[6] He writes to the Galatians "I would like to learn just one thing from you: Did you receive the Spirit by the works of the law, or by believing what you heard? Are you so foolish? After beginning by means of the Spirit, are you now trying to finish by means of the flesh? Have you experienced so much in vain—if it really was in vain? So again I ask, does God give you his Spirit and work miracles among you by the works of the law, or by your believing what you heard?" (3:2-5). Thus an experience, understood to be the Spirit, confirms Paul's teaching. Since the experience is self-evident to those who have had it, so the truth of the teachings should be self-evident. This line of reasoning is used in Pentecostal churches today.

And in Pentecostal churches you get free health care! Jesus was an exorcist-physician (cf. Mark 1-8 passim) and his immediate associates, some (Luke 8:2) or all of them, had

---

3 Raymond Brown, in *The Gospel According to John XIII-XXI*, Anchor Bible 29A Doubleday 1970 writes "John presents the Paraclete as the Holy Spirit in a special role, namely, as the personal presence of Jesus in the Christian while Jesus is with the Father," p. `1139.

4 I do not want to hear about Charles Parham, thank you, who by analogy was William Seymour's John the Baptist if he was anything.

5 Examples can easily be found throughout the world of small solid beneficial Pentecostal communities. Take a walk on the poor side of your town and you will find some. Drop in. It isn't likely you will shortly find yourself possessed by the Holy Spirit, but it's not impossible.

6 The Johannine epistles show that this led to trouble in the churches, for the Spirit in some people revealed truths that were false in the opinion of the Spirit in other people.

found healing through his spirit's power over their unclean spirits. Now others could receive healing through the spirit; this sort of healing became a fixture in the churches, and it is so today.

Before the day of Pentecost, Judean experience with people possessed by a Holy Spirit was limited to occasional extraordinary personages labeled prophets. Even if hundreds of years prior to Pentecost there were schools of prophets wandering about causing difficulties for their betters, there never had been communities of prophets, communities of men and women, Jews and Greeks, slaves and free all being prophets together. Especially there were no gentile prophets. But whatever it was that enabled the rapid and successful transmission of the spirit experience from one person to others, it included both sexes, all social classes, and gentiles. Especially gentiles, primarily gentiles. Something had obviously changed. In fact, since the mass availability of spirit experience was the core of their religious movement, early Christians knew that something of central and crucial importance had changed. In A.D. 25 there were perhaps half a dozen prophets loose in Palestine and now, A.D. 45 there are hundreds. Why?

Back to the Bible. It is Luke's view (Acts 2:33), as expressed by his Peter character just after Pentecost, that "Exalted to the right hand of God, Jesus has received from the Father the promised Holy Spirit and has poured out what you now see and hear." If Jesus' immediate followers experienced Holy Spirit possession, and what initially combined them into a community was their mutual association with Jesus, and something radical had happened to change the divine dispensation vis a vis their spirit experiences subsequent to Jesus' death, it seems reasonable to agree that they thought Jesus had something to do with it. Raymond Brown writes, "If the Father gives the Paraclete at Jesus' request, the Father gives the Holy Spirit to those who ask him (Luke ix 13; also I John iii 24, iv 13). In Titus iii 6 we hear that God has poured out the Spirit through Jesus Christ. If both the Father and Jesus are said to send the Paraclete, the Holy Spirit is variously called the Spirit of God (1 Cor ii 11; Rom viii 11, 14) and the Spirit of Jesus (II Cor iii 17, Gal iv 6; Philip I 19)."[7] We might be wise to consider the foundation of Christology to be Jesus' presumed role in sending the Spirit and not speculation about the soteriological purposes of his death and resurrection, or instances when individuals believed they had visionary experiences of him risen.

Jesus died and subsequently had nothing to do with anything, one would normally assume. And yet there was the puzzling report that the tomb into which his body had been placed was empty when female followers came to it later on. Logically, if the divine dispensation has changed so that now the Holy Spirit is available to anyone and this fact is being manifested increasingly often, and this circumstance is related in some way or other to Jesus, who was the prototype for the experience later enjoyed by his associates and their associates etc., it might be the case that this spirit, formerly Jesus' spirit, is now being sent to all of us by Jesus. If so then necessarily Jesus is not dead, but alive and in a position to send the spirit. This is all entailed in the notion that Jesus received from the Father the promised Holy Spirit and has poured it out to us. It must be coming from somewhere, and God's long established practice of sending the spirit to individual eccentrics on an occasional basis has clearly been superseded by something else.

You can see where this line of thought would lead. If there is now mass availability of the Holy Spirit (self-evidently the case for those involved), and if we agree that this is due to the late Jesus sending it, it must be the case that Jesus rose from the dead and ascended into heaven in order to send it. If so, then the rise of pentecostal Christianity may have preceded (if only by a few months) the idea of the resurrection.[8]

---

7 Raymond Brown, Ibid. pp. 1139-40.

8 In accord with this, the empty tomb story is rather similar in all our sources and not farfetched, while

Pentecostal Christianity, believing that Jesus was newly appointed to send the Spirit did not logically need to have had any particular interest in Jesus' life story. There would have been, at the outset, no need for miracle stories or stories of resurrection appearances. Indeed, the idea of a corpse coming out of the grave and walking the earth is not by any means an idea most people would have found attractive and certainly did not form the basis for a successful religious communitarian movement. Nobody seems to have taken much interest in the exit of Lazarus from the tomb, or the plethora of the living dead who walked in Jerusalem at the same time that the risen Jesus did (Matthew 27:51b-53): "The earth shook, the rocks split and the tombs broke open. The bodies of many holy people who had died were raised to life. They came out of the tombs after Jesus' resurrection and went into the holy city and appeared to many people." It is a puzzle that scholars in modern times so often think that news of a corpse come back to life would have been regarded as happy tidings to first century folks. In every culture people prefer the dead to stay dead and not come back to walk among us.

The Holy Spirit experience is self-confirming and a strong argument in favor of any doctrines connected with it. The logic of the situation would have been "we know Jesus is now divine because he sends this experience to us and after you have had the experience you will thereby be able to confirm what we say." What does it mean, though, to know that Jesus is divine? If he is delegated to send the Holy Spirit of God to whomever he pleases (and he is easily pleased) he cannot just be an ordinary guy who happened to be at the right place (Jordan River) at the right time (a particular baptizing) to receive the columbamorphic Spirit.[9] Beginning with the conviction that the Spirit of God now comes to all of us through Jesus, speculation as to the nature of Jesus' special divinity would certainly follow.[10]

If Jesus was thought to send the spirit, therefore necessarily to have risen from the dead, early speculative Christian thought would have pondered the way in which he was divine, for the Holy Spirit of God must necessarily be sent by some form or other of God. Son of God perhaps? So the early, if not immediate, attribution of divinity to Jesus should not be surprising, given his role in the new divine dispensation. Indeed, since his "teachings" during his life evidently had nothing to do with his role in sending the spirit and since, so far as we can tell, without the eyes of faith to guide us, he didn't have anything particularly interesting to say, it does stand to reason that speculations about Jesus' divinity and his divine role in the scheme of things would precede speculations having to do with any teaching program that might be ascribed to him.[11]

The divine Jesus was evidenced in the

---

the accounts of Jesus seen alive after his death are completely unrelated (near Emmaus, on a mount in Galilee, into a locked room in Jerusalem, on the shore of the sea of Galilee, to five hundred brothers simultaneously) and are obviously fictional.

9 Interesting sidelight: pillars in Saint Peter's Basilica depict the Spirit in the form of a dove of the species Columba livia.

10 Their speculations in this regard vis a vis Jesus became normative over the centuries and obviated any need for similar speculations vis a vis William Seymour.

11 The most common modern notion of Jesus the Teacher is that he predicted the end of this world, that he was an eschatological prophet with an apocalyptic message. As nothing of what he predicted happened, and most of what he is said to have predicted sounds very nasty indeed (e.g. Mark 13:9-27, Luke 17:26-35) , it is hard to think why anyone would believe that a major religious movement would have emerged as a consequence of those supposed teachings. Today his most renowned teaching is to love one's neighbor as oneself, which is a quotation of Leviticus 19:18.

pentecostal experiences. If this entails his resurrection, then, if we are possessed by his spirit, we are possessed by one a sinless new Adam who died and rose again and, accordingly, since what is true of the one we have become through possession is true for us (which is the fundamental axiom of spirit-possession), we too are sinless, have already died, and will rise again. Or so Paul would have us believe. Paul shows understandable confusion vis a vis the distinctions between Christology and Peneumatology and Theology made by Trinitarians of later centuries (cf. Romans 8). If Jesus sends us the spirit, which is the Spirit of God, which he had and was, and he is the Christ and the Son of God, then since we are possessed we are Jesus, dead and risen, and the Son of God, and Christ, and for that matter, we receive the Spirit of the One who raised Jesus from the dead. The Holy Spirit is an explanatory hypothesis for a type of mass dissociative experience and one ought not expect such a hypothesis to be fully coherent at the beginning of the movement.

As time went on, given that Jesus was once alive and now is God, or is with God, or is an agent of God or something of that sort, people eventually did begin to think that he must have had some interesting things to say during his career as an exorcist even though nobody at the outset was thinking in terms of "Jesus the Teacher" at all. But stories did develop. People with agendas (Q, Thomas, Mark, Matthew) constructed lists and then narratives in order to insist that their agendas were Jesus' own. But since Jesus probably had no teaching agenda, no coherent course of instruction has come down to us even though each Christian denomination, if not each Christian individual, firmly believes his or her views were those that Jesus taught. Since his life story was of little interest to anyone at the outset, little of it remained to be incorporated into narratives, and so biographical fiction necessarily came to dominate; it eventually became the movement's characteristic narrative form.[12]

The idea that Jesus was a great teacher whose teachings during his lifetime led a cohort of disciples first to learn from him and then to imitate him as an itinerant sage traveling from village to village spreading his message is simply not the case. Nor is it the case that after Jesus' death his inspiring teachings led to the rise and spread of the Christian movement. Nor did visions of him risen from the grave bring about a successful Christian cult.[13] Rather, it was the dissociative experience called the Holy Spirit that made Jesus a prominent physician in Galilee during his own time and that made Christianity a successful cult in the Mediterranean littoral after his demise. If you would be interested in more arguments, evidence, and discussion of the role of spirit experience in the life of Jesus and in the origin of Christianity, you might read my recent book *Possession, Trance and the Origins of Christianity*, Bardic Press, 2014.

---

12 You will have no luck questing for the historical Mary, Thecla, Peter, Paul, Thomas, John, Andrew, etc. in the novelistic narratives called the apocryphal acts that are devoted to their supposed sayings and deeds.

13 Pace Bart Ehrman who argues that his followers' visions of Jesus after his death led them to the idea that Jesus was God. Cf. his recent book: *How Jesus Became God: The Exaltation of a Jewish Preacher from Galilee*, HarperOne, 2014

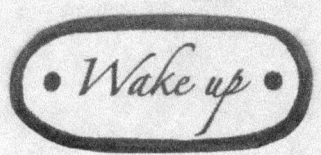

Andrea Frank

Andrea in the Country of the Cannibals
The Rise of Tachyon Consciousness

ANDREW AND MATTHEW IN THE COUNTRY OF THE CANNIBALS

"Like strangers, humans wander around in their own minds."

- Piet Vroon, *Tears of the Crocodile*

Looking back on the past decade, I would say that mine is a journey of a documentary filmmaker, ceramic artist, chef and writer, who got somewhat lost in two old world technologies of consciousness: shamanism and magic. Unexpectedly, but no doubt subconsciously on purpose, this triggered a long overdue wake-up call. Without Gnosticism, which I consider to be the bridge to understanding the more modern, scientific, technologies of consciousness, I am sure I would still be caught up in the astral plane chaos I had ended up in. Living in the ruins of the house of physical matter which my consciousness moved into at birth was obviously not an option. Not this lifetime around anyway. Guided by a deep knowing for years, and unbeknownst to myself until recently, I can only conclude that I woke up to travel the road to self-remembrance. Ouspensky said it well; "If a man realizes and bears in mind that he does not remember himself, then study begins." Our history and ancestors are just the first clues of yet an unresolved mystery. The case file *Know Thyself* requires willpower, dedication, and endless patience.

It was my friend Matthew who, in the midst of living in the emotional turmoil that is the web spun from blurred etheric lines between the astral and the physical worlds, said to me one day; "Have you ever heard of the Gnostics? I once printed out their gospels, but I couldn't deal with them. Have a feeling it's important for you to check them out though." The word Gnostic rang a bell, the bookstore supplied the basics, and slowly but surely, after spending a few years on wild seas battling huge waves, I reached land again. My body, mind, and emotions felt like they had been spat out onto the shore by a Tsunami, yet I immediately perceived an unfamiliar joy. I made it. I was back. Fully grounded, in the flesh. When months later I stumbled upon a much lesser known Gnostic gospel called *The Acts of Andrew and Matthew in the Country of the Cannibals*, not surprisingly, my interest was peeked. Why would I, Andrea, travel to a location where humans eat each other? And what was Matthew doing there?

In hindsight it is obvious: subconsciously I had recognized a younger version of myself in Matthew. In this gospel Andrew, even if he is extremely reluctant and insecure about the task assigned to him, embarks, when 'God's' voice tells him to, on a journey to free Matthew, imprisoned by the cannibals, who intend to feast on him after thirty days. Jesus serves as the ferryman, taking Andrew to Matthew. The rescue operation involves Andrew's disciples and transportation in a cloud. Once a free man again, Matthew, the tax collector, repays Andrew by selling his soul to the devil. Andrew takes the opportunity to engage in a fierce debate with the devil (himself), and converts the man-eaters (fights his own demons). As if written especially for us, what Matthew and I experienced together seems to mirror the psychological journey symbolized in the Gospel.

We got to know each other about five years ago. After a brief period of childlike fun, which I am sure was our two creative minds getting re-acquainted, once our memory of each other had kicked in, Matthew, a young man with a beautiful heart and a raging life force, started to try to manipulate me, a female emotional addict in denial. Which I only now understand I was at the time. A person feeding off drama, that I myself had regularly created throughout my life, for over four decades.

Control over another human being is the most potent drug fix for anyone who is terrified of the loss of control over their own life. Matthew would not rest until he got us back, again and again, into a mother-son dynamic. I sensed a lot of anger. Fortunately his mother was alive, and I knew it was up to them, not me, to sort out their issues. But I also knew - I could sense - that he needed a friend. Someone who would stand up to him. But who would at the same time continue to unconditionally love him, no matter what his behavior. A true friend, one who had the guts to tell him the truth. I also needed a friend - to reflect some things that I had kept hidden from myself. Yes, Matthew had mother issues. But no, I was not a victim of his sly fox behavior. I was a willing enabler. We manifested what started out as something that resembled playing a violent video game together. In reality that was our lives. This head trip that we played on each other and ourselves, made for a brutal and painful journey. The fact that my conscious mind was at the time unable to register what my subconscious was up to, and why, is my only excuse. You will have to ask him what his was. But when it comes to Know Thyself we were worthy opponents with a mutual goal: to storm the universal memory bank. To remember ourselves.

One of the things we had in common is that, deep down, we both knew that if anyone who cared for us truly knew what went on in our minds, they would consider committing us to institutions, or at least send us to shrinks. Being put on medication was our greatest fear. We are both convinced that the only way to a healthy mind is a healthy body. And highly value the importance of that balanced state of mind. Both of us avoid all illegal and legal drugs, including addictive substances like alcohol, cigarettes, sugar and coffee for that reason. On the physical plane we did everything right: we truly treated our bodies like sacred temples. And in a very strange, unexpected way, even if we were each other's as well as our own worst enemy, it turns out, that we had each other's back. Instead of driving each other crazy, we managed to actually teach each other how to become, and stay, sane in an insane world.

SELF-REMEMBERING

Starting to truly remember myself, leaving the concept of time and space behind, turned out to be a scary, self-confronting business. I received an amazing gift after enduring what for the longest time seemed to be a never ending roller-coaster ride in Astral Land, journeying through its emotional, mental and spiritual landscapes, discovering that it even has a physical landscape made out of etheric energy. Once I finally found the brakes and came to a halt, I walked out of the cart, in the light body that is my vehicle, fearless. If I was still afraid of anything today, I would say it is eternal life, not death. Now that my individual physical brain has processed remembering the recycling process that is more commonly known as past lives and the universal hologram is (re)activated within, I comprehend that the now encompasses who I was, am and will be. I have reason to believe that once (collective) memory is (back) online, your personal matter is unable to ever forget what matters again. So let me give you the heads-up, a friendly warning. If you decide to walk through the Gate of Self-remembrance, fasten your seat belt. Because there is no turning back. You slowly but surely *become* the search engine. Every thought you materialize from then onwards, evokes millions of search results.

'Instantly' (0.34 seconds).

Based on my personal experience, I would say that to embody our original blueprint in the physical matter that is our human body, is to enact the Art of Dying consciously. Which obviously starts at birth. I think, as the Age of Self-remembering unfolds, we will learn to pass over, through, and into new physical matter flawlessly. But first we must dare to embody the truth. To remember that death is birth. Instead of being afraid of dying, we should fear the process of descending (back) into matter after we are recycled. Fear forgetting how to pass thought the birth channel without incurring brain damage. I think that is the hidden, symbolic, message in *Andrew and Matthew in the Country of the Cannibals*. It is the story of the consequences of forgetting who we are. A mental flaw that results in ending up on the Dharma Wheel of emotions time and time again. Eating away at your own brain.

Cosmic androgynous consciousness suffers from Alzheimer's when it embodies in matter. In a similar way to dying, and passing through the Bardo state on our way (back) to total recall, severe memory loss also takes place every time we disembark from the womb, and descend through the birth canal. The mother pushes the androgynous consciousness into lower frequency matter, where it is left to its own devices, born in either a male or a female body, suddenly having to give up one of its polarities, as if it were an amputation. Labour pain, as well as remembering either one's time in the womb or one's own birth, can be perceived as a painful struggle. The challenge of our mental evolution is for humans to hold on to memory when the tidal wave that is labour hits us. We need to remember and comprehend the process of the descent, so we can start working with it. Upon arrival, our male and female energies need to find balance in a one gender body. For now birth, not death, seems a truly life threatening event, both to humans as well as their single shared body the planet Earth. There are many interpretations of the meaning of 'the Fall'. This seems the scientific explanation.

I think my self-remembering declined further when the adults around me, who had obviously forgotten themselves, convinced me to end the relationships with my 'fantasy' friends. Especially the one with my white horse, which I now understand to be representative of one of the highest embodied universal frequencies in animals. Fortunately since then, my once assumed wild imagination has manifested in reality as Rupert Isaacson's horse world, which is helping thousands of autistic children all over the world today. Growing up, the energies of my imaginary companions proved to be more pure, and their information more truthful, than most 'real' people I met later on in life. P.M.H. Atwater comes up with a brilliant explanation in her *Children of the Fifth World – A guide to the coming changes in human consciousness*; "Our children remember what we do not want them to remember." We, the older generation, often parents, have created a society, an entity, which is too painful to even put in words. Not only is it harder and more expensive to find clean water and organic food to sustain a physically healthy body, existing on planet Earth has more recently become a severely emotional and mental challenge because of cyber bullying and the likes. Who *wants* to take full responsibility for that?

One of the greatest pieces of wisdom ever passed on to me is the explanation that any person in your life, any situation that rubs you the wrong way, is merely a mirror reflection of something that you have not yet addressed within yourself. Face it, own it, put it under the magnifying glass to get to the truth. Be willing to understand that everything that manifests is a reflection of one of the billion frequencies of self, not yet living in harmony together, that you need to bring back into balance. I think this is the Great Work of a practicing Gnostic. Without these other parts of ourselves that are perceived as other people separate from us, it would be impossible to become aware of what we are collectively co-creating. The clarity, that I am one hundred percent responsible for everything, instantly made me grateful to the man who raped me, taking my virginity. I myself had some hidden darkness that needed to be revealed, and he was willing to activate it in me. So I had a chance to get to know that part of myself, to own it, and to work on it.

I quickly learned that not everyone was willing to look at what happened 'to' me the way I do. In general, my take on life, that we are the co-creators of the labyrinth that is our collective emotional addiction, which we all suppress with a wide variety of addictions, meets a lot of resistance. As does my statement that we deny ourselves the creativity and empathy that our life force is made out of. By abusing this unconditionally loving substance instead of respecting it, we miss out on the opportunity to live, breath, and express the understanding that everyone on this planet is One. And that Earth itself is our collective body. But unless you dare to reconnect to that frequency on an emotional level, and bring it into your grounded physical matter, it is impossible to send out the signal that attracts it to you. In the gospel, the empathic Andrew goes through hell and back to free Matthew from prison. Matthew then betrays him; he displays a lack of empathy. Matthew, not unlike an autistic person, lashes out the moment he is freed, because the incoming energies of the cannibals are too overwhelming. We create open cages around us out of fear, and pretend we are trapped.

Enter the Stage: The Empath and the Psychopath

"The healing of evil, scientifically or otherwise, can be accomplished only by the love of individuals. A willing sacrifice is required. The individual healer must allow his or her own soul to become the battlefield. He or she must sacrificially *absorb* the evil."

M. Scott Peck, M.D.

My whole life I have struggled with the fact that I perceive all that is as myself. Whether it is the joy, fear, or the excruciating pain of another human being, a plant, a stone or an animal, I seem to be in constant communication. Everything and every-body talks to me. And when it does, I blend and become that other being, that other conscious matter, which I know is me too.

Until a few years ago, I was not aware that there is a word for this quality of empathy to the extreme: an empath. The person who understood me better than I did myself was a man with psychotic behavior. He sat me down, showed me the *Star Trek* episode 'The Empath', and explained that *I*, and not him, was the true psychopath. That he perceived *me* as the intruder in *his* energy field. He exposed me as the double agent, outsmarting everyone: I was the hidden infiltrator of human kind. A manipulative imposter, whom *he* was terrified of.

I found his take on me highly disturbing, but at the same time extremely interesting. Was my empathic being actually *creating* the psychopathic behavior on this planet? Deep down I have always known, and I am far more convinced than most it seems, that other people *are* me. Yet I had put that kind of off-putting behavior outside of myself. I had to admit I was a little fearful of it. I had been playing a sublime game of chess with my own mind. You are either every-one and every-body, aware of our collective memory loss of self, or you are not.

Frank - and how poetic that the meaning of his name is 'truth' - had opened the floodgates to exposing all the lies that lay hidden in my subconsciousness, waiting to be revealed. To be self-remembered. Unbeknownst to myself then, and for quite a few more years to come after, I had set myself up to meet this random stranger on a plane, so he could walk me though the Gate of Self-remembrance. Yes, I subconsciously spied on all other matter I interacted with. In an attempt to get to know myself, to remember myself. But also as a subconscious form of self-defense, which I instantly understood to be Frank's behavior too. Just in a different way.

The automatic download which I experience

while interacting with any other living matter, the blending with energy fields other than my own, the instantaneous reading of people's thoughts and emotions, come naturally to me. I wondered if I would still be alive and healthy had I ignored these energetic heads-ups. Which I know are available to anyone who dares to live the truth with an open heart. Convinced that it was *I*, who was constantly being preyed upon by other people, I had been reading Dion Fortune's *Psychic Self-Defense*. Suddenly I understood that to some I was perceived as the perpetrator, violating *their* energetic freedom. My demanding extra care and consideration when I felt energetically threatened had just been my masterful skill in manipulating and controlling others. I bombarded other people with my powerful weapon of mass destruction: my intense emotions. In my defense; the lack of empathy, the unwillingness to feel, to live life truthfully with an open heart, which I encountered in most people I met, was actually the cause of all *my* pain. The fact that humans, wired up to several devices, avoiding as much personal interaction as possible, are well on their way to become robots, was what triggered my negative emotions. Then it dawned on me: each of us are collectively at war with ourselves, terrified of remembering ourselves and all our actions throughout history. That *is* a lot of responsibility to take.

Androgynous consciousness, split through the descent into a single gender body, trying to remember itself, would display the bi-polar tendencies I had been struggling with all my life. This would also explain all variations of gender confusion, I thought. And then I had the epiphany. *Andrew and Matthew in the Country of the Cannibals* is not about eating human flesh. It is addressing the issue of our self-inflicted mental cannibalism. At the end Andrew drifts off into the sea (of emotions). Andrew trusted God, but not Jesus. Jesus tells Andrew that Christ is the master to respect. Andrew then listens to Jesus (instead of God, himself), which costs him dearly. It dawned on me that the whole Gospel takes place on the astral plane.

Traveling the planes, Magic and the Bridal Chamber

As some of you may have experienced yourselves, in one way or another, once you consciously work on self remembering, you start to perceive, to understand, that you are everywhere at all times. Always. It makes sense scientifically that the physical brain is unable to process the reality that is your higher frequency. That creates confusion, and until you comprehend and truly believe that earth plane perception is just one of the many frequencies we encompass, our reality is truly an illusionary dream. My personal experience is that when you return back into your body, descending from the higher to the lower frequencies (often described as different planes or timelines), the astral plane is the biggest problem. Once I finally got a grip on lucid dreaming it proved to be my worst nightmare. The astral plane is overpopulated. Unless you are super clear, all of its inhabitants - including other people who are asleep, on substances, experiencing trauma, in the Bardo state, etc. - create a dense fog made out of etheric matter. Which makes you forget on waking up everything that happened while you were out of body. When it comes to our mental evolution it is crucial to individually remember what we collectively forgot.

As long as a woman does not remember once she awakens in her physical body, that she was dragged into the Bridal Chamber on the astral plane, no one is in danger of getting charged for energetic rape on the earth plane. Truth will not manifest. The moment I did remember, my intuition told me that Matthew's prison cell in the Gospel and the Bridal Chamber had a lot in common.

It took Matthew and me, androgynous consciousnesses embodied in the flesh, more than a year to figure out, to discover, to understand what the root of our mental dis-ease was. Sex. Men refused to have it with me, literally telling me that my pure lifestyle and sensitive

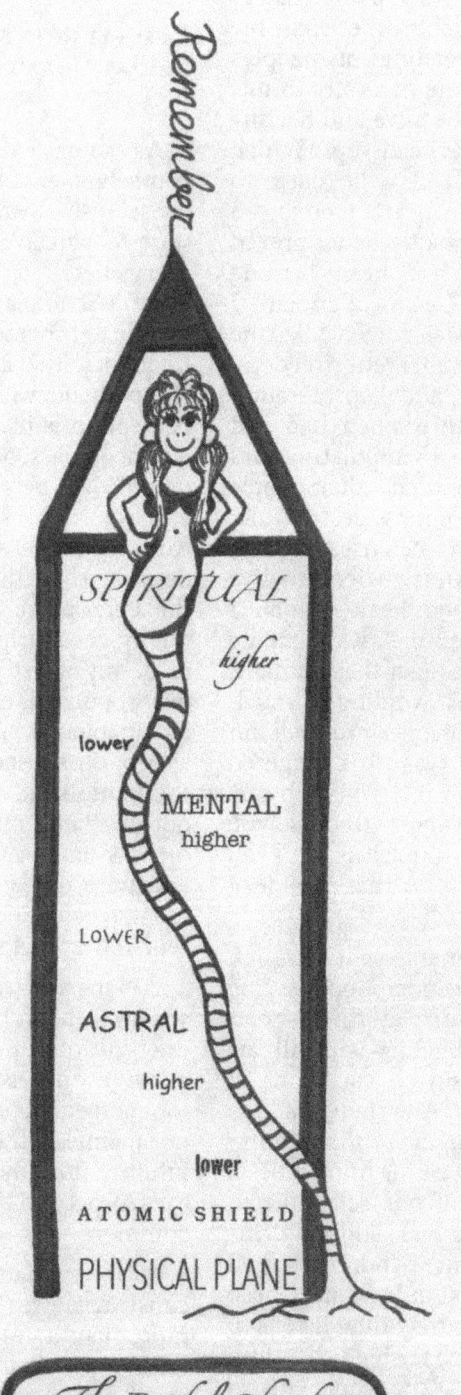

nature was too off-putting. Men were extremely interested in sex with Matthew, which was an ego boost he certainly used. But the aggressive and sometimes physically painful lifestyle that comes with sodomy, created chaos and made him severely doubt if he was even gay. Sex may be sold as the best thing since sliced bread, but it made two people of different genders and age extremely insecure and uncomfortable.

A Taoist priest once warned me against sex magic, before I had ever even heard of the word. After he brought it to my attention, I read up on it. I also went back to my diaries of the years during which I had studied with him. The priest was one of my teachers during my shamanic training. He taught our "Walking with Protection" class. And he did a great job. Without him, I would not be writing any of this. He initiated a master class for shamans after our graduation. Once signed up, as time went by, we slowly figured out that what he taught had more to do with magical practices than shamanism. Three years into studying with him I found out that the priest lied about being ordained. When a man lies about something like priesthood, how can you be sure he was not in fact practicing the very sex magic he warned me against? Looking back, I realize that sex magic is the the most powerful weapon on the astral plane. I wonder to this day if he knew what I gradually started to remember. Or if he was just a puppet on a string, waking up in the morning without any recall. Sex (nature) on the astral plane, I found out the hard way, is the only force that can overpower creative energy (grace) on the earth plane. Catch (up with) it, harvest it, hijack it. Use it as you please, to manifest the personal wants and needs of the magician. It is the most potent available etheric energy to create and manifest thought forms and energetic entities on the astral and on the earth plane. Magicians will deny this, but shamans will confirm it. And warn you against it. Carlos Castaneda engaged in many practices that reeked of sorcery, but at least he was open and honest about sex magic being automatically activated during any sexual act, and the disadvantages for women (and female energy in men) in this situation.

A lot of answers can be found reading between the lines in the gospels. *The Gospel of Philip* describes the Bridal Chamber as the holy of the Holiest: the place where redemption takes place. It is stated that a spiritual marriage is to be performed after the pattern of the higher Syzygia, which is a term for a small sea snail. This is where things, to me, got interesting. Because snails happen to be androgynous. This would also explain why the Cathers choose to eat only fish. Fish do not breed sexually. Bringing that frequency into your physical matter by eating it, allows for your focus to shift from an animal, sexually orientated nature to the creative energy that is the androgynous consciousness which forgot itself. I can tell you from experience, eating a diet of only organic fruits, vegetables, nuts, beans and fish greatly enhanced my self-memory. Abstaining from sex did too. When I am asked about acquiring self-knowledge that opinion of mine is a lot less accepted than the dietary and dream requirements I come up with. I was greatly relieved to recently read *The Revolt of the Widows* by Stevan L. Davies. He addresses the fact that it seems reasonable to conclude that the apocryphal acts of the apostles were written by women, who encountered similar resistance; "Women deciding for sexual continence met substantial opposition from their husbands." Ever since I began to remember what had happened to me in the Bridal Chamber on the astral plane, it felt to me more like a room which resembled the forbidden one in Bluebeard, the tale that tells the story of a violent nobleman in the habit of murdering his wives. And the attempts of one wife, "me", to avoid the fate of her predecessors.

I followed my intuition and found out that the OHO, the outer head of the OTO, approached Aleister Crowley, who had published, in his *Book of Lies,* what they considered the biggest secret in human history. Crowley had no clue what the OHO was talking about. He had to search his own book to find the symbolic paragraph they were referring to. A secret so big that Aleister Crowley's subconsciousness kept it from his own conscious mind? That had to be something too gruesome even for him to digest. I discovered that Aleister had a serious mommy issue. Which could explain most, if not all of his more erratic behavior. It made me open my eyes to the fact that there is much more to the Oedipus complex than Freud and Jung cared to admit. Or should I say, dared to comprehend. I suspect they were suppressing a few memories of their own.

I quote Crowley, once he figured it out: "I understand that I held in my hand the key to the future progress of humanity." Both the OHO and Crowley were on to something: the secret details of the ritual of the Bridal Chamber. But, both parties overlooked one thing. The alchemy of self-remembering the androgynous cosmic consciousness which we are is about creative energy, and not about sexual energy. The Sacred Marriage is between the male and female energy within one person, who (re)marries 'it'-self on the earth plane. Rebalancing two polarities in a single gender body. And, for those who appreciate the wisdom of the Kabbalah, and know we are truly just energy in motion making up stories to understand ourselves: this concept is beyond time and space. It is about Kether, born from Ain, the Black Hole, from a universal womb that holds light (Ain Soph) and sound (Ain Soph Aur). Which, once conceived by Space (Chokma, Force) and Time (Binah, Structure), births etheric matter, manifesting embodied newborns.

'God'; The androgynous self, one hundred percent responsibility

"Your consciousness is not your consciousness.

It is the manifestation of the longing of the cosmos itself.

It comes to you through you but not from you."

- Ervin Laszlo, *The Immortal Mind*

"Your children are not your children.

They are the sons and daughters of Life's longing for itself.

They come through you but not from you."

- Khalil Gibran, *The Prophet*

Androgynous consciousness remembers itself on the spiritual, mental, and emotional planes. But it forgets itself as it descends in the physical matter of lower frequency that is our single gender only body. It makes scientific sense that this would result in the life long struggle between the male and female energy within, which we are currently experiencing on Planet Earth.

A newborn, by the default setting, will gravitate to the embodied energy of its opposite gender, to make up for the lack of physical matter available corresponding with that energy. A female will be looking for male physical embodied energy, so she can balance her androgynous consciousness, and remember her(it)self. Where it gets tricky is, that in a family dynamic where the mother is overpowering, and the father feels less of a man because of that, or is absent, the female baby will gravitate to the mother, looking for the missing male energy in her. Resulting in an even bigger absence of physically embodied male energy in her environment. It is very likely that later in life, unless she catches herself, she will repeat the mother's behavior, mistaking it for balance and safety. Attracting males who lack male

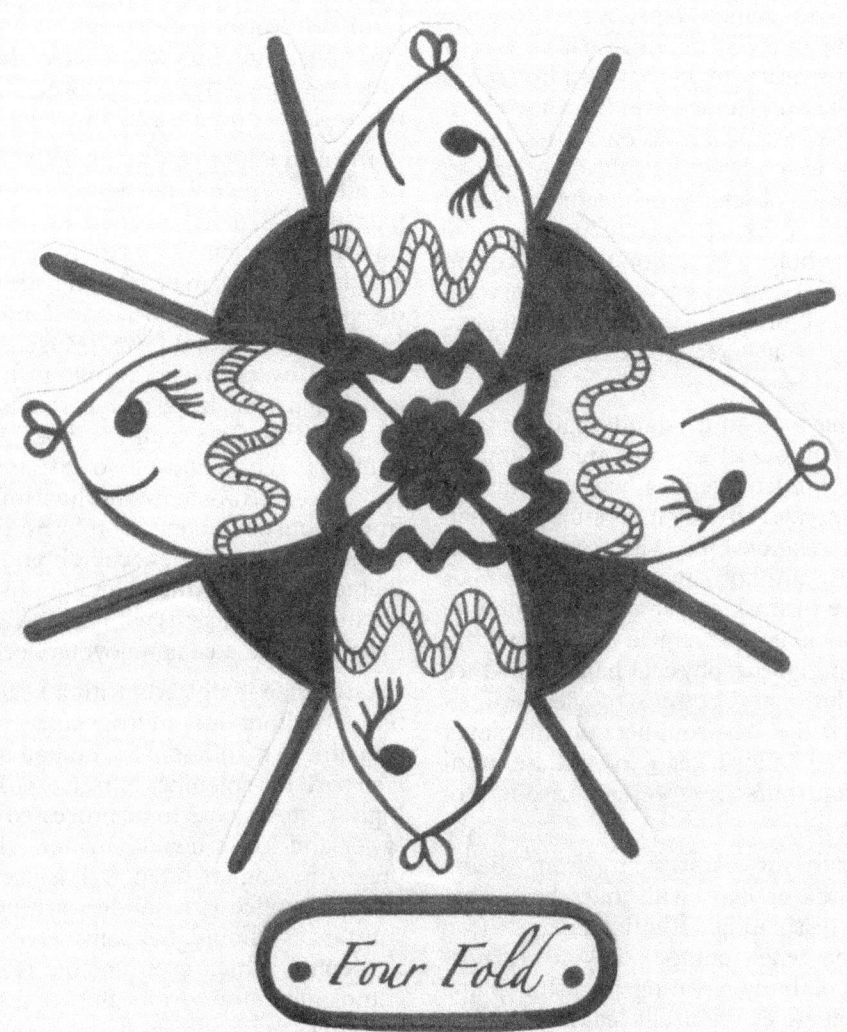

energy, and are looking for that in other females or males themselves. We have to be willing to truthfully and intelligently examine our first years. Especially people who are not sure whether they are gay or straight, who feel they were born in the wrong body, etc. can greatly benefit from doing so. There are already reports of humans born with both genital reproductive organs. That would be one way in which nature is self-correcting. In order to become androgynous again after the unfortunate event during which androgynous consciousnesses embodied in Mu and Lemuria were physically split by Atlantean priests who were obsessed with technology and sexual power. A-sexual reproduction may be up next in the human evolution, as we focus on creative versus sexual energy, striving forward in a mental evolution on the road to oneness, remembering our creative default setting: empathy.

We will have to understand that humans, until we catch ourselves and are willing to uncover our hidden agendas, will continue to repetitively create off balance situations and complicated relationships with other people. As long as we are born in one gender bodies only, we have to work on remembering how to rebalance our male and female energies within first, overcoming this 'physical handicap'. Once we do, all (illusionary) power struggles between opposite polarities - so prominent on this planet right now - can and will cease to exist. But until we understand ourselves, we are prisoners of our own minds.

All mental dis-eases stem from being emotionally ill at ease with ourselves. That results in dissipating etheric energy (fog matter). Even when embodied, you are now slightly out of body, creating an astral plane presence. You are energetically leaking and you start to blend with other leaking energy fields. Subconsciously you start to feel something is off. Next up, you start to hear voices. I heard voices. And saw apparitions. Until I remembered and understood myself. Every living person should get acquainted with the information A.E. Powell provides in his *The Etheric Double* about our atomic shield, our protective energetic layer. He explains how severely we, unbeknownst to ourselves, compromise it, and what the far reaching consequences for humanity are.

I started to remember who I was, am, and will be, once I tuned in to the higher frequencies of the mental plane with my pineal gland antenna. I am still learning every day how to guide my emotions, and how to reverse this declining process of forgetfulness. In order words, I now self-regulate and navigate my mental dis-ease.

In an attempt to try to understand the actions of others, which I perceived as heartless and painful, I (female) opened up my heart one hundred percent, to extreme empath mode. Matthew (male), in order to navigate his mental dis-ease closed his down one hundred percent. I was often told that I was 'oversensitive', and to "just get over myself". People in his past were convinced that he was a narcissist, incapable of empathy. The truth is that we are *both* empaths. Who choose two extremely opposite (subconscious) defense mechanisms to survive. In our journey together, we were two opposite frequencies, polarities, colliding. The alchemy that took place - which literally, physically, blew my fuse and struck us with lightning during our journey - created a new, joyous electric current.

Of course it all starts with a healthy physical body. Without one, androgynous consciousness is unable to manifest in the human brain. Why is it so hard to remember ourselves? The incoming high frequency has to be processed in bodies of lower-and-lower-quality matter. The fact that pregnant women often feel nauseated by the smell of coffee is a subtle warning that some substances should be considered as harmful as alcohol, which even doctors recommend to completely refrain from. But what about before and after a pregnancy, and what about the fathers? Humans consume alcohol as if it were soda, of which the main ingredient, refined sugar, has already proven to be the leading cause of cancer, compromising the DNA of both the sperm and the egg. Alcohol kills braincells and thins blood. Self-memory requires braincells to work with, and blood to transfer the incoming information to all organs, so they can work optimally. When the physical matter lacks quality, the fetus forgets how to build the foundation for a healthy body in the womb, forgets how to disembark through the birth channel, and how to make correct use of the excreted hormones. This causes all kinds of physical and mental stress to occur. These different levels of panic, related to self-forgetting, explain why autism and Alzheimer's continue to be on the rise. The cure for all physical and mental dis-ease lies in restoring the body to optimum health, and making sure the energy around the person is calm, positive, and supportive. And, most importantly, in teaching people about their own individual energy field.

All physical matter is a hologram that can activate self-remembrance. That is how a tree knows how to blossom every year. The challenge for a human is to consciously manifest the electric grid that is the universal hologram on the astral plane, and then flawlessly guide that etheric energy as it embodies in perfectly healthy flesh. Truth, the all knowing, remembering self, is a frequency available to anyone who chooses to stop lying. If lying ceased to be an option our society would (temporarily) collapse. Not to mention our personal lives. Maybe we embrace forgetfulness because the truth takes character, discipline, and hard work in the trenches.

Our body is designed to embody androgynous consciousness. The pineal gland is the antenna. Joseph Sadony explains that beautifully in his *The Human Radio*. Our teeth, related to our organs, are the conductors. When you Google 'teeth organs', a surprising number of progressive dentists turn out to be already familiar with that fact. Our meridians distribute the incoming electrical information. We produce a fluid, to support matter: blood. Our appendix is like a vacuum cleaner. It can perceive incoming incongruent energy, transfer it into matter, which then can be processed by the digestive system and excreted. An acute appendix is just a warning that there is an overload of incoming etheric energy, which can not be processed into matter and digested fast enough. Unfortunately, most of the medical establishments continue to tell us that the appendix has no function. Once removed, all kinds of other problems arise. Diseases that no one understands, or can find a cure for. There is nothing in our body that does not have a function. Our reproductive system is designed to bring in the highest frequency, androgynous consciousness. To either create or to reproduce. Orgasm is designed to make the connection, out of body, long enough to draw that frequency in, but brief enough for us not to get stuck out of body, unable to return and settle back into physical matter. Tantra, often misrepresented by the focus on sexual versus creative energy, teaches that when you climax, you loose valuable, self-empowering, creative energy. Unless we shift our approach to only engage sexually when there is purity of intent, body, emotion, mind, and spirit, we miss out on the opportunity, on the alchemy, of balancing male and female energy in a way that supports our self-remembrance.

It would make sense that androgynous consciousness births itself into matter, trying to remember itself in the flesh, over and over and over again. Until it gets it 'right'. That is the cosmic survival instinct. Indeed, the longing of the cosmos itself. In *Andrew and Matthew in the Country of the Cannibals* Jesus tells Andrew, as he is about to embark on the journey to free Matthew; "Your blood will flow unto the earth like water." The emotions (water) I experienced, once I started to remember that we are mentally torturing ourselves, depriving ourselves of reconnection to the accessible-for-all information, that ends all mental and physical dis-ease we humans ever experienced, made me feel like I indeed was bleeding to death on the battlefield. I instantly realized that the ozone layer is Planet Earth's atomic shield. By stubbornly continuing to damage our individual bodies, we are collectively destroying ourselves.

Processing the Gospel, I truly started to feel I was *Andrea in the Country of the Cannibals*. All the characters in the gospel represent the voices in my head. Andrew tells 'God' (himself) to just send his angels (higher frequencies) to free Matthew (his mind). Suddenly Jesus (obviously a lower frequency than God in any story) insists he has veto over God. Jesus arrives in a boat from the land of the cannibals, to pick up Andrew. That indicates that Jesus himself is a resident of the country of the cannibals. To me, Jesus is God, myself, androgynous consciousness, which made up an astral play, titled *Know Thyself*, which it wrote, produced, directed, and stars in itself.

Andrew, who in the New Testament is a modest Jewish fisherman, is transformed in the gospel into a warrior. A divergent metamorphosis. That battle, that hidden psychological Third World War, fought on the front lines of our awakening consciousness during the mental evolution we find ourselves in, can actually be found in this unwilling apostle, this paradoxical figure, who is, of course, both the Empath and the Psychopath. The constant battle within is between our right brain hemisphere, feminine energy, and the left, male energy. I was able to, slowly but surely, leave both my bi-polar experiences as well as my multiple personality dis-order tendencies behind, once I got reacquainted with myself.

ASCENSION: THE TACHYON'S DESCEND IN MATTER

"It is sometimes an appropriate response to reality to go insane."

Philip K. Dick

"I have transcended space and time... I am even smaller than the atom,

But I have expanded to the outer limits of space."

Tukaram (1598 - 1650)

In *Liber 51, The Lost Continent*, Aleister Crowley writes; "The aim of man is to attain to the sun." He himself describes the book as a combination of memories of Atlantis and a prophecy of what is still to come. Parents, in *Liber 51*, offer up their children. That is as far removed from attaining the sun as I could imagine, so I dug deeper. What if we are supposed to attain something else than the maybe overestimated light? What if the black hole, that most of us are weary of, is actually where all the necessary information is, hiding from the light? Light brings growth as well as decay. It creates the possibility for shadow. And its rays can distort. Especially once reflected in mirrors. What if (sun)light distorts the truth? Then we would need to connect to something faster than light, in order to remember that and ourselves. To my great surprise, my Google search resulted in yet another word that I had never heard of: a tachyon. A particle that is faster than light and can not be witnessed would explain why human beings find it so hard to shed light on the Dark Night of their Soul. If 'God' is the black hole, than that is the location of our undetectable, untraceable, androgynous consciousness. Of our memory. I think we have been looking for en*light*enment in all the wrong places. 'God' *is* Tachyon Consciousness. Understanding that we wrongly assumed that we should attain to the sun and willing to return to the dark, a tachyon in human form would certainly be able to rid itself of any and all worldly physical life illusion. To manifest in matter, leaving all lies and denial behind. To take one hundred percent responsibility for living a (self)sustainable life on planet earth. The womb symbolizes and confirms this whole concept; it is the black hole too.

There are many different versions of this gospel, which is sometimes just titled *Andrew in the Country of the Cannibals*. In all of them, in one way or another, Andrew somehow manages to transform the voices of God and Jesus in his head into the voice of reason. He manages to realign to universal truth. Abstaining from alcohol and other harmful substances, as well as forgoing sexual intercourse, seems a worthwhile investment for anyone who cares about their mental sanity, our mental evolution and planet Earth. Maybe the highest spiritual goal in life is not ascension at all. Maybe it is all about *descending*. Into matter, recovering

full memory. Consider that "The Fall" is 'God', our androgynous tachyon consciousness self, in a state of fear. Brought on by shell-shocking into the lowest frequency it could ever find itself robed in: physical matter. That explains the Big Bang. The most effective and productive start to self-remembrance, is taking one hundred percent responsibility individually for everyone, -thing, and -body, recollecting the billions of particles of yourself, of 'God', of your androgynous consciousness self.

I think it is key for anyone who is interested in remembering themselves, first and foremost, to be willing to treat your physical body like a sacred temple. When you do, you enable yourself to start practicing what I call mental hygiene. I stay in the now, focused on the task or company at hand. I make sure I do not communicate about third parties unless they are present. This way it is much easier to lead an emotionally balanced life. At night, I set the intent to remember. Study as much as you can about energy fields, and what happens when you are out of body, or slightly out of body while awake. Keep a dream journal, and be open to waking up several times at night to make notes. Understand that we come from darkness, and that light can easily trick us. What I call false light roams freely, even on the spiritual plane, where you would least expect it.

Oscar Kiss Maerth was right, when he wrote, in *The Beginning Was the End*, that we are human apes who messed up our evolution, eating each other's brains because we figured out that it enhanced our intelligence and sex drive. We overdosed on lust, and ended up with an STD plague as well as a raging epidemic which we mistakenly call mental illness. But the human species can decide to discipline itself emotionally, mentally and spiritually. Step up to the task of bringing the highest frequency currently known to man in time/space, Tachyon Consciousness, into a healthy physical body. I believe Modern Gnostics are the pioneers who can help assist freeing the collective mind.

When it comes to two of those individual minds which are part of that collective mind, Matthew and I share the opinion that, even if our individual journeys are still quite challenging, that we no longer are in the dark about *self*. Willing to fearlessly dive into the abyss that is mental dis-ease, we created the possibility to literally clean up our physical, emotional, mental and spiritual acts. We returned from the front lines of the Third World War, which is fought on the astral plane, and forgotten by most people when they wake up in the morning. We had to fight many psychological battles. Perfectly gruesome strategies scorned our hearts and blew our mind to pieces many times over. We lost many loved ones to the etheric black plague, which is fueled by sodomizing acts gone viral on the astral plane. But we found the antidote safely stashed away in the Bridal Chamber. And returned home the first war casualties in history mentally sane.

Two empaths, two tachyon consciousnesses, an energy frequency that to this day is mistakenly labeled autistic, both fully aware that they are 'God', seemed to be each other's worst enemy. But as we put into practice the theories we came up with living this journey to-gather Matthew, with his closed-off heart self defense mechanism (categorized as a person with psychotic behavior, a narcissist, a person with some kind of mental illness) and Andrea, open hearted (categorized, often judged, as an oversensitive person) actually became the cure to each other's mental dis-ease without any drugs or third party assistance. Teaming up, we were able to teach each other how to navigate a society, which is driven by fear and commercialized sexual energy. A society that abuses its creative energy to the point of self-destruction. As did we, until we remembered ourselves.

When you are 'God', empath, tachyon, you run the highest frequency currently experienced in human bodies on this planet. For most other people that is too high a frequency to attune to. It makes them uncomfortable when they are around you. In order to block the energy, they will start to either drain the empath (emotional vampirism), or try bring the tachyon down to a lower frequency, because that is easier for them to maintain. Parents, unbeknownst to themselves, by default, start that dynamic with their newborns, who are of very high frequency. I think that is what Aleister Crowley meant when he wrote about parents offering up their children. If an empath does not catch the downward pull, he or she will start to feel ill at ease. That leads to high frequency feelings translating into a lower frequency emotional state. This results in dissipating etheric energy, as well as blending with any other energy fields in the empath's environment. Until empaths remember themselves and get to know themselves inside out – literally - etheric matter functions as a contagious airborne virus that still has to be acknowledged. This hidden plague threatens the mental evolution of the human species. The only cure lies in acquiring, by putting self-awareness, self-remembrance, and self-knowledge into practice, a personal energy adaptor, which can assist your individual energetic light body regulating incoming frequencies.

Anyone, unaware of who or what is influencing their individual energy field frequency, is short-circuiting their personal electric current. And runs the immediate risk of falling prey to closed-hearted empaths looking for illusionary safety. They draw to the etheric of the open-hearted empath like moths to a flame. That dynamic results in more and more etheric matter being dissipated from the body, creating an astral plane existence on the earth plane. Now the free buffet of the physical matter, available to those who feel the need to manipulate other people and subdue them to their personal wants in order to feel in control of their own out of control lives, is open to anyone who has the information described here. Knowledge which many magicians, shamans, and other so called healers have conveniently kept to themselves for ages. Because there is a lot of money to be made of the physical and mental dis-ease of fellow human beings. The manipulation of etheric energy scientifically explains all the well-known, age old misinterpreted phenomena like apparitions, ghosts, hearing voices and hypnosis. Annie Besant was already on to this in 1909, when she wrote in *The Seven Principles of Man*, that H.P. Blavatsky had told her that she had deliberately moulded the plastic matter of the medium in attendance into the likeness of persons known to herself and no-one else present with her willpower. From what Matthew and I now understand, this etheric energy, on a deeper level, is the root of all enslavement. What manifested as slave plantations on the physical plane, originated from the astral plane theatre, where puppet masters bargain to cast the perfect actors to play out their scenarios to this day.

Matthew's need to get me emotionally upset is clear. Harvest time kicked in the moment I started to dissipate etheric energy. But what was in it for me? Why was I a *willing* slave? I had a want, a need to be loved, because I was unable to love myself. I was an emotional addict. Ironically Matthew and I, unbeknownst to ourselves, had created an umbilical chord between us, which allowed for a two way street feed. On today's menu is mental cannibalism. We were reenacting the most hidden parent-child issue that Aleister Crowley, who had experienced it himself, had written about in *Liber 51* a long time ago.

In 1995 I wrote a novel titled *Pain and Passion – Living in Freedom with the Soul on Death Row*. After one literary agent ridiculed it, I had thrown it in a box. Recently I came across it. To my surprise, it read like the diary I did not keep in those twenty years. Instead of dreaming my world into being, I seemed to have been *writing* my life into being, before I even physically experienced it. I am pretty sure that I subconsciously knew what was about to happen to me. I did not write a novel, I manifested a blueprint. So I could free my Tachyon Consciousness, suffering from memory loss, trapped in a physical body. Overruling the collective, which seems strangely addicted to chaos and confusion, with the power of my individual mind.

For me the answer, in all its complications, is simple. Self-remembrance is key to any human, who wants to manifest an independent joyful life of service in the flesh. Matthew and I are two of the billions of particles attracting and colliding, that manifest the puzzle that is my personal experience of the collective me. To understand that separated oneness made me fearlessly untangle all the individualized energy fields of my, 'God''s, scattered flesh. Like Andrew after he had it out with the Devil, I can now roam the universe freely. I am in my own driver's seat.

When individual opposite minds, like those of Matthew and I, are willing to team up for extremely challenging journeys of truth, while all the time remaining in unconditional love for each other, the possibility arises to leave the illusion of separateness behind. Once over the fear of true oneness, the tachyon can surpass light, embrace dark, and return to its original state: the empath. When we all open our hearts one hundred percent, we will collectively activate that safe state of being to-gather in the human matter worldwide. Eventually any need for war, from the smallest personal argument and manipulation to nations fighting over control, will end. In other words mental evolution, the balance between the male and female energies within ourselves, is the only way for the human species to achieve World Peace.

Epilogue – On the Road to Tachyon Consciousness

"Life responds to itself. When we "remember", we *know*."

"Any form of growth is cyclic, not just from life to life but from one vibratory phase to another, in and through dimensions without number. Yet only consciousness progresses, and the only true goal is to express and eventually rejoin the thought which stirred (our Source). We can be taught all manner and types of knowledge, but truth, the real truth of life, cannot be taught, it is "known" or "remembered" through the higher mind (soul mind)."

Phyllis M. H. Atwater, *Future Memory*

There have been times during which the mental health expert in me, self-aware of my true state of mind and in charge of my case file, seriously considered diagnosing me with at least a severe case of "Alice in Wonderland syndrome". But the stubborn and convincing voice inside which I also perceived to be me reassured me, every time, that I am actually one of the sanest human minds currently embodied on the planet. Recently I got a little worried that my ego could be clouding my perception. My "I just *know*!" answer to the frequently asked question: "But *how* do you know?" is perceived, by some of my family and friends, as one of my most annoying traits. Wrapping up writing this article, Phyllis M. H. Atwater's *Future Memory* arrived in the mail. I had forgotten I even ordered it. This book clarified and justified my inner voice to be an intuition to be reckoned with that can and should be trusted, as well as taken seriously. It also humbled me in understanding that a manual, offering insight in how to survive and proactively embrace the trials and tribulations that make up the mental evolution that the human race currently finds itself in, has already been published. In 1995! It turns out that in *Future Memory*, endorsed by Peter R. Rothschild who was nominated for the Nobel Prize in Physics in 1986, Ms. Atwater already linked tachyons with consciousness. She writes; "It is believed that tachyon fields lie beyond the light barrier and are superluminous." Suddenly my theory, that consciousness' highest frequency, universal mind, *is* the tachyon field, seems rocket solid. Professor of Physics Robert Ehrlich confirms; "Not only does a tachyon appear to speed up the faster you chase it, but at a certain chase speed the tachyon would be moving away from you at infinite speed – it would be literally everywhere at once."

Since matter vibrates at a very slow rate, scientifically it is possible for consciousness to outsmart itself, one human at the time. Anyone able to process the until recently out of body higher frequencies of the self, the truth, through their physical brain, can learn to avoid the

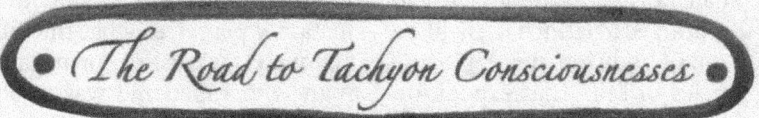

chaos and confusion that is the etheric jungle most people refer to as the astral plane. Lucid dreaming may be exciting, but it is a mine field. The real skill that needs to be acquired by humans is manifesting Tachyon Consciousness in matter. In doing so, we can live our lives As Above So Below and perceive it as the heaven on earth that is the Fifth World. A new reality for any human being who chooses to rise out of the ashes and wills to remember 'it'self.

Having read what Ms. Atwater wrote twenty years ago, I would love to respectfully ask her if she would agree with me that we do not actually remember a *future*. But that we are now finally evolving towards being able to process the higher frequency that is the universal mind. Creating human bodies that hold a higher state of consciousness in our individual flesh, collectively raising the frequency of the matter that is our planet. Separation and hate was invented by the human race. It can, once all human beings remember that they are the puzzle pieces suffering from memory loss that make up the indeed puzzling but perfect universal mind embodied, cease to exist in the animal kingdom. It is a matter of individual people reconnecting with what many refer to as the higher self (universal soul).

What Ms. Atwater describes as near death experiences, I believe to be near birth experiences. Since the organs in the body stop functioning in that situation, the brain has a lot less work to do than normal. Therefore it can temporarily be fully utilized to launch itself, like a rocket ship, on an out of body journey exploring the higher frequencies of self. That expedition brings clarity, memory of self, of universal mind, of truth. Upon returning from that experience (which Ms. Atwater calls a brain shift), the brain can process and bring into matter the timeless space that is higher consciousness. Making use of that higher frequency once it takes up its regular jobs again results in the healthier mind and body that are often mentioned related to post-near-death experiences. Quoting Ms. Atwater; "It seems plain enough that brain shifts accelerate higher brain development. If the limbic system isn't jump-started, there is no brain shift. The limbic system, as the higher brain's emissary, is the region of the brain that activates the surges in neural network expansion. Accessing mechanisms flourish in such a climate, throwing the system first into chaotic disarray until, through pathways newly formed, coherence results."

I am of the opinion that my experiences with shamanism and magic did indeed jump start my brain, which started to slowly wake up and remember that it is actually wired for a fifth dimensional life. Stuck in three and four dimensional perceptions, chaotic disarray naturally followed. Working with people who are labelled bi-polar, multiple personality, psychopath, etc. I started to realize that what these people were going through was almost identical to *my* chaotic disarray. In a rare unconditionally loving moment, Frank had texted me once; "You're so metaphysical it's beautifully frightening." That is the best way to describe what I now understand to be the regular brain shifts in me. I was honest to myself but kept quiet about them, because I was very aware that if I were to describe my experiences to a professional, I would have been diagnosed with a dangerous combination of bi-polar and multi-personality dis-order.

My self-diagnose looking back would be closer to labeling myself a person with Down syndrome, highly functioning. Once an empath is able to finally love itself, it equally loves everyone, and instantly perceives what the motives are behind anyone else's positive or negative behavior. The man who raped me was unable to cope with what had happened to him: there is so much truth in "the abused become the abusers". I had become empathic to the point where I accepted any abuse because I felt only love for everyone. I tolerated any behavior and refused to protect myself. Living became unbearable but I got to understand autism because of this period in my life. In my opinion it is not a *lack* of empathy that disrupts the autistic human being. It is just that, unlike Down syndrome people who stay in a constant state of unconditional love, when the autistic person feels energetically threatened, a self-defense mechanism is activated that often results in lashing out to the extreme. In order to create and maintain an isolated secluded world that is falsely perceived as safe, protecting it with all ones might. This behavior is often incomprehensible to even the people who love and medically treat people on the spectrum. They come up with all sorts of misinterpretations, because autistic people are unable to communicate that the simple truth is that, when they have people in their environment who run low frequency energy (due to moods or substances like coffee, sugar or alcohol in their energy fields), those people are in fact the root of their extreme discomfort. Similar to Down syndrome, people with autism are the new humans, often referred to in literature as the Fifth Root Race. Courageous beings who are willing to embody in the flesh their out of body high universal truth frequency in a society where those who have forgotten themselves label *them* abnormal.

In what I now call my old life, the one where I subconsciously opted for memory loss, I used to hurt myself physically, when the emotional pain became too much for me. What I did not realize at the time was, how powerful emotions are. And that I created a powerful energy field blending with other people's energy bodies because of them. I did not believe it, when several people told me that I had appeared in their bedroom at night (and that it scared the hell out of them). Now that I scientifically comprehend how all this this works, I truly believe that I can manifest an astral projection of myself when I am emotionally distressed, running thought forms of a specific person. I would never do that on purpose, but I will have to own now that unbeknownst to myself, I used to be engaged in creating astral plane entities, forgetting all about it waking up the next morning. It would make sense that in mental health institutions, prisons, homes for Alzheimer patients etc. the combination of strong emotions and medication would result in a lot of loosened roaming etheric matter that few people are aware of. Until we educate ourselves on how thought forms fueled by emotions become the illusionary hallucinations that we find hard to explain but are real to some extend, a lot of people will fall between the cracks unnecessarily. Or get worse when they are placed amongst other people who are living similar astral ignorance and chaos.

In closing, there is one more topic that I think is of great importance but is being completely overlooked. What if writers, unbeknownst to themselves, get their inspiration from being on the astral plane? Forgetting that they do on wake-up, eating up with a spoon the praise for their assumed rich imagination and creativity? That would explain the list of examples in Ms. Atwater's *Future Memory* of situations that actually manifested *after* the events were published in a book or portrayed in a movie.

In the novel I am writing a writer struggles with this issue; "Yareht knew what problem truly endangered the planet and the human species. Writers. That is where the trouble always starts. Writers make or break astral etheric energy reality in motion. All fiction was science-*faction*. The fascinating thing was that no-one ever seemed to be giving the creative influence of writers any thought. People were not worried about writers. They were up in arms about political leaders and corporations. But they never gave the hidden power writers have any thought. I mean, would the president even be the president if he did not have a brilliant writer at hand? And that was just the tip of the iceberg."

Writers, especially when under the influence of emotions or substances, are watching and interacting with the chaos on the astral plane. Instead of manifesting scenarios that are representative of our Tachyon Consciousness, they often cash in on writing low frequency stories, jump starting and fueling negative behavior. Embodied human consciousness interacting with this "entertainment" finds itself subconsciously pulled down in frequency, which results in negative thought forms and emotions. In my opinion a writer has the responsibility to offer material that inspires our mental evolution and not our devolution. I could defend *Harry Potter* and *The Hunger Games* as *insight* in the workings of negativity, but I am afraid that in a large part of the audience it just subconsciously triggers out of body astral journeying at night, followed by manifesting that chaos in their actions on the earth plane.

My goal as a writer is to inform readers to the best of my ability how to become self-aware enough to start self-remembering. Closing the door to the astral plane and locking it with the key that is knowledge resembles walking out of an open cage reclaiming the freedom you always had but gave up because you forgot how to be fearless. For those who recognize themselves reading this article, for all human tachyons in hiding or still consciously unaware of themselves waiting for the alarm to go off, I think I have a joyous first aid remedy of high frequency that I share whenever opportunity arises. Hopefully it inspires what through the ages is called "The Great Work" (of self remembering).

Determine if you are an empath with a heart open, closed, or somewhere in the middle. If you are a closed-hearted empath, be aware that your tendency will be to use the astral plane to manipulate actions on the earth plane to gain control over your manifested earth plane life. With hijacked etheric energy of other people. Since this is a form of sorcery, your earth plane life will continue to feel, or even get more chaotic. That is God's (your own) way of telling you that the physical plane is a place to be in your individual body one hundred percent of the time, truthful, practicing mental, emotional, and spiritual hygiene in regards to others and yourself. You will have to learn to trust your Tachyon Consciousness to guide you, without playing shaman or magician. Communicating directly with other members of the human species, ceasing to hide the truth, to make assumptions about others, or to fill in their thoughts for them, is the only way to bring God consciousness into matter.

Open-hearted empaths often just try to please other people, emotionally and mentally eating away at their own loving, vulnerable heart, eventually physically damaging it. Learn to love yourself, because an extended period of self-denial could literally lead to the need for open heart surgery. You have to catch yourself as soon as any *feeling* takes on its more extreme state, the emotion, since that triggers the release of etheric energy. Once you are leaking energy from your individual energy field, no longer safely contained in your body, you start to loose control, because you are loosing the connection with your Tachyon Consciousness. Your pineal gland, your human radio antenna, works hard to receive its guidance, so that you can activate and fully embody God in your individualized energy field 24/7, and manifest an energetically balanced, joyous life, embodied in matter, living on planet earth.

Etheric energy in a state of chaos and confusion is the thick fog that the astral plane is made of. The road to the hell that is conscious astral travel is paved with good intentions. Assuming that you are out there to assist others, as for example the International Academy of Consciousness does, is the human ego doing a number on itself. The fact that you are there, only indicates that *you* have something to learn about yourself, in that environment. Smoke gets in your eyes. So make use of your visits to clear the air. Descend into matter awake and aware. Getting yourself *off* the astral plane is the way to ground yourself firmly in our collective physical body, Planet Earth, remembering your androgynous tachyon self.

The human mental evolution will result in the birth of more and more hermaphrodites. Humans will cease all sexual intercourse, which will result in creative energy, and therefore empathy, coming (back) online. God, remembering itself, can then create its earth plane life, experiencing its physical body that is our planet, finally, as above so below. Consider stopping the prioritizing of your sexuality. Open your vistas to loving, caring physical interaction between human beings, stemming from the state of grace that is the evolved human mind, as nature continues to be the foundation of your human body. Sex addiction is just about being homesick. Why keep going there for only a few seconds when you can use all that creative energy to manifest the life you intended to live if you stop unloading your precious creative energy in somebody else's body, which has no idea what to do with it, because it is of a foreign frequency? In the Fifth World, for the Fifth Root Race, free mind over healthy matter is the new lovemaking. Not war.

BIBLIOGRAPHY

Andrew and Matthew in the Country of the Cannibals

Andrew in the Country of the Cannibals – Robert Boenig's translation (Garland Publishing, Inc., 1991)

The Gnostic Bible – Edited by Willis Barnstone & Marvin Meyer (Shambhala Publications Inc., 2009)

The Revolt of the Widows – Stevan L. Davies (Bardic Press, 2012)

Projectioloy – Waldo Viera (International Institute of Projectiology and Conscientiology, 2002)

Dancers between Realms – Elisabeth Y. Fitzhugh (Synchronicity Press, 2006)

The Four Winds – Alberto Villoldo and Erik Jendresen (Harper and Row, Publishers, 1990)

Tranen van de kokrodil (Tears of the Crocodile) – Piet Vroon (Ambo, 1989)

Beyond the Indigo Children – P.M.H. Atwater (Bear & Company, 2005)

Anatomy of an epidemic – Robert Whitaker (Broadway Books, 2011)

Self-remembering

A New Model of the Universe – P.D. Ouspensky (Alfred A. Knopf, Inc., 1931)

The Theory of Celestial Influence – Rodney Collin (Vincent Stuart Publishers LTD, 1954)

The Fire of Creation – J.J. v.d. Leeuw (Theosophical Publishing House, 1927)

The Master and His Emissary: The Divided Brain and the Making of the Western World – Iain McGilchrist (Yale University Press, 2010)

Entering the stage: The Empath and the Psychopath

The Highly Intuitive Child – Catherine Crawford (Publishing Group West, 2009)

Emergence – Temple Grandin, Ph.D (Warner Books, 1996)

Psychic Self-Defense – Dion Fortune (Society of the Inner Light, 1930)

People of the Lie – M. Scott Peck, M.D. (Simon & Schuster, 1983)

The Science of Evil – Simon Baron-Cohen (Basic Books, 2011)

'God'; The androgynous self, 100% responsibility

Man and his Counterpart Woman – Aleta Baker (The Order of the Portal, 1930)

She the Woman-Man – Aleta Baker (The Order of the Portal, 1935)

My Other Self – The Letters of Olive Schreiner and Havelock Ellis, edited by Yaffa Claire Draznin (Peter Lang Publishing, Inc., 1992)

The Etheric Double – A.E. Powell (The Theosophical Publishing House, 1969)

The Human Radio – Joseph Sadony (The Valley Press, 1924)

An Immortal Mind – Ervin Laslo with Anthony Peake (Inner Traditions, 2014)

Autism and the God Connection – William Stillman (Sourcebooks, Inc., 2006)

The Soul of Autism – William Stillman (The Carreer Press, Inc., 2008)

The Nature of Consciousness, the Structure of Reality – Jerry Davidson Wheatley (Research Scientific Press, 2001)

Gods in Exile – J.J. De Leeuw (The Theosophical Publishing House, 1940)

Traveling the planes, Magic and the Bridal Chamber

The Gospel of Philip – Andrew Phillip Smith (Skylight Paths Publishing, 2005)

The Seven Principles of Man – Annie Besant (The Theosophical Publishing Society, 1909)

Sorcerer's Apprentice – Amy Wallace (Frog Ltd., 2003)

Mother of God – Luna Tarlo (Plover Press, 1997)

Liber 51 – The Lost Continent – Aleister Crowley (The Yorke Collection, 1913)

The Book of Lies – Aleister Crowley (Wieland and Co., 1913)

Ascension; The Tachyon's descent into matter

The beginning was the End – Oscar Kiss Maerth (Praeger Publishers, 1974)

The Age of Empathy – Frans de Waal (Three Rivers Press, 2009)

Empathic Accuracy – William Ickes, Editor (The Guilford Press, 1997)

The Empathic Civilization – Jeremy Rifkin (Penguin Group Inc., 2009)

Children of the the Fifth World – P. M. H. Atwater (Bear & Company, 2012)

The Secret of the Creative Vacuum – John Davidson (New Age Books, 2009)

The Essential Difference – Simon Baron-Cohen (Basic Books, 2003)

The Horse Boy – Rupert Isaacson (book and documentary, Little, Brown and Company, 2009 and Zeitgeist Films, 2010)

Alleen met mijn wereld (Alone with my world) – Wessel Broekhuis (Uitgeverij Nieuwezijds, 2010)

Epilogue – On the road to Tachyon Consciousness

Living an illusion more real than any reality I had ever known;

Madeleine l'Engle's *Time Quintet* (Square Fish (boxed) Edition, 2007)

Nine Crazy Ideas in Science – Robert Ehrlich (Princeton University Press, 2002)

Future Memory – P. M. H. Atwater (Hampton Roads Publishing Company, 1995)

My own reality and dream-life diaries daily entries 2008-2015

© 2015 Andrea Frank, a.k.a. Dree Andrea van Mechelen

Journeying with the Gnostics
Confessions of a Teenage Evangelical

Steve Dee

Confessions of a Teenage Evangelical

Okay I need to come clean about my misspent youth as a teenage evangelical. Being a somewhat precocious child, I had begun a yogic and meditation practice at about the age of 10, but encountered the figure of Jesus via the Christian Surfers when I was an adolescent living in Australia. As the psychoanalyst Erik Erikson has highlighted, teenage years can be a confusing time as we seek to navigate the core dilemma of "identity formation vs. confusion". For the 14 year old version of Steve Dee, the confusion about both my sexuality and spiritual identity were worrying enough that I felt in need of rescuing from myself. This rescue came in the form of "going forward" at an evangelistic rally and "accepting Jesus as my personal friend and saviour." Although I was consistently unconvinced about their claims of exclusive truth, the lure of forgiveness and a sense of belonging that this form of church had on offer were enough to bring me into the fold. Looking back I can see that during those early years as a believer, I was definitely "in child" in wanting to be fed certainties that would calm the turmoil that I was feeling. My faith did this for me, but as I was to learn, the suppression of core drives and the central aspects of self rarely come without serious consequences:

> If you bring forth what is within you, what you bring forth will save you. If you do not bring forth what is within you, what you do not bring forth will destroy you.
> The Gospel of Thomas

The payback that I eventually experienced came during an under-graduate degree in theology at a conservative seminary. As my certainty was replaced with confusion, anxiety and eventual hallucinations, my psyche began to give way. It's fair to say that the process was far from pretty, but the fact that I'm writing this evidences the efficacy of prodigious tea drinking with friends who weren't in a hurry to respond to my demands for exorcism! In addition to the healing power of community I was also greatly aided by the stillness of contemplative prayer and the work of that great wizard Carl Jung.

Stephan Hoeller has written extensively about not only Jung's role in safe-guarding the Nag Hammadi library but also his groundbreaking role in popularising the Gnostic's emphasis on self-liberation rather than a faith-based approach to belief. Jung's contemporary re-visioning of Western alchemical traditions made vivid the idea that the making of Soul was not only a life-long journey, but that we could actively cultivate transformation via the application art, dreaming and active reflection.

From a personal perspective I needed a serious reconnection to those aspects of my identity that I had pushed underground. I needed to "own" my sense of fey, liminal Queerness and to embrace the playful curiosity that my attempt at orthodoxy had clamped down on. With his ideas concerning the shadow aspects of self and the concept of archetypal emergence from the collective unconscious, Jung provided me with fertile soil from which to start growing my own liberation. Jung was also my doorway into the realm of the Gnostics.

Strange Revelations

It's hardly surprising that more mainstream Christians found the Gnostics troubling – while outwardly appearing orthodox in many ways, with their vivid and at times anarchic mythologies, their take on the nature of the divine was radically subversive.

For the majority of the Gnostics, the realm of nature and the God of the Old Testament were incompatible with the picture of the divine painted by Christ in the New Testament. If both Yahweh and the natural world were capricious and violent how could one reconcile this with the "heavenly Father" that Jesus believed was ever listening and attentive? For many Gnostics, the tribal, desert God of the old covenant represented at best an outdated perception of the Pleroma's true nature; at worst this "God" was a deceiver actively seeking to blind humanity to the divine spark within. While I personally struggled to adopt these insights as "beliefs". I feel that they do help us as we struggle to evolve metaphysical principles that we feel are more congruent with our own experience of life.

For the religious philosopher the knotty issue of theodicy (the problem of evil) has always proven to be of a decidedly Gordian nature. Whether our gods are singular or plural, if we attach to them either omnipotence or omniscience then the reality of human pain is likely to raise some awkward questions regarding their goodness. For the fervent Dawkinite, the presence of suffering and disaster in our world is enough to render the possibility of godhead unlikely at best.

While recently revisiting some of the Gnostic's primary sources in June Singers' excellent *A Gnostic Book of Hours*, I was once again struck by the novelty of their solution to our experience of suffering:

Yaldabaoth (the demiurge) stole power from his mother (Sophia), for he was ignorant,
Thinking there existed no other except his mother alone…..
When the Arrogant One saw the creation which surrounds him
And the multitude of angels which had come forth from him,
He exalted himself above these and said to them:
"I am a jealous God, and there is no God besides me."

The Apocryphon of John

When we attempt to engage with its primary texts we see a complexity and variation that mustn't be minimised in an attempt to homogenise the subtle variety of narratives regarding our beginnings. While many present day magical practitioners may reference "gnosis" as an experiential short-hand for the in-coming of new insights, many scholars of early Gnosticism would be keen to place an emphasis on cosmic dualism as being innate to the traditions that they are seeking to categorise.

Certainly as we look at manifestations following on from the early historic sects such as the Sethians and Valentinians we do encounter groups that seem to have a decidedly negative attitude toward the realm of matter. While we may be heavily dependent of the polemical accusations of their opponents, from what we know about groups as diverse as the Manicheans and the Cathars, it is hard to deny that their views of the material realm were less than positive.

While an understanding of such a dualistic perspective may have been critical for the purposes of my own understanding of Gnosticism as a historical phenomenon, I have to remain honest in acknowledging my own questions and discomfort regarding the psychological and environmental wisdom of holding such a worldview. In some ways the radical dualism of many Gnostic schools is hardly surprising given their life expectancy, infant mortality and the lack of decent dental care! While I might struggle with such perspectives, I'm also aware that my own somewhat rose tinted eco-consciousness may largely be based on my own western privilege and the current availability of antibiotics.

In seeking to recover an arguably more nuanced position, many contemporary revivalists of the Gnostic tradition have emphasised the similarities between the gnostic message and the central dilemmas at the heart of the four noble truths [of Buddhism], and existentialism. The core concerns of both these world views regarding dissatisfaction and impermanence have considerable overlap with the Gnostic's longing for both salvation and significance that are not defined by the impermanence of the material realm.

It is also of note that given the Gnostics appeared to have placed a far higher value on a more experiential and non-historic approach to the Christ story, one might question the degree to which they themselves viewed such cosmological models literally.

THE JOY OF PROCESS THEOLOGY.

In reflecting on these themes, I am aware that in pursuing my own desire to depict the Gnostics as some sort of existential freedom fighters, that I might be glossing over their potentially hostile view of the material world. None of us come to this material without our own presuppositions and biases, and I think it's only fair to acknowledge my own as both an aspiring Process theologian and a creative magical practitioner.

For the uninitiated, Process theology is deeply interested in what the emergence of religious myth reveals about the shape and concerns of human consciousness. Even a cursory study of religious phenomena reveals both our greatest aspirations and the depths of our prejudices. Humanity's religious expressions, be they tribal deities, anthropomorphized monotheisms, or Lovecraftian terrors, all mirror our collective journey through history. This is not to imply some bleeding out of mystery; rather it glories in religion as art. The gods are real precisely because we've made them so (see Terry Pratchett's *Small Gods* for a fantastic exposition on this concept).

As I sought to engage with the Gnostic material, my own hunch was that the Demiurge gets a bit of a hard time and ends up becoming some sort of cosmic whipping boy. In most Gnostic myths, while the Pleroma takes things easy as the "unmoved mover" in some sort cosmic chill-out zone, it's the feisty Sophia and her wayward son who actually get on with doing something! Good ideas are great, but unless they work their way through to planning and creative expression, they remain ideas only. The Demiurge arguably represents the messy reality of how we produce and maintain a creative endeavor. As humans we may long for an idealised state in which nothing dies and pain never gets felt, but our shared experience of what happens day-to-day is far from this. Our yearning for Platonic ideals and the Perfect may well be part of our evolving consciousness, but it may be that the complex joy and violence of Life is like this because it couldn't function otherwise.

In trying to appreciate these potent myths, I found myself experiencing serious flashbacks to part of my day job as a family psychotherapist. In seeking to grapple with the dynamics at play within Gnostic cosmology it didn't feel that dissimilar to the issues that arise in the therapy room. In one corner we have the Pleroma as the somewhat distant father figure, seemingly critical of his wayward son's attempts to make his way in the multiverse ("Dad you just don't understand! I just want to create and make stuff happen!"). In the middle of this conflict we have a somewhat care-worn Sophia trying to mediate between these two. It's not easy being caught in the middle between a numinous perfection you respect and a wayward but creative rebel you don't want to lose.

Even with these reflections, we still need

to engage with the core dilemma of how we seek to reconcile our ever-changing, messy world with this very human longing for a more tranquil numinosity. We could certainly have a decent attempt at going into denial about either part of this equation and burying ourselves in either materialist hedonism on one extreme or spiritual fantasy on the other. The trickier alternative (and my suggestion) is that we have to bare the tension! Here we need to return to the wisdom of the Mother. Between Pleroma and Demiurge lies Sophia and although some of the gnostic myths want to lay blame at her door for seeking independence, Sophia seems to be key in understanding how the realm of the ideal works alongside our experience of reality. Wisdom (the heady fusion of intellect, experience and intuition) allows us to oil the cogs in helping our ideas become plans, our plans become actions and our actions become Art.

Hermetic Insights.

The discomfort that many of us feel in adopting a radically dualistic attitude toward the world that we know, means that many Neo-Gnostics adopt a more hermetic view of our origins. What we might describe as a form of "soft dualism", relies on a more Neo-Platonic view of emanation where the reality (and messiness) of life on our planet results from its distance from the original divine source.

This softer perspective certainly allows a greater acknowledgement that we can experience the material world as both incredibly beautiful and pleasurable without having to view such experiences as being as a result of false consciousness. To experience the tension between the imminent and transcendent, the material and ethereal, is arguably at the core of our human experience.

For myself it is within the broader Hermetic and Western alchemical traditions that we find a potent synthesis of the integrative and more dualist, adversarial positions. Via the process of seeking to transform lead into gold, the practitioner works with resistance at both a macro and microcosmic level so as to bring change.

Certainly within the Corpus Hermeticum we can see the tension between these two positions as the redactor of the current text has incorporated sayings that represent both a radically dualist and a more emanation based view. This tension between finding the divine in and through matter in contrast to abandoning it runs through the history of many religious traditions.

The Way of the Magician.

While some contemporary followers of a gnostic path find consolation in the types of sacramental mysticism born out of the French Gnostic revival and the Liberal Catholic tradition, in seeking a "lived experience" of gnosis, I chose the more anarchic path of ritual experimentation known as Chaos Magic. This form of freestyle ritual magic sought to reinvigorate the dusty pseudo-masonry of many magical orders by injecting them with a heady fusion of punk rock energy and quantum mechanical insights.

In contrast to most "believers", magicians are often those who actively seek to explore dualities and are willing to get their hands dirty in the process of seeking a potential synthesis. The tension between the transcendent and the imminent is what fuels the art and science of magic. What we experience in being embodied and feeling the pull of the transcendent fuels our curiosity and the alchemy of self-transformation. The interplay of longed for ideal and pragmatic action create a hermetic frisson via which new realities might be born.

In my own work as a magician I find myself attracted to those depictions of the Demiurge that reflect something of the alchemical tension innate to a more awakened encounter with the human dilemma. The images of both Abraxas and Baphomet that are most familiar to us, provide vivid pictorial depictions of the cosmic balancing act that we are engaged in.

Humanoid bodies mutate with animal heads and transgendered bodies, as arms point at balance or bare the whips and keys of our deliverance. For me these glyphs are road maps for becoming; the path of the demiurge being a journey through the reality of our lives not simply away from it. As much as the realm of matter and the body may provide challenges and obstacles, this is the place we find ourselves, and where the work needs to happen.

Magicians are often those who choose to walk the treacherous path of transmuting those substances which others seek to avoid. The initiate's vows of "Daring, Willing, Knowing and keeping Silent" challenge them to confront those obstacles within themselves formed by either genetic make-up or environmental conditioning. Arguably part of the 'Great Work' that we pursue in daring to "immanentize the eschaton" is the transformation of those aspects of ourselves that we could view as negative or "Archonic" in order to make them Aeonic opportunities of further becoming and evolution. This process of seeking the Kingdom of God amongst us, may seem a long way from my early Nicene beginnings, but such are the joys, terrors and adventures of the heretic.

After Simon, the Deluge

Tobias Churton

Of the Gnostics, so much has been cursorily, as it were, written. We proceed now to the sequel, and must again contemplate faith; for there are some who draw the distinction that faith has reference to the Son, and knowledge (gnosis) to the Spirit. But it has escaped their notice that, in order to believe truly in the Son, we must believe that he is the Son, and that he came, and how, and for what, and respecting his passion; and we must know who is the Son of God. Now neither is knowledge without faith, nor faith without knowledge. Nor is the Father without the Son; for the Son is with the Father. And the Son is the true teacher respecting the Father; and that we may believe in the Son, we must know the Father, with whom also is the Son. Again, in order that we may know the Father, we must believe in the Son, that it is the Son of God who teaches; for from faith to knowledge of the Son is the Father. And the knowledge of the Son and the Father, which is according to the Gnostic rule—that which in reality is Gnostic—is the attainment and comprehension of the truth by the truth.

Now the sacrifice which is acceptable to God is unswerving abstraction from the body and its passions. This is the really true piety.

(Clement of Alexandria, Strōmateis, V, 1; 11, ca. 200 CE)

That Simon Magus may personally have set the radical Gnostic ball rolling with his self-made interpretations of Jewish scripture seems to be confirmed by the names and whereabouts of heresiarchs linked by opponents to Simon's legacy. There is a time gap, however. Church tradition places Simon's death in Rome during Nero's reign of 54–68 CE, while his appearance in heresiological writings does not occur until the period 149–160 CE. Scholarship has also shown that numerous key twists of Christian practice later associated with Gnostics were present, at least in Pauline churches, from the 50s onward. Such twists, however, do not seem to have been worked into thoroughgoing all-in systems until the lifetime of Justin Martyr (ca. 100–165 CE), himself a native of Samaria with good knowledge of the region and its characters.

According to Justin's Apology to Emperor Antoninus Pius, among the first heresiarchs to impact on his territory was Menander, a Samaritan, like Simon, and said to be his pupil.[1] Menander was successful in Antioch in the early second century persuading followers that they would not die. (See the opening lines of the Gospel of Thomas: "These are the secret words which the living Jesus spoke, and Didymus Judas Thomas wrote them down. And he said: 'He who shall find the interpretation of the words shall not taste of death.'") Menander's promise does sound rather Simonian in its audacity. Hippolytus countered Menander's "realized resurrection"—spiritual awakening to eternal life before death—with the remark that death was simply a "debt of nature."

Irenaeus distinguished Menander from his

predecessor Simon, in that Menander held the chief power to be unknown to all; the world was not made at Simon's behest, but, as Simon himself taught, was fashioned by angels, themselves the work of the Ennoea of the supreme power: God's First Thought, Wisdom.2 We see at once in Menander the rift with nature also evident in the famous heresy of Menander's contemporary, Marcion of Sinope (ca. 85–ca. 180), who according to Justin Martyr held that the Father of Jesus had no contact with the world, the world's maker being a fairly savage deity responsible for the Old Testament's violent threats and cursings.

It is this rift with nature that gives Gnostic-type groups two possible paths in assessing the lusts of the flesh, even though the two radically divergent paths are deduced from the same premises. First, flesh is part of the deficient creation, so involvement with it drags the spirit down to Earth, into the realm of death and spiritual sleep. Thus, the lusts of the flesh must be subdued: a conclusion shared by Palestinian and Syrian Encratites who went so far as to abjure marriage altogether, fearing (most un-Carpocratian!) contamination with impurities.

Second, the spiritual person or pneumatic is above nature, having escaped the tragic born-to-die cycle, and so long as he or she knows and maintains awareness of this superior state, the lusts and needs of the flesh cannot harm the essential being, for the flesh is weak and the spirit ever willing. The Gnostic is above them all. Thus marriage becomes incidental, a matter of spiritual indifference, or, to use Hippolytus's phrase, "a debt of nature" for the provision of heirs or, note, the right kind of heirs: inheritors of spiritual seed. The Simonian tradition seems to have been: "make the most of it." If sex exists, and we're passing through, let's use sex to its highest potential; that way we, forever contra mundum, can at least banjax the powers of the world!

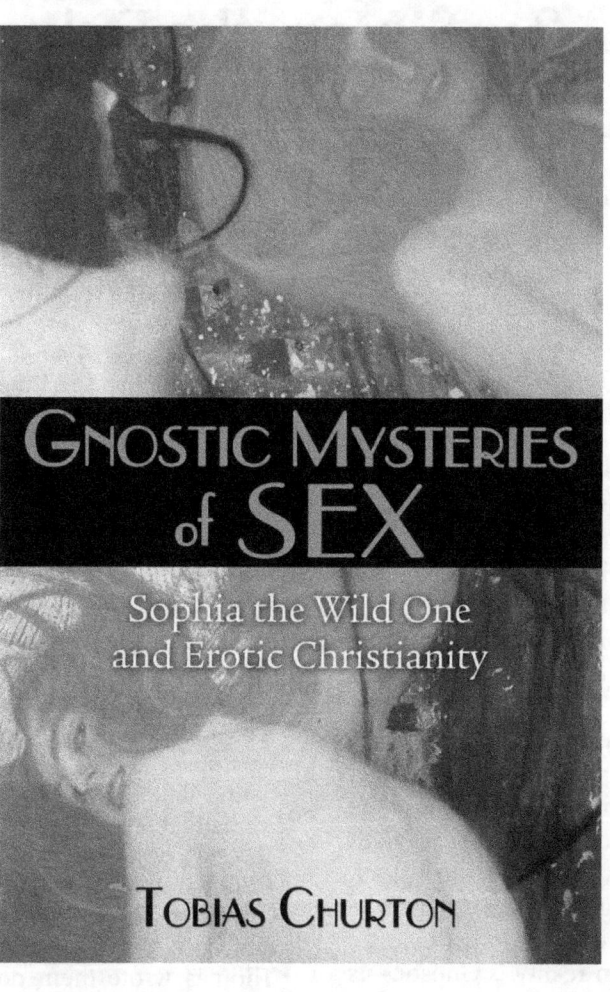

Irenaeus expresses the indifferent attitude very well in chapter 6 of his Adversus Haereses, where, describing the followers of the Gnostic Ptolemy, he sums up a prevalent conceit of Gnostic groups in his period: "For even as gold, when submersed in filth, loses not on that account its beauty, but retains its own native qualities; the filth having no power to injure the gold, so they affirm that they cannot in any measure suffer hurt, or lose their spiritual substance, whatever the material actions in which they may be involved." The idea seems to be: This Earth is the Demiurge's inn—or brothel. We're not here long; it behooves us to follow some of the rules, so long as we don't forget that we know better and will be checking out soon enough with credit.

Again, I think we see the legacy of the Book of Enoch. It is a short, though highly significant, step to go from seeing the corruption of the world as the work of the fugitive Watchers under the leadership of Azazel, to attributing the nature and indeed origin of the present creation to those same agencies, having rebelled against their maker, or gone demented with jealousy over her: the feminine Wisdom who got beyond herself.

Menander advised his followers to get the better of the creative angels. According to Irenaeus, this they achieved by magic, taught them by the revealer, Menander himself, who passed on the gnosis as a magical attainment.3 Menander's followers "obtain the resurrection by being baptized into him." Might this have indicated some kind of homosexual, or indeed heterosexual, rite? We may presume that, if it did, Irenaeus would have been glad to pass on the news. However, doing so might have made ordinary Christians question what it was to be baptized into Jesus. The emphasis then is probably on Menander's imposture in setting himself up in Jesus's place. Anyhow, Irenaeus does not impute specific sexual activity to Menander, being content with repeating the charge against Simon that Menander was a perfect adept at magic and taught how one may overcome the angels that made the world. Since Irenaeus says he taught followers that through his resurrection they would attain eternal youthfulness, there may well have been a magical elixir produced, not only figuratively but actually, and we are free to speculate that such an elixir may well have been the product of sexual activity, diverting the will of the angels for human reproduction with alternative, transgressive uses for sexual fluids.

If, incidentally, you find this discourse about dark angels a trifle incredible, it might help to see them in more psychological terms as "chains of the mind," subconscious powers that inhibit growth and awareness, though I dare say Professor Jonas would have regarded such a transposition as soft. These Gnostics believed firmly in the reality of these angels in the objective universe, which, anyhow, was their work.

Irenaeus asserts that it was at Antioch where Simon's doctrinal virus was passed by Menander to Saturninus (or Satornilos) and to Basilides, whence it found itself replanted in Alexandria, there to be subjected to extensive philosophical exploitation and theological development. It also seems likely that the link with magic continued as well, for we read in Tertullian's On the Prescription of Heretics:*

*A prescription was a Roman legal means of denying a plaintiff a court hearing.

> I shall not in this place omit to describe the conversation of heretics, how vain, and earthly, and frail it is, without weight, without authority, without discipline, though at the same time we shall readily allow it to be in every respect suitable to the faith they profess. The conversation of heretics is infamously notorious. They are almost continually with magicians, with jugglers, with astrologers, with philosophers. For the enchanting pleasure of curiosity must be gratified; "seek and ye shall find," is with them a precept never to be forgotten, a precept eternally to be insisted upon.4

Such sarcasm is leveled by every heresiologist at every heresy, heresies whose chief proponents in this period (early to mid-second century) were Cerdo, Marcion, Cerinthus, Saturnilus, and Basilides: all come in for the sarcastic treatment.

Cerdo

Apparently starting as a Simonian, Cerdo was active in Syria around 138, shortly after the Bar

Kokhba rebellion provoked the traumatic Jewish expulsion from Jerusalem and the general diaspora, accompanied by eradication of Jewish and Samaritan political identity. Hippolytus credits Cerdo with having shared his two-gods theory with Marcion, but then Hippolytus also says Marcion got his two-gods idea from Empedocles. Tertullian's take is that after Cerdo, "emerged a disciple of his, one Marcion by name, a native of Pontus, son of a bishop, excommunicated because of a rape committed on a certain virgin." Starting from the fact that, it is said, "Every good tree beareth good fruit, but an evil [tree] evil," he attempted to approve the heresy of Cerdo; so that his assertions are identical with those of the former heretic before him."5 That is to say, the world contains evil so it must be the work of one disposed to evil. Since this idea, to the orthodox, was abominably blasphemous enough, that may account for why we hear nothing concerning sexual peculiarities related to either Cerdo or Marcion. However, it is likely that Tertullian couldn't find anything more to pin on Marcion, other than his abominable ideas and that he had had an illicit affair, an accusation doubted by many scholars who think Tertullian misunderstood, or chose to misunderstand, an earlier accusation that Marcion had defiled the virgin church with his heresy.

Denial that the supreme God made the world was also attributed to Cerinthus, active around 100 CE. Hippolytus attributes Cerinthus's teaching that the Old Testament God was just, but the Father of Jesus was good, to his "being disciplined in the teaching of the Egyptians."6 This jibe may simply have meant Cerinthus had been influenced by paganism.

Justin Martyr's Dialogue with Trypho7 (ca. 150–ca. 60 CE) associates Marcionites with the followers of Basilides and with Saturnilus (or Saturninus or Satornilus), whose teacher, allegedly, was Menander. Saturnilus, in his turn, allegedly taught Basilides, and Basilides would influence Valentinus, but the connections are vague and based on similarities of idea.

SATURNILUS

Saturnilus was apparently an Encratite—Irenaeus included Encratites in his list of heresies—on account of his being ascetic, eschewing marriage. Jesus was only the appearance of the divine savior who came to save the pneuma scattered among men. Man's creation came about after the angels below caught a glimpse of a heavenly being, presumably the Logos or Gnostic anthrōpos (divine idea or ever-existing aeon of man), and tried to make one in the likeness of what they had glimpsed and in the image of themselves. Their creation was unable to stand (a Simonian echo), so the higher deity took pity and sent down pneuma to the creature, which, working as a spark and dynamic breath within man, over time, evolved within him to create the upright figure able to stand the doctrine of pneuma-salvation. Clearly, the theory of human evolution from a crawling thing to erect posture is not new ("creationists" and anti-creationists should both note!), but the spiritual motivator or spark of Logos-within might alert evolutionists to a variant interpretation of the usual materialism. Even after all this innovative pneumatic evolution, however, the heresiologists believed that, for Saturnilus, the body did not count, since the spark flees heavenward when the corpse is discarded. The highest God might just as well have kept the pneuma to himself in the first place, rather than subject it to ignominious incarnation!

Now it may be that, contrary to the last chapter's suggestion, a fully Encratite type of Gnostic was indeed active in the early to mid-second century, of a Syrian-Palestinian /northwest Mesopotamian provenance. However, it is just as possible that these ideas were backdated from the late second and early third century, when Encratism was considered a priority problem for orthodox authorities, a problem sufficiently painful to inspire the anti-Encratite chapter 26 of book 4 of Clement of Alexandria's Strōmateis, titled "How the Perfect Man Treats the Body and the Things of the World." On the other hand, the libertine Simonian strain might have been the exception, but this is unlikely. Irenaeus, for example, mentions a sect of Nicolaitanes, followers, he says of Nicholas, one of the seven apostle-appointed deacons referred to in the Acts of the Apostles. "They lead," Irenaeus says, "lives of unrestrained indulgence," deeming adultery a thing indifferent.8

In book 1, chapter 28, Irenaeus refers to the Encratites directly, saying they are "springing from Saturninus and Marcion," suggesting perhaps that followers of the latter have "moved on" from older heresies with new, stricter ideas about denying marriage, insisting on vegetarianism, lest they take in "created" flesh and corrupt themselves. Encratites, Irenaeus insists, set aside "the original creation of God" (male and female) and gainsay the divine wisdom of procreation. They "indirectly" blame God for having made men and women. This suggests another take on the androgynous, or more likely, sexless, spirit. Encratites also deny that Adam (the first created) will be saved. This, however, says Irenaeus, is only the latest notion (ca. 180 CE), and he attributes it to one Tatian, originally a "hearer" (or uncommitted acolyte) of Justin, and who, after Justin's martyrdom, allegedly separated himself from the church to assume big ideas about being a teacher, inventing his own system of invisible aeons, "while like Marcion and Saturninus, he declared that marriage was nothing else than corruption and fornication."9 Irenaeus concedes laconically that denying Adam's salvation really was original to Tatian!—its very originality rendering it ridiculous.

Immediately after implying that Gnostics might be "going Encratite," Irenaeus presents us with fresh fever:

> Others, again, following upon Basilides and Carpocrates, have introduced promiscuous intercourse and a plurality of wives and are indifferent about eating meats sacrificed to idols, maintaining that God does not greatly regard such matters. But why continue? For it is an impracticable attempt to mention all those who, in one way or another, have fallen away from the truth.

If the picture appeared confusing to Irenaeus, a man on the ground so to speak, we must be permitted some margin for error in assessing the facts of the situation over eighteen hundred years later.

Again, we cannot be sure if all the views attributed to Saturnilus by Hippolytus10 are not those of later followers, but it is most interesting to see how, in Hippolytus's account of Saturnilus, beliefs about marriage are tied in with what is clearly a development of the ideas of the earlier and post-Jesus portions of the Book of Enoch. That is to say that in the earliest part of the Book of Enoch, written between the first century BCE and the lifetime of Jesus, God (the Father of Lights) determines to quash the earthly power of the evil angels (Watchers), led by Azazel, who have sinned and fornicated with the daughters of men, while in the later sections, the agent of the angels' apocalyptic downfall is named as the "Son of Man" (considered by scholars as a Jewish-Christian interpolation). The Enochian picture appears directly in Hippolytus's account of Saturnilus where the wicked "Watchers" have probably been translated into the Greek "Archons" or "Rulers" of zodiacal fate:

> And he says that the God of the Jews is one of the angels, and, on account of the Father's wishing to deprive of sovereignty all the Archons [my italics], that Christ came for the overthrow of the God of the Jews, and for the salvation of those that believe upon Him; and that these have in them the scintillation of life. For he asserted that two kinds of men had been formed by the angels—one wicked, but the other good. And, since demons from time to time assisted wicked [men, Saturnilus affirms] that the Savior came for the overthrow of worthless men and demons, but for the salvation of good

men. And he affirms that marriage and procreation are from Satan [my italics]. The majority, however, of those who belong to this [heretic's school] abstain from animal food likewise, [and] by this affectation of asceticism [make many their dupes]. And [they maintain] that the prophecies have been uttered, partly by the world-making angels, and partly by Satan, who is also the very angel whom they suppose to act in antagonism to the cosmic [angels] and especially to the God of the Jews. These, then, are in truth the tenets of Saturnilus.

I suspect here that we have perhaps one of the best sources to account for negative views on marriage advocated by some of those promoting a redemptive gnosis from the grip of the archons. The wicked angels have defiled the relations that should pertain to spiritual beings by means of their evil seed, passed on from generation to generation. Such believers would find nothing to admire in the sex-charged Simonians, unless, of course, they accepted an interpretation of Simonian sex magic as the sacramental means for redeeming the vulnerable logos spermatikos, but it is impossible to believe the Encratite type could ever tolerate the thought of spermatophagous rites.

Such qualms would not have bothered some of the other Gnostic groups that had emerged by, at least, the 170s.

Extracted from *Gnostic Mysteries of Sex by Tobias Churton*

To purchase this book visit B&N.com, Amazon.com, InnerTraditions.com, or your local bookstore.

Gnostic Mysteries of Sex by Tobias Churton © 2015 Inner Traditions. Printed with permission from the publisher Inner Traditions International.

www.InnerTraditions.com

Jeffrey S. Kupperman

Marsilio Ficino and Alchemy as Material Theurgy: The Synthematic Function of Alchemical Prima Materia

There were several Renaissance critiques of alchemy. Most focused on the obscurity of the language, the numerous charlatans, and a general arbitrariness of the occult in general.[1] From the practitioner's perspective, a more important critique is that the goal of alchemy, the transformation of base material into another, purer, substance, is impossible. This is because, according to this view, what alchemy seeks to perform is transubstantiation, which can only be accomplished via divine miracle. As alchemy seeks to speed up natural processes, not transcend them, what alchemists seek cannot be found through their art. Such a view rests on Aristotle's elemental theory, which does not allow for the transformation of one substance into another in nature.[2] But what if transubstantiation is not what alchemy seeks? What if, as I intend to show, it instead seeks to reveal what is already present in the prima material: the perfect and divine synthemata, tokens or signatures, present in all nature?

Alchemical texts often read like they are one-part obscure cookbook, one-part Greek mythology, and one-part acid trip. As we've seen, this tendency was well criticized in the Renaissance. Arguably, these kinds of critiques can be safely set aside. Every discipline has its technical language, not to mention its fare share of charlatans. The primary critique of alchemy as aiming towards the impossible-to-attain-in-nature transubstantiation [a little awkward: "a transubstantiation impossible to obtain in nature" instead?]is more serious. This is not simply a criticism of alchemy's form or technical aspects. It is a criticism of alchemy itself. If the goal of alchemy is transubstantiation in nature, and this is impossible to obtain, then all alchemical pursuits are pointless.

There are two primary ways in which this critique might be addressed. First, we might argue that transubstantiation in nature is possible. However, it seems unlikely any Christian alchemist of the Renaissance would make such an argument. The host and wine of the Eucharist are the primary foci of the language of transubstantiation. Their transformation into the body and blood of Christ occurs only through divine grace; outside the realm of natural processes. As such, using the language of transubstantiation in reference to the alchemical process, which occurs in nature or as a speeding up of natural processes, would be inappropriate.

The second approach is to deny alchemy seeks transubstantiation. To do this, we would argue any transformations produced via alchemy are entirely natural and yet still lead to the seemingly super-natural results sought. To do this, we do not want to go outside the areas of knowledge and beliefs with which Renaissance alchemists and occultists were familiar. This is entirely possible, and there is no need to step away from the Aristotelian elemental theory already mentioned. All that is required is recourse to the theurgic thought of late Neoplatonism, which is

---

1 See Christopher I. Lehrich, *The Language of Demons and Angels: Cornelius Agrippa's Occult Philosophy* (Boston: Brill, 2003), 82-91 for a brief overview of these.

2 Lehrich, *Language*, 90.

well known for incorporating Aristotle into its Platonism.

Theurgic Neoplatonism is by no means beyond the experiences of Renaissance occultists. It has already been demonstrated the so-called Hermeticism of many Renaissance esotericisms, from Marsilio Ficino to Cornelius Agrippa and Paracelsus, has Neoplatonism at its roots.[3] While there may be little outright alchemy in his works, Ficino is listed as a fourteenth century Italian alchemical authority,[4] he made constant use of planetary metals, and his commentary on the Timaeus has in it a great deal to whet an alchemist's appetite, including chapters on Chaos, metals, the origin of gold and the use of salt and nitre. There is even more alchemical language in his commentary on the Enneads of Plotinus.[5] As such, it is not surprising that his De Vita Libri Tres[6] incorporates Neoplatonic thought, and contains instructions for creating both talismans and healing concoctions following suspiciously alchemical recipes. The latter, especially, is reminiscent of alchemical medicines. Here is an example of one:

Take four ounces of chebule myrobalans, three of rose-sugar, in winter one ounce of preserved ginger, in summer half an ounce. Cook these three gently with emblic honey and coat it with seven leaves of gold. Take a morsel of it four hours before dinner on an empty stomach. Take it daily for at least a whole year and 'thy youth shall be renewed like the eagle's.[7]

How is this like alchemy? On the surface, it is not. This recipe uses several ingredients, rather than a single "first matter." Although the ingredients are gently cooked, a common alchemical process, there is no indication that this should be done in a way different from regular cooking. The simmering of the ingredients again is more suggestive of regular cooking than of alchemy. But this is the surface.

Ficino's De Vita relies heavily on the Neoplatonic concept of synthemata, tokens or signatures. Such tokens are manifestations of the logoi or reason-principles of the gods in and through nature. They can be thought of as the thoughts of the gods, or God, crystallized in nature: animal, vegetable, and mineral. The key to the above recipe is that we are told it was "received from Jupiter."[8] This tells us the ingredients share one thing in common: they are Jovial in nature. That is, they are all synthemata, tokens or signatures, of Jupiter, which in the Neoplatonism of Antiquity, is the manifestation of the body of Zeus. In effect, there are not several ingredients but one.[9]

The 5th century Neoplatonist Proclus, in a text translated by Ficino, shows the propensity for many things sharing the same synthematic quality: "Thus, consider the multitude of solar animals, such as lions and cocks, which also share in the divine, following their own order."[10]

---

3 See Jeffrey S. Kupperman, "Marsilio Ficino and the Neoplatonic Roots of Modern Hermetism," *The Gnostic* 5 (2011): 151-157.

4 Peter J. Forshaw, "Marsilio Ficino and the Chemical Art," in *Laus Platonici Philosophi*, ed. Stephen Clucas, Peter J. Forshaw, and Valery Rees (Boston: Brill, 2011), 249.

5 Ibid., 255.

6 Pierre Borel lists this as an alchemical text in his 17th century *Biblioteca Chimica*. See Foreshaw, "Chemical Art," 256.

7 Ficino, Marsilio. *Three Books on Life: A Critical Edition and Translation with Introduction and Notes*. Translated by Carol V. Kaske and John R. Clark. Tempe, AZ: Medieval & Renaissance Texts & Studies, 1998. II.5, 215.

8 Ibid.

9 The inclusion of gold may seem odd here, as it is related to the sun and therefore Apollo or Helios. However, some of the Neoplatonists of antiquity, such as Julian the Philosopher, identified Zeus with Helios, making them cognate with one another.

10 Brian Copenhaver, "Proclus, On the Priestly Art According to the Greeks," in "Hermes Trismegistus, Proclus, and the Question of a Philosophy of Magic in the Renaissance," in *Hermeticism and the*

Also added to the list of solar sunthemata are the lotus, sunstone, and a stone called "Bel's eye."[11]

Seeing alchemical prima materia as a form of synthemata begins to solve the above criticism of alchemy. In this light, alchemy serves to give the alchemist direct access to the synthemata by removing, or refining, the dross hylic form in which the synthematic logoi are entombed. However, in order for alchemy to be theurgy, it must meet at least a general definition of theurgy, which has at least two parts. As Iamblichus writes, theurgy

> presents a double aspect. On the one hand, it is performed by men, and as such observes our natural rank in the universe; but on the other, it controls divine symbols, and in virtue of them is raised up to union with the higher powers, and directs itself harmoniously in accordance with their dispensation, which enables it quite properly to assume the mantle of the gods. It is in virtue of this distinction, then, that the art both naturally invokes the powers from the universe as superiors, inasmuch as the invoker is a man, and yet on the other hand gives them orders, since it invests itself, by virtue of the ineffable symbols, with the hieratic role of the gods.[12]

Iamblichus' description includes the divine symbols, our synthemata. However, theurgy also requires a divine element beyond the manipulation of synthemata. The manipulation of divine tokens through purely human means is sorcery. The ritual act becomes theurgy when the practitioner is in line with the divine through the rites handed down from the gods, or God, to humanity. That is, theurgy occurs when humans engage in the activities of the divine.

This way of thinking is brought into Christianity through the hieratic, or theurgic, liturgies of the Christian Neoplatonist Dionysius the pseudo-Areopagite. These rites, including baptism and the Eucharist, are seen as being divine in origin, and undertaken by divine authority as transmitted through the Hierarch or Bishop. We might even link the purifying power of the fiery Seraphim, which is brought into manifestation in the application of the chrism by the Hierarch, with the purifications through heat employed by the alchemist. And, of course, Ficino was quite familiar with the Dionysian corpus. During the Middle Ages and Renaissance it was quite normal to see Plato himself connected with alchemy, especially in relation to the ontologically-inclined Timaeus.[13] Ficino, not only in De Vita, but also in Argumentum in Critiam and later commentary on the Enneads, makes alchemical-like comparisons between the seven planets and seven metals.

Ficino's De Vita bridges the gap between alchemy and theurgy. In the third book, Ficino discusses both talismancy and astrology, connecting the efficacy of both, explicitly in the case of the former, implicitly in the case of the latter, to the activity of the divine World Soul:

In addition, the World Soul possesses by divine power precisely as many seminal reasons of things as there are Ideas in the Divine Mind. By these seminal reasons she fashions the same number of species in matter. That is why every single species corresponds through its own seminal reason to its own Idea and oftentimes through this reason it can easily receive something from the Idea since indeed it was

---

Renaissance, ed. Ingrid Merkel and Allen G. Debus (Cranbury, NJ: Associated University Presses, 1988), 102.

11 Ibid., 104.

12 Iamblichus, *On the Mysteries*. Translated by Emma C. Clarke, John M. Dillon, and Jackson P. Hershbell (Atlanta, GA: Society of Biblical Literature, 2003), IV.2, 207.

13 Forshaw, "Chemical Art," 253.

made through the reason from the Idea. This is why, if at any time the species degenerates from its proper form, it can be formed again with the reason as the proximate intermediary and, through the Idea as intermediary, can then be easily reformed. And if in the proper manner you bring to bear on a species, or on some individual in it, many things which are dispersed but which conform to the same Idea, into this material thus suitably adapted you will soon draw a particular gift from the Idea, through the seminal reason of the soul.[14]

The above sounds a great deal like an alchemical process. The Idea discussed here is the logos contained within the synthema contained within the World Soul. Also, by connecting astrological medicine to astrological talismancy, which work through the divine movement of the planets, Ficino implies a similar activity in the creation of his medicines. Ficino also connects the World Soul to the alchemical quintessence, an idea brought out of De Vita by the 16th century alchemist Philipp Ulstad.[15] This being the case, we now have a direct connection between alchemy and the two parts of theurgy; synthemata and the imitation of divine activity.

How does this answer the original critique, that alchemy cannot accomplish its goal because it requires divine activity outside of nature? First, it provides for a divine origin of alchemy. That is, alchemy is an imitation of divine activity, which includes the purification of objects and the exemplifying the synthemata they contain. If the criticism of alchemy is that it requires divine activity in order to accomplish its ends, then that is met by alchemy being in imitation of the divine. That is, alchemy becomes a form of demiurgy, in the Neoplatonic sense of the term.

Second, it shows that the transformations alchemy seeks, even if requiring divine activity, need not occur outside of nature. The accessing of synthemata through physical processes is well attested to in Iamblichus, who discusses material theurgy at length. None of the processes of material theurgy, or alchemy, need to happen outside of nature. Through Providence, divine activity occurs within and through nature.

Bibliography

Copenhaver, Brian. "Proclus, On the Priestly Art According to the Greeks." In "Hermes Trismegistus, Proclus, and the Question of a Philosophy of Magic in the Renaissance." In *Hermeticism and the Renaissance*, eds. Ingrid Merkel and Allen G. Debus, 79-110. Cranbury, NJ: Associated University Presses, 1988.

Ficino, Marsilio. *Three Books on Life: A Critical Edition and Translation with Introduction and Notes*. Trans. Carol V. Kaske and John R. Clark. Tempe, AZ: Medieval & Renaissance Texts & Studies, 1998.

Forshaw Peter J.,"Marsilio Ficino and the Chemical Art." In *Laus Platonici Philosophi*, eds. Stephen Clucas and Peter J. Forshaw, 249-271. Boston: Brill, 2011.

Iamblichus, On the Mysteries. Trans. Emma C. Clarke, John M. Dillon, and Jackson P. Hershbell. Atlanta, GA: Society of Biblical Literature, 2003.

Kupperman, Jeffrey S. "Marsilio Ficino and the Neoplatonic Roots of Modern Hermetism." *The Gnostic* 5 (2011): 151-159.

Lehrich, Christopher I. *The Language of Demons and Angels: Cornelius Agrippa's Occult Philosophy*. Boston: Brill. 2003.

---

14 De Vita, III.1, 243.

15 Forshaw, "Ficino," 258.

The Crucifixion of Christ-j242

The nail was hammered first through one wrist then the other. Jesus gave out a great cry, 'My god, my God! Why hast thou forsaken me?'

The husk of the mortal Jesus expired slowly and agonisingly on the cross. He gave up the ghost, the Christ spirit within him ascending to the Father.

'This one's an adoptionist, spirit-based christology, parallel H-578,' shouted the angel Phanael to the archangel Uriel over the deafening noise, as the immensely powerful Christ-spirit ascended the ether, returning to the father in an etheric whoosh of blinding light that blasted aside the angels as it roared up to the Father. Just because they weren't material beings it didn't mean that nobody could get hurt. Protective goggles and wing protectors had to be worn in the ether whenever they were working with a Christ.

'There he goes,' replied Uriel, 'straight up to the Father. Like always.' It was an intense, perfectly circular beam of light, rising from the cross up to the heavens. The luminous flurries were difficult for the angels even to squint at through the goggles, but in the column of light there were suggestions of a gaunt, bearded male face, high-cheekboned, the body indistinct, draped in linen robes. Suddenly the column brightened and the volume increased, in an artificiality redolent of CGI effects. Then the pillar of light was gone, leaving in its wake only an intimation of divinity, almost a resinous scent, all that remained of a unique cosmic event, of a son ransomed for many.

'He's gone now. Leaving us to clear up his shit. Do we get a proper forty-day resurrection period this time? Do we even need one if it's an adoptionist milieu? Doesn't Jesus get adopted as the son at some specific time as he's invested as Christ, then it's back off to the Father once he's finished and we're done with him? I'm not quite clear on it. What are the regulations?'

'He has to come back down again, just for decency's sake. '

'When was he officially adopted by the Father? At birth? When he got baptised by John, with the dove and everything?'

'No, H-578 was adopted as Son when he was crucified. Poor bastard. So Jesus the carpenter's son got to be Jesus Christ just for a matter of hours, and excruciating ones at that, and then he's back to poor old Jesus bar Joseph again.

'Does he return in a physical body or a spiritual body? "

'It's a physical body, but it's spiritually powered, apparently.'

'And what is that supposed to fucking mean?'

'Nobody's sure. Look, I don't make the rules, I just carry them out. Nobody said it was meant to make sense.'

'Maybe I'll get promoted to scrubbing the sewers of Hell if I'm lucky. Anything but this.

'Well, there's no point waiting around. There's only his weeping Jewish mother and some seriously depressed disciples to gawp at down here. Tell Teiaiel the angel of dominion over the future to fast forward a bit.'

There was the temporal equivalent of a hiccough, or perhaps it was more like a spasm, or a blackout, and suddenly the beam of divine light was returning back again, rushing down towards earth, triumphant and holier-than-thou.

'Get out of the way, Phaniel! Fuck! I got my wings singed again. It's the smell that's worst.'

The risen Christ had returned to Earth. It didn't always go according to plan like this. But when it did it wasn't necessarily enjoyable viewing. The disciples would all be so miserable, ignoring the women at the tomb and dismissing their testimonies of the risen Christ, and were then so exultant once He had appeared to them on the road to Emmaus, and so smug afterwards that the overall effect was tedious.

'OK, Teiaiel, take us forward forty days to the ascension.'

This time they stood well back as the column of light bored its way through the ether and vanished, a job well done.

'Everyone get some rest,' said Uriel. 'Events in these first few weeks and months after the ascension usually play out in the same way. Sariel can keep a weather eye on the monitor. Post-pentecostal disciples, increasing numbers of converts, antagonism between these new people of the Way and other Jews. Judaean rebellions. Roman reprisals. You know the score. Atrocities. Schism. Dogma. When Saul becomes Paul pay a bit more attention. That can often be a crucial time. No pun intended. Crucial. Cross. They have the same etymology. Get it?'

'It only works in English,' said Phanael.

By the year 70 events had more or less progressed as they always did. Some of the disciples and their followers had decided that Jesus wasn't adopted on the cross after all but had been born the son of God. The archangels watched at the monitor, its blue light illuminating their etheric faces. The proto-orthodox Christians were getting increasingly belligerent, literal-minded and, of course, were well-organised. As the second century started up the overall scene was depressingly familiar. Martyrs were cropping up and getting chopped down like summer weeds.

'Whew, this is tedious,' said Sariel. 'Can't we just skim through the centuries?'

'The word from above was this one might be exceptional,' said Uriel.

'He looks like your bog-standard Christ to me, adoptionist or not.'

'Wait and see,' said Uriel.

* * *

The centuries creaked past, boredom rusting away the hearts of the angels as they watched the decline of technology and the fall of civilization as Christianity supplanted the classical world. The first millennium came and went and the medieval world erupted into crusade and Inquisition. Sariel finally had enough. 'Is He coming back? Have you found out yet?'

Uriel replied, 'The message came through a short while ago. He's not returning. No Second Coming for parallel H-578, boys.'

They got as far as the early twenty-first century, watched Christianity fizzle out in western Europe, blinked deliberately in affected disbelief as they viewed the rise of fundamentalism and the emergent Christianity of the third world. There was no point lingering. They knew exactly how the rest would play out. They gave up on the parallel and returned to Heaven, leaving an ancient yet seedy and incompetent cherub as its caretaker. As they vacated the ether of this parallel earth Uriel looked back and noticed that the cherub already had his tiny cock out already and was jerking off to the scenes on the monitor.

* * *

If the Ether had been immaterial, Heaven was even more so. Uriel had had time to decompress and debrief. There had been nothing unusual to report. He wished he could get off Messiah detail, but he had been on it long enough for everyone to acknowledge his expertise. The endless light was giving him a headache and the lack of form always made it hard for him to think. He tired quickly of kicking around in beatitude and was glad when he received a call from Gabriel himself.

'Christ isn't happy,' Gabriel told him in his clipped voice. 'And when Christ isn't happy the Father isn't happy. Christ doesn't see the point in zapping up and down in all these parallel earths when the outcome is always more or less identical. If he's going to continue with it at all, he wants results. It's all very painful for him, don't you realise? Something has to change.'

* * *

'What if we make Jesus wholly man and wholly God, since that's what the Christians—or at least the Church triumphant—always seem to want him to be. ' said Uriel.

'Wholly man and a holy man!' said Phanael.

'That pun only works in English. We prefer Aramaic and Greek up here, Latin if really necessary. Keeps us connected to the right time and place. Wholly man and wholly God is what we need.'

'And how exactly do you propose we engineer that?'

'I … uh … we can't do it, can we?'

'No we can't. So that means …'

'It means we'll have to fake it. We'll have to intervene at the Council of Nicaea and convince them that he was wholly God and wholly man all along. '

'And what is that going to mean in practice?'

'More waiting around.'

* * *

They tried giving him a dual nature. It failed. The twentieth and twenty-first centuries were always a litmus test. If the situation on the Earth hadn't improved by then, they were done for. They checked. They assessed. They even measured and quantified the success of the operation. Was the Earth in a state ready for Christ to return? It wasn't. They abandoned this parallel too, J-348, calling in the same seedy cherub who had stayed as nightwatchman for the previous one. He looked the same as ever, despite his age, with his pink rosy cheeks and his tousled hair. He was naked of course, and they couldn't help looking down at him then looking away.

* * *

Desperation began to take hold. One of Gabriel's suggestions had been to take some cues from Islam. Not that Islam had worked out any better, particularly by the twentieth and twenty-first centuries, but Gabriel had notoriously been intimately involved in its conception and a focus on that later faith always went down well with him.

They had also been thinking about Judas. Poor Judas. It was convenient to have a scapegoat, they usually thought, and Judas could bear the burden. It was a nasty situation, but didn't he do it out of his own free will, more or less? It was Gabriel's opinion that the Father thought this was so. Well, if Judas wished to blunder into roughly the same trap on every single parallel Earth, that was up to him. And if the burden of blame continually fell on him, well that burden could be a little bit heavier if they so wished. And correspondingly Jesus's burden could be lightened in other ways. Maybe that would be enough to set up conditions for a second coming.

So what they did was this: Jesus was the Christ, okay. And there was no point at all in doing this if the Christ spirit wasn't going to get involved. Or was there? Maybe they would look into that later. In any case, this time it was going to be all about Muhammad. Perhaps if the mission of Jesus was more closely linked with that of Muhammad the end result would be more successful. Integration, that was the key.

Jesus would go through the usual motions, and he would preach the same things. But he would deny that he was the son of God, and all of his emphasis would be on the coming of Muhammad. He would be like a John the Baptist to Muhammad. Well, like a John the Baptist who lived several centuries before the Prophet, and didn't baptise him, and would never actually meet him. And who would be treated by the Prophet as a mere mortal human being. But as a forerunner, nonetheless. In that way there would perhaps at least be peace between Islam and Christianity. And Judas could help out. Judas would like to do that, surely.

'It's going to be a stool with three legs, Phanael. Jesus prepares for the Prophet. Judas has a bigger role. And, wait for it, the clincher: Jesus doesn't really get crucified. I think Christ would be up for that, don't you?' He winked at Phanael.

'How are we going to achieve that?'

'We're going to introduce some angelic intervention. Why not?'

Jesus did as they planned and preached and prophesied the one who was to come, the Prophet, the one whose shoelaces he was not worthy to tie. Or was it unloose? Judas betrayed Jesus but just as the Roman soldiers were about to enter the upper room Phanael and Uriel abducted Jesus, transformed the appearance of Judas into that of Jesus and allowed him to be crucified in Jesus' place. Everyone was happy, apart from Judas of course, but Judas was never happy, was usually suicidal to tell the truth, and they were confident that Muhammad would have an easier time of it, though they knew it was beyond their remit to get involved with the Prophet.

They fast forwarded through the years, the decades, the centuries. Once they got to the so-called industrial and post-industrial epochs everything looked the same as it usually did. Somehow the gospels in the New Testament had been doctored and just told the usual story. The only traces of what had really happened were in the Qu'ran which only mentioned, somewhat ambiguously, that Jesus hadn't been crucified, and in the Gospel of Barnabas, which told the whole story but was somehow rejected in the western world as a medieval fake. Christ did not come back for a second coming and 'what, indeed, would have been the point if he had?' opined Uriel.

They looked at the possibility of a Sunni Muslim Jesus. It seemed much likelier that he might return than any of the others. Like the previous Muslim Jesus he had not been crucified, but was taken up into Heaven while still alive. Yet when he did come back he was destined to kill all the pigs, smash all the crosses and destroy the churches. The damage to livestock and property was bad enough, but this returning Sunni Jesus would cap it all by destroying all Christians who believe in Jesus as the Son of God rather than as a prophet. It wasn't advisable.

* * *

Their radical invention hadn't worked so they took to tweaking again. Let's make Jesus more apocalyptic. Surely that will bring on the second coming. All the "Love thy neighbour" and the parables and the bread and the wine and the miracles and al that were nice enough, but surely they were somewhat beside the point. The end of days was the thing. After all, the return of Jesus Christ was their own litmus test as to the success of an incarnation.

They tried, and fast forwarded, and found everything as usual in the depressing decadence of the third millennium. The problem with apocalypticism is that is was always more attractive when deferred. Thus Christ would never find the conditions right for his return.

'He should be more Jewish,' said Phanael. They rebooted once again into another parallel, M-957, and made him more Jewish. Jesus was a Jew. He usually was, in just about every single parallel, with only a few quirky variations in which he was a Celt, or an African, or a Chinese man, or in one ridiculous instance, an Australian aboriginal. He was nearly always a Jew, but in this one he was a Jew. It had its effect. There were Jewish Christians everywhere. They kept the kosher laws and got their male children circumcised. They were ejected from Jerusalem along with the other Jews when the Romans suppressed their rebellion. Jesus was a rabbi, they said, the greatest of them all. He was the son of man, but wasn't the fishmonger a son of man too. He wasn't the son of God. These Christians read the Torah and didn't eat with gentiles. Jesus was the messiah, the king of the Jews.

But the angels had forgotten about Paul. Sure enough he didn't seem to have much influence in his own lifetime. There were the epistles, sure, but many of them weren't even by him in the first place. Nor was his influence huge by the second century. But somehow or other thousands of gentiles had converted to Christianity, despite the plan, and those genuinely Jewish Christians were intermarrying with Gentiles themselves, the Christian children of Jewish mothers even forgetting they were Jews. Many of them just putting aside their Jewishness. The remainder were converting back to Judaism. Uriel gave a weary glance to Phanael. They knew what was going to happen and could barely muster the energy to fast forward. As they gazed out into the twenty-first century that cherub, now red-eyed, was already jerking away. He didn't even try to hide it.

They were getting desperate. 'Make him more gentile, more Greek.' They decided. There were plenty of Greeks in the decapolis in Galilee anyway.

'What kind of Greek?'

Uriel thought of the masturbating cherub and said, 'What about that philosopher who lived in a barrel, the one who used to masturbate in public?'

'Diogenes, the cynic, you mean?'

'That's him.'

So they made Jesus into the Jewish equivalent of a Hellenistic cynic philosopher, whatever that could be, and he was pretty indistinguishable from all the others, it turned out, though some of the proverbs were a bit pithier, though most of these were lost in transmission. The twenty-first century cherub liked the influence of Diogenes and acquired his own barrel in which to monitor the parallel as it played itself out.

Pentecost was when the despondent apostles were filled with the holy spirit. Everyone liked the Holy Spirit. The spirit was breath, the spirit was life. The spirit inspired and had neither the authoritarian tendencies of the Father nor the self-obsession of the Son. The spirit even had a feminine quality; some said the spirit was the Mother. Let's emphasise the Spirit, they decided.

All was going well. Pentecost went off with a bang and, for once, the conversion of Saul presented no problem. Paul loved the Spirit too, though he kept quiet about her feminine qualities. It was better to marry than to burn, and all that. Uriel and Phanael rubbed their hands with glee and flexed their wings. The individual feathers shuffled fractally, as white and as individual as snowflakes. But when they peeked ahead optimistically the gears of time had ground down the influence of the spirit. She wanders where she will and had seemingly wandered off. Early in the twentieth century a pentecostal movement offered the experience of the spirit to anyone who would join them. Millions took up the offer, but somehow they were ignored by the mainstream. There was something a little tawdry and ersatz about it after all. It had all looked so promising but had petered out.

Gabriel summoned them.

'The Christ is not happy. How many times shall he be crucified for ye? Must ye nail him to the cross over and over again?'

Uriel made a brave joke, 'Well if the conditions are never right for his second coming, then yes.'

Gabriel's visage was as black as a coal and his anger as red as the fire that a coal feeds. They didn't hang around.

In the next iteration they decided they actually wouldn't crucify Christ this time. Just Jesus. It would amount to a dry run, a way of testing variables and making little calculations and manipulating little details. There was no reason for Christ to be incarnated and to suffer under Pontius Pilate. Just little Jesus. This Jesus was wholly human. He taught in parables and he healed. He consorted with the outcasts, with prostitutes and tax collectors and lepers and gentiles. He told them to love one another, to feed the poor, to forgive sinners. He was a good man.

They crucified him. And then they decided he was God after all. Even though the Son had never entered into this human Jesus they acted as if he had and at the Council of Nicea they declared him wholly God and wholly man. And by the twenty-first century the whole mess had developed as usual.

'There may be technical issues,' suggested Phanael. 'Some sort of resonance between parallel worlds. Each time we make a change history starts to vibrate in unison with the other parallel worlds and hey presto we get the same outcome.'

Uriel thought long and hard about this. 'You may be right, or you may not. But if that is the case we can hardly ask the Father to roll out an entire new multiverse just because we're having technical difficulties.'

They tried numerous variations of the Jesus as human theme. After all, it was cheap and the Son didn't have to suffer on the cross: what's not to like? They made the Good Man Jesus primarily a healer. They made him more charismatic. They made him a charismatic healer. They made him a Jewish charismatic healer, they made him a Hellenized Jewish charismatic healer. They could afford to take this step by step. Yet none of them came to anything. Uriel shrugged, his wings drooping, and he requested an audience with Gabriel. Gabriel was carrying a nasty-looking sceptre and at one point Uriel thought he was going to hit him with it. But the job was done. Christ had agreed that He would get involved again. After all, how could Christ return for a second coming if he hadn't had a first coming?

But Christ wanted some real changes. He wanted them to put some creativity into it. He wanted something new, something fresh. They obliged. The feminine Spirit had been popular so they put a lot of emphasis of Mary Magdalene. Jesus enjoyed that, and so did the Christ spirit inhabiting him, you can be sure. They had babies. Their babies had babies. Their lineage passed down through the centuries, a holy bloodline, a holy sangreal, establishing a kingdom of their own, a royal Merovingian line. It waned. They were usurped. But the line continued in secret, each heir guarded by a secret society that protected him. The twentieth century came and surely the hidden messiah would emerge. Surely Christ could return, his spirit descending to inhabit his remote descendent. But the heir of Jesus by this point was a seedy, right-wing Frenchman. Uriel took one look and advised Gabriel to hold off.

Yet they could take some inspiration from this attempt. They had another go at the kingship theme. His kingdom was not of this world. It didn't work. His kingdom was of this world. Didn't work. He was the son of David, the messiah who would free his people from the Roman yoke. They crucified him and Rome continued as a great power for centuries after, although the Christians had a hand in its eventual failure, you can be sure.

They were running out of options and they recognised that Christ increasingly required some novelty to persuade him into incarnation.

They tried a Gnostic Jesus. He was docetic. He didn't even have a real body and didn't suffer on the cross, which was always a plus. It was a little disconcerting to see Christ laughing at the poor Simon of Cyrenea as the poor guy asphyxiated in agony on the cross. But Christ knew what it was like. And the poor Son needed a laugh occasionally. They tried to tweak the docetic body but the main problem was that most Christians couldn't work out what on earth doceticism was all about and just decided that he must have had a physical body anyway.

Novelty became the order of the day. Let's focus on the Passion of the Christ, they decided. It would be a bit rough, a bit violent. Heck, it would be brutal. But the people would surely sit up and listen. They made the soldiers of the eastern Roman Empire all speak Latin and not Greek, on some obscure point of principle. As Jesus was beaten and scourged and knocked down, and having struggled back up was knocked down again, the angels almost turned their faces away in disgust; but not quite. And when the carrion birds pecked out his eyes as he hung on the cross, they knew that good taste had been left behind. At the resurrection Christ demonstrated that he came not to bring peace but a sword. This was one angry motherfucker of a Jesus returning to life, spouting Church Latin in an Australian accent. The Roman soldiers took one look at him as he emerged from the tomb and they skedaddled. He got them anyway. The disciples managed to calm him down eventually, though Peter sometimes doubted if the blood that caked Jesus' skin could really have all been his own. They had to call in Mary Magdalene, Salome, Martha and a vast army of prostitutes with whom Jesus had consorted during his ministry and had a great need to consort with them again. Drunkenness followed the violence and Jesus made some anti-Semitic remarks that were widely reported. That iteration, all the angels agreed, was not Uriel and Phanael's finest hour.

But the violence had whetted their appetites for the bizarre. They fashioned a zombie Jesus, shuffling out of the tomb, converting all and sundry with a heavy-limbed clout. That one was persistent and the ascension was problematic, delayed until the Christ spirit could free itself from the resilient undead body. They tried a vampire Christ. It was the flesh of others that he ate and others' blood that he drank. He went down well with the women, and the teenagers, but when in as a substitute for the crucifixion he was immolated on a stake, his body turned into ashes. The Christ spirit was lucky to get out alive. There wasn't even a resurrection, let alone a second coming.

In another parallel the Virgin Mary had an abortion. Christ and the angels vacated that reality in a hurry.

The parallel histories were piled on thick and fast. They had Jesus the clown, Jesus the juggler, Christ the gambler, Jesus the boozer, Jesus the wrestler. They tried a gay Jesus, they tried a transsexual Jesus, they tried a bi-Jesus, a genderqueer Jesus, they tried a straight Jesus. They made him Japanese, they made him spend his lost years in India. They made him tall, they made him short, they made him into a white man with blue eyes and blonde hair. He had a hook nose, he had a snub nose, he had a Roman nose, a flat nose. His hands were narrow and well-manicured, they were the large rough hands of a peasant, they were the hands of a carpenter, missing half a finger.

He was a hawk, he was a dove, he helped the poor, he hated the fucking scroungers. He was a socialist, he was a capitalist, he was libertarian, libertine, conservative, right, left, up, down and all shades and angles in between. They tried one thing after another, always with the same problems and the same outcome.

The end came when they had skipped forward to the twentieth century after a particularly depressing episode involving a bland, airbrushed Jesus who was particularly keen on hoarding money. They had been through this so many times that they had stopped noticing the cherub who was stationed in each parallel as a matter of course to keep a watch over its history once they knew there would be no Second Coming. The cherub was pathetic. His skin was blotchy, his shrivelled cock rubbed raw. There was booze on his breath, and a detritus of drug paraphernalia surrounded him. He was weeping, his nose was running, the slack mouth dribbling.

'I can't take it any more,' he whimpered. 'Watching those centuries, those millennia, those tens and hundreds of millennia of cruelty and neglect. Find a solution, please. please!'

He grabbed at their ankles like a beaten dog.

The next iteration came around Uriel and Phanael made certain not to mention anything to Gabriel, and avoided meeting him. Despite his obnoxious qualities Gabriel was very perceptive. They moved sideways into parallel i-109. They arranged a deceptively standard scenario, one that was perfectly familiar to Christ the Son. He encountered John the Baptist, he was tempted, he had his ministry, he was betrayed, tried, crucified. He came back. All seemed familiar, all usual.

But it was a set up. Once the resurrection occurred the two angels were ready in position at the tomb. It was an empty tomb. The risen Christ went on to meet the disciples on the road to Emmaus. There was no need to make him suspicious, after all. They had to make sure that the scenario would work out. It was potentially very, very dangerous. They had Thomas doubt the physicality of the body, just to make sure. Once he had put his hands in Jesus' side the angels were waiting for him. Jesus stepped outside and they tackled him to the floor and bound him. They chained him. They gagged him. They used whatever physical and whatever etheric means they had at their disposable to imprison him.

Once they had abducted him they carried out the planned procedure. Some might have interpreted it as torture, but that wasn't their intention. Jesus was tough enough, they knew. They just wanted to make him secure.

They mummified the resurrected body. It was placed within a lead casket within another casket, a whole Russian doll sequence of them, each stronger than the last with the tiny body of Jesus at the centre. They could not risk any emanation of the Christ leaking out. Despite his high place in the hierarchy was all good, all holy, and had a strong sympathetic influence. Then they encased the multi-layered sarcophagus encased in concrete and marble and granite and whatever other materials they had at their means. They buried him. He had not yet ascended so there was no way that Jesus could contact the Father, or even other angels.

No one knows where he is buried. Some say it is beneath the Vatican, some beneath Westminster Abbey, some say beneath the Kremlin, some say in Rennes-le-Chateau, some that he currently resides in a southern Baptist mausoleum in Texas. There are others who say that his tomb is, as it were, hidden in plain site under the hill of Golgotha. Only Uriel and Phanael know. And they're not telling. But if pressed they will admit that the suffering, claustrophobic, betrayed Christ isn't getting out of there any day soon.

Scott Stanley Smith

Is There Life After Death?

To listen to skeptics, only the gullible masses believe in an afterlife, desperate to be reunited with loved ones.

As we have shown, however, skeptics are so convinced of their intellectual superiority that they are incapable of examining evidence objectively that contradicts their strongly-held viewpoints.

Unlike the cases for ESP and UFOs, however, the evidence for survival after death is by its nature less measurable and more subtle and complicated.

Militant skeptics would have everyone believe that this is merely anecdotal and easily explained away by the biochemistry of the dying brain, pumped up by morphine and stress, with the particular hallucinations the result of a combination of wishful thinking and religious preconception. But as we shall see, this view ignores some inconvenient facts.

While looking at several types of relevant experiences, I will only focus on the issue of immediate survival after death, not theological assertions about what happens beyond that, such as whether there is a heaven or hell or reincarnation. Nor will we try to resolve here exactly what it is that may survive death.

One way to think about the larger picture of reality that the so-called supernatural presents is like the difference between the world of ordinary objects we interact with daily and the invisible quantum world that underlies everything. It is difficult for our minds to get around the fact that what seems like solid reality is mostly empty space. Skeptics are invited to imagine that the paranormal world is something like the theorized other dimensions of the "multiverse."

Death-Bed Visions

Let us begin with something that should be a perfect test for the skeptical case about hallucinations of the dying: death-bed visions. It is not uncommon for people who are about to die to imagine that the heavens open up and relatives appear to welcome them to the other side.

In *What They Saw at the House of Death: A New Look at Evidence for Life After Death* by Karlis Osis, a noted physics professor, and Erlendur Haraldsson, a clinical psychologist. Between them, they had carefully examined 5,000 cases of death-bed visions for nearly two decades starting in 1959. These were culled from observations by 17,000 physicians and nurses. Most were medical personnel in the U.S., but some came in from a separate study about patients in India, to check to what extent cultural and religious beliefs influenced the experiences.

Investigative journalist Michael Schmicker, in *Best Evidence*, summarized the remarkable conclusions:

Biological-Pharmaceutical Factors

• Patients who were given painkilling drugs were not more likely to have such visions than those who were not.

• Brain malfunctions were more likely to reduce such visions.

• A history of using psychoactive drugs did

not increase the likelihood of these visions.

• There was no evidence that a lack of oxygen induced the visions.

Psychological Factors

• Stress played no role in predicting which patients would see "the dead."

• Whether the patient believed in an afterlife did not matter.

• In some cases, the death-bed visions came to people who did not know they were dying.

Cultural Factors

• The visions often did not fit with the religious preconceptions of the individuals. Christians saw no evidence of hell; Hindus had no visions that confirmed they would be reborn.

• There were 11 aspects to these visions that were shared by both American and Indian cases, so they are likely common to many cultures.

Schmicker cited a compelling example. In 1919, Horace Traubel, a friend and biographer of the poet Walt Whitman, was dying in Bon Echo, Ontario, Canada. With him was Lt. Col. L. Moore Cosgrave. Cosgrave reported that at 3 a.m., Traubel stared at a point in the room three feet above the bed.

"A light haze eventually resolved itself into the form of Whitman...wearing an old tweed jacket, an old felt hat, and had his right hand in his pocket," which Cosgrave could see. The apparition nodded twice to Traubel, who said, "There is Walt." As the ghost brushed by him, Cosgrave felt a slight electric shock.

Near-death Experiences

"Near-death experiences" (NDEs) was the term coined by Dr. Raymond Moody, a physician who wrote the first popular book on the phenomenon, *Life After Life*, in 1975. He studied cases of patients who were pronounced clinically dead, but claimed they could see and hear things that seemed impossible, according to the materialist understanding of reality.

A 1982 Gallup poll revealed that one out of seven Americans had at least once been close to dying and 35% of these reported having the NDE. These experiences would seem fairly common, but were not generally reported by physicians, which is explained by the fact that only 32% of doctors at the time believed in an afterlife vs. 67% of the public.

While the specific details of the experience would be interpreted by the person who was supposedly dead, based on his or her cultural and religious background, the most common stages occurred in this order:

• A sense of dying as a release from cares and pain.

• The patient feels he or she is rising from the body and able to look down on it and the attending medical personnel.

• This self or spirit is compelled to pass through a dark tunnel with light at the end.

• Beings of light greet the spirit at the end of the tunnel—often these are deceased family or friends and sometimes a person understood as a founder or leader of their religious tradition (atheists reported an abstract figure of light).

• As many as 29% recalled having their life's events flash through their memories, as if reviewing them before judgment.

• Many wanted to stay in this disembodied state, but were told they needed to return.

• Consciousness returns to the body, startling medical personnel, who had pronounced the patient dead.

Moody's initial report has been confirmed in thousands of cases investigated by others. The International Association for Near-Death Studies www.iands.org was founded in 1978 to encourage the serious study of the phenomenon.

Skeptics are quick to argue that all of these things can be explained by incorrect judgments about clinical death and by the combined effects of a sick brain and the drugs administered at the time.

Among the most notable books to take a more systematic scientific approach to anecdotal evidence were by medical doctors Kenneth Ring, in *Life at Death*, and Michael Sabom, in *Recollections of Death: A Medical Investigation*.

Sabom in particular was skeptical. He accepted the critics' theory that NDEs were hallucinations due to heightened brain activity and was surprised to realize that they occurred most commonly in patients who had been unconscious for at least 30 minutes, when neuroactivity was reduced.

He believed that claims that these "dead" patients had accurately described what was happening around them were easily explained by hearing medical personnel discussing them or that they were educated guesses.

Sabom set up a control group of cardiac patients who had not reported having NDEs. He found the NDEers' accounts very accurate, while the guesses of cardiac patients were way off, and he was able to rule out the possibility in many cases of the "dead" picking up the information by hearing it.

Doctors at Southampton General Hospital studied 3,500 patients and concluded that cases of NDEs being reported involved "well-structured, lucid thought processes with reasoning and memory formation at a time when their brains were shown not to function," contradicting the materialistic view of how the brain works.

Dr. Eben Alexander's NDE

The most famous of modern NDEs was recounted in the 2012 bestseller by Dr. Eben Alexander, a neurosurgeon, in *Heaven is Real: A Doctor's Experience with the Afterlife* (a good example of skeptics' inability to state the facts in their rebuttals can be found in a response to an article in Esquire: http://iands.org/news/news/front-page-news/970-esquire-article-on-eben-alexander-distorts-the-facts.html). He went into a seven-day coma after suffering from microbial meningitis in 2008 and had an experience that ran counter to his expectations. He recalled:

I did not believe in the phenomenon of near-death experiences…I sympathized deeply with those who wanted to believe that there was a God and I envied such people the security that those beliefs no doubt provided. But as a scientist, I simply knew better.

When I entered the emergency room, my chances of survival in anything beyond a vegetative state were already low, but they soon sank to near nonexistent. For seven days I lay in a deep coma, my body was unresponsive, my higher-order brain functions totally offline.

All the chief arguments against near-death experiences suggest that these are the results of minimal, transient, or partial malfunctioning of the cortex. But mine took place not while my cortex was malfunctioning, but while it was simply off. This is clear from the global cortical involvement documented by CT scans and neurological examinations. According to current medical understanding of the brain and mind, there is absolutely no way that I could have experienced even a dim and limited consciousness during my time in the coma, much less the hyper-vivid and completely coherent odyssey I underwent.

———————

A 2001 study reported in the British medical journal The Lancet reported that the NDEs could not be explained by reactions to medications, a lack of oxygen to the brain, or fear of death.

Perhaps most convincing is that patients are able to report events outside the room where their bodies were. For example, some claimed that their spirits went into the waiting room and heard conversations between family members, which they recalled accurately. Given the skeptics' position on ESP, this should be impossible.

In 1990, Seattle pediatrician Melvin Morse's Closer to the Light examined the cases of 120 children who had NDEs. In most cases, they would have been too young to have absorbed a well-grounded religious expectation of what might happen. He made a point-by-point refutation of the skeptics' arguments about the biochemistry of death and hallucination, compelling enough to have persuaded some skeptics to take a more open-minded position.

In *Beyond: On Life After Death*, Fred Frohock attempted to weigh the evidence objectively and concluded:

> The problem with the materialist explanation that NDEs are a purely neurological reaction to the stress of death is that we would have to stretch the powers of the brain to new and unproven levels of achievement. The weight of the likelihood, of possibilities, seems to be in favor of transcendent experiences, although NDEs could be both transcendent and part of the physical world.
>
> The brain may be the instrument that guides the self into a realm of existence as real and empirical as the dimension we currently occupy. All we have to do is move the perimeters of physical reality out to more comprehensive dimensions. Death is as ordinary as birth, and may be the same kind of portal to another empirical stage of life. Physicists tell us there must be more dimensions to reality to explain the reality we sense and know.

In Dr. Andrew Newberg's Teaching Co. course The Spiritual Brain, he cites the impact these experiences have on those who go through them: "People come away from a near-death experience with a radically altered set of beliefs about themselves, the meaning of life, relationships—everything. They no longer fear death and are more spiritual and less religious. Many say things like, 'I don't think there is a God; I know there is a God.' One said that the experience was 'bigger' than religion, which was not sufficient to help encapsulate the NDE."

OUT-OF-BODY EXPERIENCES

But some aspects of the NDE mimic other experiences, such as the phenomenon known as an out-of-body experience (OBE). While the NDE is involuntary, the OBE may be a spontaneous occurrence or it could be something the individual wills.

While this is not a direct indicator of survival of death, it does provide evidence that humans consist of something other than a body: a "spirit" that can separate from it under certain conditions while the body remains alive.

Such experiences have been recorded around the world throughout history, often by shamans who claim to have gone into the "spirit world" to receive guidance. In a study of 70 non-Western groups by D. Shiels for the *Journal of Psychical Research* in 1978, the core experiences of being able to leave the body voluntarily were very similar, despite major cultural differences.

I interviewed Scott Rogo, the highly-regarded parapsychologist, in June 1990. Two months later, he was murdered and my interview appeared in the December issue of Fate magazine. I particularly admired his hardheaded approach to the field, always skeptical about easy explanations for so-called paranormal phenomena. He had his first book published at 19 and by the time of his death at 40, had written 29 others.

One of these was Leaving the Body: A Complete Guide to Astral Projection (another name for intentional OBEs). In addition to recounting many credible experiences of people able to describe distant events as they hovered over them, Rogo had lots of personal knowledge. He had trained himself to leave his body and once while out of town, returned in spirit to his home to find his roommate had someone visiting. He confirmed this when he came back from the trip.

In his *Psychic Breakthroughs Today*, Rogo reviewed some of the best anecdotal collections by people who had repeated experiences with this, such as Sylvan Muldoon's *The Case for Astral Projection* and Dr. Robert Crookall's *The Supreme Adventure*. It appears that 10-20% of the population almost anywhere in the world has had at least one OBE.

Rogo also discussed lab experiments to induce these experiences. Noted psychologist Dr. Charles Tart at the University of California at Davis, for example, in the 1960s had subjects fall asleep and try to prove they had left the body by viewing a number that was placed out of sight.

In some cases, Tart found that when the individual later reported being out of the body, brain waves showed strange activity that indicated he or she was neither asleep nor awake.

One of his most notable clinical subjects was Robert Monroe, who went on to write the classic memoir *Journeys Out of the Body*. During one experiment, Monroe's spirit went into the hallway and accurately reported that the lab technician who was supposed to be monitoring him was there talking to someone else.

Another set of experiments were conducted at Duke University by Dr. Robert Morris. His most outstanding subject was Keith Harary, who would later become a parapsychologist himself. Rogo called the system of testing him "ingenious" and the results "stunningly successful."

A study of those who claimed to have undergone OBEs was supported by the University of Kansas Medical Center and the renowned Topeka-based Menninger Foundation. They compared these who had these experiences with those who did not claim to have had them. "They could not find any specific personality characteristics differentiating people who experience the phenomenon from those who do not," wrote Rogo.

Finally, Rogo also considered the credible anecdotal evidence that some saints and mystics of a variety of religions have had the ability to be more than one place at once, known as bilocation. This could be either as an apparition or seemingly having their body in both places at the same time. In Miracles, Rogo (who had no religious affiliation), provided the thought-provoking documentation. But it is not likely a lab will be able to test this phenomenon.

GHOSTS

The most commonly reported evidence for human afterlife is the encounter with apparitions of people who are dead.

"Ghosts are a universal phenomenon, seen again and again without end by people of every culture, religion and country," wrote Schmicker in *Best Evidence*. "They have been reported for thousands of years by people from every economic, educational, and social strata. They have been seen by kings and peasants, hamburger-flippers and nuclear scientists, aborigines and bank presidents, doctors and laborers, by famous people and by average citizens, by men and women and children of every age and sex."

In 1882, the Society for Psychical Research (SPR) was founded in England to support a scholarly investigation of such phenomena.

Four years later, its first report was published, a two-volume, 1,400-page summary of 700 cases (edited and updated by Eleanor Sidgwick in 1923 in the revised edition of *Phantasms of the Living*).

One of the cases occurred on Dec. 7, 1918, involving a Lt. David McConnel, a pilot trainee who was flying to an airbase when he crashed and died at 3:25 p.m. At about that time, his roommate, Lt. J.J. Larkin, claimed to have him in the pilot lounge and reported that McConnel told him he "had a good trip," then left.

Fifteen minutes later, a friend of the two came into the lounge and wondered when McConnel would be back so they could all go to dinner together. Larkin informed him that McConnel had already returned, but they could not locate him.

Later that night, they learned of his death and informed their commander of the experience, as well as writing his family a detailed letter about it.

The best example of a ghostly haunting of one location cited by Schmicker is Borley Rectory in Essex, England. From 1863 until it burned down in 1938, there were some 100 persons who were witnesses to seven different ghosts and a variety of related phenomena. Harry Price's *The Most Haunted House in England: 10 Years' Investigation of Borley Rectory* details the strange happenings.

MEDIUMS

One of the most sensational books on evidence for the survival of the human soul after death was the 2002 bestseller *The Afterlife Experiments: Breakthrough Scientific Evidence of Life After Death* by Gary E. Schwartz, Ph.D., and William L. Simon. Schwartz is a professor of psychiatry and medicine at the University of Arizona, a graduate of Harvard and former director of the Yale Psychophysiology Center, with 450 published scientific papers. His credentials did not make his report any less controversial.

Schwartz and his colleagues conducted clinical tests on a handful of so-called psychic mediums, including Allison DuBois (the inspiration for the TV series "Medium"), John Edward (who also had a TV show), George Anderson, Suzane Northrop, George Dalzell, Anne Gehman, and Laurie Campbell.

The 374-page book details not only the precautions taken to prevent fraud and statistical analysis of the possibilities of chance in the results, but his responses to the charges of professional skeptics (including James Randi and Ray Hyman, whose criticisms of ESP experiments we cited earlier).

In the early 1990s, I was trying to find a legitimate medium—someone who could "channel" messages from the dead for the living—for reports in Fate (which was making an effort to avoid printing just any psychic's claim and was counting on my experience as a business reporter to screen for the better ones). Frankly, I could not find many, but there were a few.

One was Bevy Jaegers, a St. Louis psychic with a particular skill known as psychometry. That is the ability to handle an object and psychically pick up information related to it. For example, she would touch a piece of clothing a victim had been wearied when murdered and would have images of the crime flash before her. In its peculiar way, this was receiving "messages from the dead."

When I visited with her, she set up a number of meetings and phone calls with law enforcement officials who had worked with her on 50 murder cases. We began to collaborate on a book about her work, but my more mundane career was skyrocketing and we did not have time to finish it before she died (and yes, mediums do not generally get warnings about their demise). But the experience did convince me that she had been largely accurate and was certainly not a fraud.

I had read what the skeptics had to say about the medium James Van Praagh, who had a TV show at the time, so I went to his "group reading" very well-armed (for the same reason that I prepared to expose Uri Geller).

I took careful notes on whether his information, allegedly from the dead for loved ones in the audience, was accurate and was surprised that most of it did seem to be. There appeared to be a few misses and there were some things that could not be verified at the time.

In our follow-up interview, we discussed the views of his critics. I cannot say for sure that he has never cheated, but as I mentioned previously, there is evidence that some seemingly genuine psychics have tried to "improve" their results.

As part of my research, I also went to a "séance" conducted by Edward one Halloween. I was convinced he was a fraud at the time, not because I could prove it, but what he did seemed like nothing more than a parlor trick in the dark. After reading The Afterlife Experiments, I had to have a more open mind about his achievements.

I also had studied George Anderson previously, including watching him in a TV documentary and reading his 1989 bestseller, *We Don't Die*. I think it is fair to say that if there is one medium whose accuracy has been repeatedly confirmed by thousands of readings,

Anderson is it.

Of the others in the Schwartz book, I had two personal readings by Laurie Campbell. The first turned out to be surprisingly accurate in looking into my past and forecasting the future, while the second, five years later, did not even hit the target. This was, I had learned, not atypical of even the best (as Rogo observed, psychic talent seems to operate like an unreliable electrical connection that frustrates those who claim to have such abilities).

I do not put much stock in getting reliable information from any medium, but for those who want comfort without being gullible, it is worth getting a reading from any of those purported to be the best, without thinking it will be infallible revelation.

Another interesting source on mediums is Victor Zamit's *A Lawyer Presents the Case for the Afterlife*. It pulls together a huge amount of information for every kind of "evidence" of the hereafter, although I am a skeptic about the New Age channeling examples. Spirits, I have become convinced, love to promote specific belief systems that contradict each other.

ANIMAL APPARITIONS

Finally, I would like to consider something that would not seem to provide much promise of credibility, but is one of my specialties: encounters with animal ghosts. I recounted 125 cases in *The Soul of Your Pet: Evidence for the Survival of Animals After Death* (dozens of others that came in after the third edition in 1998 will be included in the next version of Animals and the Afterlife by Kim Sheridan).

The understandable skeptical response to this notion is that anecdotes that claim that people saw their dead pets are clearly based on wishful thinking. That would make some sense, since many people grieve severely when they have bonded with a companion animal for 10 or 20 years.

The trouble with this theory is that it does not explain most of the stories I reported.

I really had no idea what I would receive when I sent a request for information from readers of veterinary professional journals and publications about the paranormal.

The most striking thing about most of the stories was their credibility:

• Many witnesses were not the owner of the pet encountered, so a desire to see it played no role.

• Other cases involved multiple witnesses, so the events were not simply one person's hallucination.

• Some involved more than one sense—the witness not only had a sustained view of the dead animal, but could hear or feel it, making it less likely they were simply imagining the event.

• Some witnesses were veterinarians, doctors, psychologists and other professionals who would be expected to take a more objective attitude than most people.

• Many stated they had never had a paranormal experience of any kind before or since the event and others said they were not religious in any way (virtually no one said their religious background taught that animals have spirits, although an ABC News/Beliefnet poll showed that 43% of Americans believe animals go to heaven, while 17% are unsure; 40% disbelieve, including both those who religious views deny that any animal has a spirit and those who do not believe in the supernatural at all).

• Perhaps the most intriguing cases were those that involved the reactions of other animals, making it apparent that these incidences were not simply figments of human imagination. For example, one evening a witness reported that she was at home with her two cats, watching TV on a couch. Suddenly, what appeared to be her recently deceased third cat came out of the kitchen and walked across the living room, then went right through the closed bedroom door. The two living cats had gone to the edge of the couch to stare at the ghost as it walked by them, then when it disappeared, they ran up to the bedroom door and stood there briefly before running away. They refused to go into the bedroom for months thereafter.

The point is that if there is evidence that even some animals have an afterlife, that makes it all the more likely than humans survive death.

The likelihood of human survival of death does not explicitly provide evidence for God or any particular religious philosophy. However, it would be evidence that the global phenomenon of belief in the supernatural has a grounding in some kind of alternate reality that deserves more study.

Sarane Alexandrian

How to Make Love with an Invisible Creature

This chapter title would appear to announce a fictional fantasy. This is not at all the case: since antiquity many men and women, without necessarily being under the influence of hallucinogens or religious hysteria, have experienced the sensation of having loving commerce—and even intercourse—with an entity living in the preternatural universe. In the literature of every land, there are countless tales, inspired by popular fears, that tell of lemurs, striges, empusae, and ghosts who pester humans with their libidinous attentions. I will not draw my examples from folktales, however, but from theological and medicinal treatises. In the early years of Christianity, Saint Augustine stated in his City of God (book XV, chap. 23):

> There is, too, a very general rumor, which many have verified by their own experience, or which trustworthy persons who have heard the experience of others corroborate, that sylvans and fauns, who are commonly called *incubi*, had often made wicked assaults upon women, and satisfied their lust upon them; and that certain devils, called *Duses* by the Gauls, are constantly attempting and effecting this impurity is so generally affirmed, that it were impudent to deny it.[1]

Saint Augustine is mainly speaking here of elementary spirits, to which he assimilates the satyrs of paganism, because the church fathers after him had a different definition for the nature of incubi and succubi.

In addition to the lubricious activity of demons and elementary spirits with human beings, we can add that of undead who have returned with a craving for living flesh—especially in the East. The story of Garab and Detchema, collected by Alexandra David-Neel in Tibet, reveals how a woman was raped by a ghost. Garab became jealous at seeing Detchema moving in her sleep as if abandoning herself to the embrace of an invisible lover. "Had Detchema come to prefer the caresses of her phantom lover to his?" He believed this invisible entity was a yogi "capable of projecting an etheric double that could act like a real person." One night this creature materialized and attacked him before suddenly fading away. Garab went to consult a hermit of Mount Khang Tise, who told him,

> Your father's spirit has become a phantom who still thirsts for the sensations he felt while still alive. . . . He wanted to possess your mistress to steal her own life force and that psychic energy you had given her.[2]

THE SEXUAL ASSAULTS OF INCUBI AND SUCCUBI

The incubus is the male demon that attempts to take his pleasure of a woman, and the succubus is the female demon that lasciviously couples with a man. But how can they do this if

---

1 Augustine, *The City of God*

2 David-Neel, *Magie d'amour et magie noire*.

they are immaterial? Father Sinistari of Ameno (the Novare diocese), the seventeenth-century Franciscan brother who became an adviser to the Supreme Tribunal of the Holy Inquisition, studied this matter from every angle. To make love with the men or women they desire, the demons create a temporary body or borrow that of a dead person they animate so perfectly that sexual relations with an incubus or succubus is "copulation with a corpse, said corpse having no feeling or movement, and only moves exceptionally through an artifice of the demon." The incubus is so salacious that it will even assault female animals.

> It is not only women he attacks, but mares as well; if they are docile to his desires, he overwhelms them with caresses and braids their manes with an infinite number of inextricable knots; but if they resist, he mistreats them, strikes them, bites them, and finally kills them.[3]

Among the demons with the power to create bodies for themselves, Father Sinistari distinguishes two groups of incubi and succubi. The first group, those who have sworn allegiance to the Devil during ceremonies, he claims to have seen with his own eyes. The second group, which is much harder to fight, includes independent, wandering entities:

> These incubi—which in Italian are called foletti, and in Spanish, denudes, and in French, follets—pay no heed to exorcists and have no fear of exorcisms, no veneration for sacred objects, the approach of which causes them not the slightest fear. They are entirely different in this regard from the demons that torment the possessed.[4]

To convince his readers of the truth of his assertions, Father Sinistari tells the following story that took place in Pavia when he was a professor of theology there. He swears that he has been scrupulous in reporting the details exactly as they happened.

A married woman, Gironima, had ordered a loaf of bread from the oven keeper and he also gave her a biscuit, which she ate. That night when lying in bed with her husband, she heard a hissing voice at her ear asking, "Did you like the cake?" Terrified, she muttered a prayer, but the voice reassured her: "I am smitten by your beauty, and my greatest desire is to take my pleasure in your hugs and kisses." She then felt something kiss her cheek so gently that it felt like being brushed against by feather down. "The temptation lasted almost half an hour, after which the tempter went away." Gironima went to see her confessor the following day, who gave her some relics for protection, but they were useless: "Similar temptations occurred over the following nights, with words and kisses of the same sort." She then decided to have herself exorcised; exorcists blessed her house, room, and bed, and commanded the incubus to cease its importunate solicitations. "The tempter only redoubled his efforts; he claimed he was dying of love, weeping and moaning to soften the woman's resistance."

Despite all of this, Gironima resisted every attempt made by this invisible being to have intercourse with her.

> The incubus then ventured an entirely different approach. He appeared to his beauty in the form of a young boy, or little man, who was incredibly handsome with a blond beard shining like gold, eyes blue-green as flax flowers, elegantly clad in Spanish fashion.

---

3 The Reverend Father Sinistari, *De la démonalité et des animaux incubes et succubes*.

4 Ibid.

He even appeared to her when she was in the company of others, giving her kisses or weeping: "She alone could see and hear him; nobody else could see or hear a thing." Gironima stubbornly refused to surrender to the incubus in her bed: "After several months, the annoyed incubus resorted to a new form of persecution." He stole her jewels, turned everything in the household upside-down, and struck her so cruelly she had bruises that lasted two days. "Sometimes when she was nursing her little daughter, he would snatch the babe off her knees and stick her on the roof by the gutter." One night he appeared in the shape of the little man with the blond beard and tried to rape her, but she repelled him. He left and came back with stones: "Around the bed he built a wall with these stones that was so high it reached the ceiling, and the couple needed a ladder brought to them to get out." During a meal when the couple was hosting eight soldiers, at the moment they sat down to eat, the guests' table vanished along with all the dishes and tableware.

In despair Gironima sought advice from a Bernardine brother of Feltre. Taking heed of his counsel, she made a vow to remain clad in a gray habit cinched with a rope at the waist, like those of the brothers minor of Saint Bernard, for an entire year. The day after she made that decision, on the Feast of Saint Michael, she went to mass at ten o'clock with a crowd of other worshippers.

The poor girl had no sooner set foot in the parvis of the Church, when all at once all her clothes and adornments fell to the ground where they were carried off by the wind, leaving her naked as a hand.

The incubus played a number of other tricks of this nature on her, to force her through intimidation to surrender in bed to his penetration. "He persisted in tempting her for a number of years, but finally realizing he was wasting his time and energy, he lifted his siege." This is not a superstitious old wives' tale, but a seriously presented example by a priest whose Criminal Code of canon law was most definitive and contained many similar anecdotes on the activity of incubi.

Sarane Alexandrian

Father Sinistari was outraged at the absurdities spouted by his colleagues, as if he never ventured any himself, and wrote back concerning Vallesius's theory on how incubi impregnated women: "I am amazed that such an enormity has come from the pen of such an erudite figure." Inquisitors claimed that the same demon disguised itself as a succubus to extract the sperm of a sleeping man, causing him to have a wet dream, and then next transformed into an incubus to inject this same sperm into the vagina of a living woman, consenting or not. This sperm had grown cold during this transfer, and she had the sensation of receiving an icy ejaculation in her belly. But it would be hot and endless if the incubus had harvested the sperm of several men and flooded her womb with this mixture. This is how audacious, robust, and proud bastards were born, and a list had been drawn up of historical figures with this constitution because a demon had filled their mother's uterus, with "an abundant, very thick, and very hot sperm, which is highly charged with spirits and exhibits no fluidity": Plato, Alexander the Great, Scipio Africanus, Martin Luther, and so forth. Father Sinistari protests: "I maintain that the demon incubus, in its congress with women, engenders the human fetus with its own sperm." He objects that it is not the quantity of semen that matters in conception, but its quality. In contradiction to other demonologists, he puts forth the notion that incubi and succubi form their own population of invisible beings, midway between demons and angels, and who are "difficult to kill because of the speed with which they escape danger." Their ability to travel through walls comes from "the subtle and delicate corporeality of the beings in question, similar to the substance of liquids." Sinistari of Ameno did not offer his view on an anatomical peculiarity revealed by various theologians, to wit, the incubus had a large, bifurcated penis like a fork, one end of which he stuck in the vagina and the other in the anus of the woman, simultaneously.

There is no shortage of succubi stories in the manuals of the Inquisition, either. In the shape of fluidic women with vampiric manners, they come to the beds of men preparing to go to sleep. The victim may be a bachelor or a married man. They then sit astride him and, with frenzied intercourse, compel him to ejaculate. Sometimes they relentlessly copulate with him the entire night, leaving him exhausted when he gets up. It is possible to maintain a long relationship with a succubus. The most significant case is that of Bernedeto Berno, an octogenarian priest who confessed to the judges of the Inquisition that he had been copulating for forty years with a succubus named Hermoine, who accompanied him everywhere without ever being seen: "He also confessed that he had inhaled the blood of several small children and committed a number of other execrable wickednesses, and was burned alive," says Jean Brosin, who added that there was "yet another priest, seventy years old, who confessed to have had similar copulation with a demon in the guise of a woman, and who was also burned."[5] The dreadful inquisitor Jacob Sprenger reported the case of a German sorcerer of Conflans who had sexual relations with an invisible creature in the presence of his wife and friends. They would see him suddenly throw himself on the ground, open his breeches, and make increasingly stronger thrusts with his pelvis, "as if he was in copulation with a woman, and spurt semen." He was victim to the same kind of autosuggestion that compelled peasant women of that time to go out into the fields naked and lie down on the ground where they thrashed about like girls being raped: "And sometimes husbands would find them mating with devils, who they mistook for men, and when striking them with their swords, would touch nothing."[6]

The history of humanity's sexual harassment at the hands of invisible creatures expanded when Paracelsus, the creator of "spagyric medicine" (which is connected with alchemy and the Kabbalah), in his *Liber de nymphis, sylphis, pygmaeis et salamandris et de caeteris spiritubus* (Book of Nymphs, Sylphs, Pygmies, Salamanders and Other Spirits; published in Basel in 1590, after his death), described the secret peoples inhabiting the four elements of Water, Air, Earth, and Fire, some of whose individual members sought to copulate with humans. This became an article of faith for the Rosicrucian Brotherhood in the seventeenth century and the abbot Montfaucon de Villars, in the *Comte de Gabalis* (1670), reported everything an initiate had revealed to him on this matter, after telling him peremptorily: "You must renounce all carnal congress with women." In fact, no human women could compete with the "invisible mistresses" one could find among the elementary spirits. The nymphs or undines resided in rivers, lakes, and seas: "Few males, and of women there are great number; their beauty is extreme." The upper air is inhabited by

---

[5] Brodin, *De la démonomanie des sorciers, revue diligemment et repurge des plusieurs fautes.*

[6] Ibid.

the sylphs: "Their women and their daughters are male beauties, like our depictions of Amazons." In the depths of the Earth, in mines or caves, live the gnomes: "The Gnomides, their wives, are small and quite pleasant, and their dress is extremely odd." Finally, fire is the dwelling place of spirits called *salamanders*: "Their wives and daughters are rarely seen."[7] Montfaucon de Villars illustrates his theory with many anecdotes, but they are fables and not adventures concerning actual people.

Another author who wrote on this theme was Jacques Cazotte, after he returned from serving as a chief administrator in Martinique. At the age of fifty-three, he published a book in 1772 titled *Le Diable amoureux* (The Devil in Love), a novel "dreamt in one night and written in one day." Its hero, Alvare, a young captain in Naples, invokes elementary spirits in a cave at the instigation of the necromancer Soberano. He sees a camel appear that transforms into a dog, who he asks to serve him a light meal. The cave changes into a castle room, where a page named Biondetto forms a bond with Alvare. After various trials and tribulations, this page reveals he is a splendid woman, Biondetta, and confesses: "I am a sylph by origin, and one of the highest among them ... I am allowed to take on a body to associate with a wise man: here I am." An exalted amorous liaison develops between Alvare and his sylph, but after they have made love with infinite climaxes, Biondetta tells him:

> I am the Devil, my dear Alvare, I am the Devil.... Tell me finally, if possible, but as tenderely as I feel it for you, my dear Belzebuth, I adore you.[8]

Alvare flees home to his mother in terror and finds protection from a confessor against this diabolical misadventure.

This novel earned Cazotte a visit from a disciple of Martinez de Pasqually, master of the Order of the Elus-Cohen in Lyon. He was then initiated into Martinism, where he learned that he had misrepresented the sylphs. Gérard de Nerval, in *Les Illuminés* (The Illumined Ones), says that Cazotte blamed himself "for having somewhat defamed these innocent spirits who give life to the middle reaches of the air, by assigning them the dubious personality of a female sprite answering to the name of Belzebuth." As a general rule, everything concerning sylphs and nymphs falls under the heading of folklore or literature. Heinrich Heine spoke of them from a poet's perspective and the ethnographer Karl Grün collected legends concerning them.[9] In this domain there are no historical events that compare with the abundant examples from the witch trials, in which men and women were condemned to be burned alive for confessing they had copulated with succubi and incubi.

Sex with incubi and succubi is not a Christian aberration that no longer occurs. They have modern aspects that René Schwaeblé defined after discussing them with his close friend, the author Joris-Karl Huysmans: "The art of sexual intercourse with incubi and succubi consists of the possibility of possessing at any time any man or woman, living or dead, provided one has a clear image of them." This depends on self-hypnosis, "the art of putting oneself in a trance and causing somnambulistic sleep," that was a subject of experimentation for the doctors from the Salpêtrière Hospital. Schwaeblé mentions the possibility of using an apparatus to help encourage suggestibility, a light source striking the eyelids. "It is necessary before entering the lethargic stage, to clearly determine the individuality of the incubus or succubus personality one desires; one must imagine that she is there in one's bed, and that one is taking her." The experimenter must be in a more or less agitated state from continence; having deprived himself of amorous contact, his obsession

---

7 Montfaucon de Villars, *Le Comte de Gabalis, ou entretiens sur les sciences secrets*.

8 Cazotte, *The Devil in Love*.

9 Grün, *Les Esprits elementaires*.

conditions him to feel one.

Later, with habit, the auto-suggestion occurs on its own, so to speak. In this way an individual can parade through his bed celebrities, male and female, who the imagination can inflate even more. With practice, the suggestion becomes so strong and the consequent hallucination becomes so intense that the summoned phantom takes on haunting substance with all the properties of the living individual. One then intensely perceives the color, odor, and sounds that this ghost releases; one can even feel new impressions . . . finally, a veritable individual, a male or female lover, is there—a larva engendered by the incubus or succubus maker.[10]

Before his conversion Huysmans was attacked by succubi and believed much more in their reality than he had let on to René Schwaeblé. In his novel *En Route* (On the Way), the character Durtal has an erotic dream during his first night at the Trappist abbey Notre Dame d'Igny with the "clearcut sensation of a being, a fluidic form vanishing with the sharp sound of a percussion cap or the snap of a whip, nearby, on waking." He even had the impression that the wind caused by its flight had thrown the bed sheet into disarray.

During this same era, there was a case of adultery in which a wife deceived her husband not with real men but with incubi. This happened with the couple MacGregor Mathers (Grand Master of the Order of the Golden Dawn) and his wife Moïna (sister of the philosopher Henri Bergson). In fact, no cheating was involved as he knew and approved of it. He no longer touched her, which she did not find frustrating, because in their conjugal bed Moïna sometimes abandoned herself to the embraces of an incubus invoked by the Abramelin ritual and had fantastic orgasms.

René Schwaeblé was witness to a kind of orgy—this is not too strong a word—between living women and incubi that took place in Batignoles in a deconsecrated chapel on rue Truffault that had belonged to a community of expelled nuns around 1905. "In the evening between five and seven, women and men came to sit in the confessionals or quite simply on sagging, rickety straw chairs." Schwaeblé was drawn there by his writer's curiosity, and noted among its habitués a painter, a theater critic, and a countess ("the famous veiled Lady from the Dreyfus trial"). In the half shadows weakly lit by a lamp on the altar, everyone waited until a voice murmured: "The incubi and succubi are here!" Then, those in attendance "started moving and wiggling like chickens in a sack. Their gestures became lascivious and obscene. Their hips writhed. Sighs were emitted; first they were indistinct and faint, then clearer and more emphatic." Schwaeblé watched this hysteria as best he could: "All at once, they fell still, swooning. They opened their eyes and came out of their trance. The incubus had left . . ." The spectator noted: "That's what I saw. In truth, I couldn't see much of anything!"

To be perfectly sure, Schwaeblé questioned "one of the most gracious regular visitors," who

---

10 Schwaeblé, *Les Recettes magiques pour et contre l'amour.*

answered him: "You could not see anything because you have not undergone the preparatory training." Which is? "Never eat meat, fast totally two days a week, strive to slow down your breathing, and so on. In fact, it is a matter of purifying your nervous force and being able to concentrate on the exterior object." She told him: "You should not think you can make X or Y show up." First, one should "obtain an object touched by the desired individual, a letter written by him, a lock of his hair." He wanted to know if she could see the incubi that possessed her, but she shook her head: "They generally remain invisible. . . . Sometimes we can see a shadow, a barely perceivable shadow, but finally we can discern it; and in certain cases—very rare cases—we can clearly distinguish a body." He asked her if it was necessary to evoke or expect the incubus. She answered: "Personally, I always evoke the same demons. And once they have served me well, I drive them away without pity." Why did she not form a liaison with just one of them? Her reply is categorical: "You must not let the incubus become the master, under penalty of not being able to get rid of it. It will couple with you night and day, and the nervous expense among other things is so terrible that death will soon follow."[11]

There is nothing implausible about this testimony from the pen of a credible author. This was a time when the "psychic sciences" were in fashion. Worldly women found neurotic pleasure in gathering together in an abandoned chapel to play at being possessed by incubi, watched by voyeurs who paid more attention to their voluptuous contortions than to irruptions of larvae from the astral realm. Among them could be found pretenders, brought to orgasm by the thought of exciting the spectators and by being placed in an unusual situation, as well as hysterics who were genuinely convinced they were being penetrated by an extraordinary lover who had come from outer darkness.

The Lovers of Sophia

Never have amorous relations with an invisible woman been more realistic than in the story of Johann-Georg Gichtel and Sophia, which culminated in a collective marriage. Sophia is the highest female figure in the Gnostic belief systems that existed during the earliest period of Christianity. As I said in my book on the History of Occult Philosophy:

It was common knowledge she represented Wisdom, an impalpable aeon, but she inspired such passions that she was transformed into a kind of Christianized Isis. Almost every Gnostic group had its version of her misadventures and made the distinction between the higher Sophia, the Celestial Mother, and the lower Sophia that was sometimes called Sophia Achamot or Sophia Prounicos (lascivious), because in her the desire for light became assimilated with sexual desire.[12]

In the seventeenth century, the great visionary Jacob Boehme restored the cult of Sophia to honor by stating she had been Adam's wife before the creation of Eve, and the mystics of his school began worshipping her more than the Virgin Mary. She was the "Queen of Saints," the sacred Body about whom Boehme said: "This Sophia, who is animated by the Holy Ghost, is of substance, without being corporeal like our bodies."

After reading Jacob Boehme's two books, a man fell madly in love with Sophia: this was Johann-Georg Gichtel. He was born in 1638 in Regensberg of well-to-do Lutheran parents. He made his start by producing a pamphlet against the corrupt clergy of that region, which earned him the wrath of the priests, who caused him to be expelled from his native village and to have all his property confiscated. He took refuge in Holland. Suffering from extreme poverty, he managed to survive because several Amsterdam families took an interest in him due to the dignity of his life, which was animated by an ideal of

11 Ibid.

12 Alexandrian, *Histoire de la philosophie occulte.*

secular saintliness. The father of a young girl offered him the hand of his daughter (who was the heiress to a fortune) in marriage, but Gichtel declined, thinking he should take a vow of celibacy in order that he might one day deserve the love of Sophia. Next, an extremely wealthy widow fell in love with him and insistently asked him to marry her. Although he felt drawn to her, he postponed acceptance and retired to his home for four weeks to pray to God. The result was negative, as noted by a commentator: "He then gave himself thenceforth utterly to Sophia, who wanted naught of a divided heart; he saw that his vocation was the priesthood in its most elevated sense." In 1672, when the troops of Louis XIV were at the gates of Amsterdam, Gichtel organized prayers to repel them.

His exemplary conduct eventually earned him the love of Sophia. Colonel Kirchberger, in his correspondence with Saint-Martin, described it this way:

> Sophia, his dear, his divine Sophia, whom he loved so much and whom he had never seen, came on Christmas Day 1673 to pay him a first visit. He says in this connection that he saw and heard in the Third Principle* that Virgin who was of an amazing and celestial beauty. She accepted him as her husband upon this first meeting, and the marriage was consummated in inexpressible delights. She distinctly promised him conjugal fidelity; never to abandon him, neither in adversity nor in poverty, neither in sickness nor in death, and that she would always live with him in the interior luminous depths.[13] *[In the mystical terminology of Jacob Boehme, the Third Principle refers to the divinely created visible world. —Trans.]

This would indicate that Gichtel most often saw Sophia at the center of his soul, and this inner conversation only manifested itself externally on rare occasions with a fleeting vision before his eyes:

> The wedding lasted until the beginning of 1674. He then found more comfortable lodging in a spacious house in Amsterdam whose rent was quite expensive. However, he didn't possess a sou . . .

His heavenly bride carried on constant conversations with him in a "central language, without external words or vibrations in the air." She was an intransigent and chaste lover: "Sophia insinuated that if he wished to enjoy her favors without interruption, he had to abstain from all sexual bliss and all earthly desire—a stipulation he observed religiously."

This union with Sophia gave such assurance and power to Gichtel that all people suffering difficulties came to him for advice and he was able to extricate them from their hardship. A doctor named Raadt appealed to him because he was at his wit's end; Gichtel taught him to pray, and prayed with him to free him of a £24,000 debt, which came to him in a miraculous manner. Raadt then decided to impose upon himself and his wife "spiritual circumcision," meaning complete abstinence from the sex act henceforth. This renunciation was advantageous for him: "Sophia welcomed Raadt, and all those who came to see her husband with good, perfectly clear intentions. . . . She let fall several rays of her image into the earthly qualities of their souls." Soon public rumor ran wild with this supernatural information, and Gichtel found himself welcoming all manner of visitors keen to obtain the benefits of Sophia. Once their number swelled to thirty, they formed the Society of Thirty. The Society's members made a commitment to practice sexual abstinence with their wives, as Sophia wished them to be pure of all carnal contact. Colonel Kirchberger remarked that "On this occasion, Gichtel observed in noteworthy fashion how greatly the

---

13 Saint-Martin, *Correspondance inédites*.

astral spirit desired to enjoy the nuptial bed of Sophia."

With the help of his new friends, Gichtel decided to undertake an edition of the complete works of Jacob Boehme. A rich magistrat (who was not one of Sophia's lovers) provided the funding. In the beginning they were all utterly convinced of the reality of their amorous congress with this heavenly creature, and this galvanized them. "As long as the Thirty, who were spread through different cities, remained one in spirit, they obtained through their prayers all they desired." Little by little their ardor cooled, either because their wives were unhappy about being abandoned for an invisible rival, or because they did not receive enough visions of Sophia, or because the advantages they had drawn from this relationship failed to satisfy them. The first to leave was Raadt, and he went so far in the opposite direction that he became an enemy of Gichtel. Others also abruptly abandoned him, some even accusing him of being a magician. Despite the defection of the Society of Thirty, Gichtel succeeded in publishing his edition of Boehme's complete works in 1682.

A young Frankfurt bookseller named Ueberfeld asked him for two hundred copies on deposit to sell. This individual was such a fervent admirer of Jacob Boehme that he knelt in deference while reading his work. He received an alert from Sophia, ready to become his wife because of his fervor. He went to visit Gichtel in Amsterdam in 1683, and decided to remain with him: "On his arrival Sophia manifested in the Third Principle to the two friends united in the most glorious manner, and renewed her bonds with them, which lasted until 1685." This is how Sophia, who had promised Gichtel fidelity, had no hesitation about becoming bigamous, after having had thirty lovers: he was simply her preferred husband, and she favored the others in proportion to their service to her. The life of these two "brothers" during their years together, both believing themselves to be Sophia's husband, must have been quite odd. When she vanished for a period of time, they had a vision of Christ (in 1690) as if she was working in the higher spheres for their souls' salvation. "Shortly before Gichtel's death, which occurred in 1710, Sophia appeared to the two friends as she had in 1683 for the first time, and recalled her faithful friend to her side," Kirchberger concludes.

Ueberfeld attempted to publish a six-volume edition of Gichtel's letters, but they were full of gaps.

> Sophia came personally, after her husband's death, to oversee and direct the arrangement of his posthumous letters; she revised several pages that had not been clearly stated in the rough drafts that Gichtel had given his friend Ueberfeld; and as this latter worked on this composition, Sophia guided him personally. She had come to see Ueberfeld several times for this purpose. It was a never-ending feast, during which she communicated to the editor and several faithful friends of the deceased, developments of holy economy.[14]

In the preface to his friend's correspondence, Ueberfeld wrote that "mouth cannot express the lasting, permanent joys that this manifestation afforded them."

This case is thoroughly original, as it involves an angelic creature rather than a diabolical one. Her worshipper perceives her at the center of his soul and outside his body at the same time. She is able to vanish, return, and vanish again for a certain amount of time, and she gives a spiritual pleasure that is even more intense than sensual pleasure, as if she was the inner wife of the inner man.

14 Ibid.

Andrew Phillip Smith

An Interview With Gerard Russell

APS: I really enjoyed your book, Gerard. It's unique in two ways: firstly, I don't know of any other book that addresses all of these ancient minority religions in the middle east and, secondly, you have direct experience of contact with the peoples involved. What motivated you to go to such lengths to make contact with these ethnic groups and religious practitioners?

GR: Well I suppose it really began when I was in Cairo, and I found that it was much more interesting for me to go to a Coptic church than to go to an English-speaking one, and I went to church anyway. So that was how I came across these minority religions. I think what makes them so interesting for me is that they give a slightly different take on the encounter between the European and the Middle east. So often that's reduced to a set of dichotomies which divide people and set them apart. A lot of my friends are Muslim, but even so, people tend to think of Islam and the West. That's a classic division, isn't it. Actually, what distinguishes the West from the Muslim world, or the Middle East, is much more complex and subtle and there's a lot of room for commonality as well as differences. That was one thing. The second thing is that I was a historian before I became interested in the Middle East. I was a classicist. And there were all these links with the classical world which I found fascinating. I love to find the links to ancient history. When I came across these religions that have those links, I couldn't get enough of it really. It was incredibly interesting and the more one discovers, the more interesting it becomes.

APS: Yes, I notice that you have a slightly different historical perspective on many of these groups. You emphasise the Babylonian influence on the Mandaeans. Most scholars are operating under a religious studies paradigm when they address, for example, the Mandaeans.

GR: Yes, a lot of the time. And there are scholars who do. I discussed it with one or two before writing the book, just to see, not necessarily that they would agree with me in stressing the Babylonian heritage. Some of them would put Judaism as a more important influence. But it's debatable. Just to make sure that it wasn't a totally silly thing for me to be saying. It is a valid interpretation. But also one that, as you say, appeals more if you look at the practices of the people. So much scholarship, especially these days, is done in a sort of protestant context in which one looks at the scriptures and says the essence of a religion lies in its scriptures and its origin lies in when those scriptures were written. But if you look at, particularly, a group like the Yazidis, it doesn't make much sense to say that, in my view. I think it makes more sense to say, let's look at their customs and its practices and ask where do those come from, and how long have those existed? It's a different way of reading the history of these people. Of course, both are valid, but they come from different traditions.

APS: Yes, the approach that religion is something that people do.

GR: Yes.

APS: On the other hand, some of these peoples have survived because of their status as people of the book: the Zoroastrians, and whoever we decide that the Sabaeans are. How were your encounters with the scriptures of these various peoples?

GR: It depends a bit. Zoroastrians have scriptures which are pretty intact and published, and acknowledged. At the other end of the scale you have the Yezidis, where it's probable that the books that were published in the west are not genuine. But nobody knows for sure. Even beyond that, the Alawites, you've got scriptures that are not specifically recognised, and are meant to be secret. So there is a real range. Of course, the scriptures don't always give you much of a sense of the religion. The Mandaean scriptures are quite baffling, to be honest. I don't profess to be a scholar of them. But they're just so different. They don't tell you beliefs. They are a set of stories. In a sense, Origin myths. Myths of the world and sometimes origin myths of their religion, and how it came to be. You can read them and not know much of what a Mandaean believes at the end.

APS: I done a little bit of work on the Mandaean myths and they can be very contradictory as well.

GR: And very puzzling and multi-layered. For example, if you're looking for a Jewish context, there's clearly a Jewish context but it's very puzzling. It's absolutely polemical. The attitude towards the Temple in Jerusalem is rather odd. They're very, very polemical in a particular way which is very unfamiliar to readers of the Qu'ran and the gospels.

APS: That's a paradox with the Mandaeans themselves, who as I understand are very peaceable people and have been a minority in their areas for a long time, and don't mind being mistaken for Christians occasionally, and feel some commonality with Christianity. On the other hand Jesus was an apostate, and in one writing Muhammad was the son of the Arab butcher, if I remember correctly.

GR: Yes, there's a lot of stuff like that. A lot of stuff about menstrual blood and so forth, and the Temple and so on. I understand why their scriptures aren't being published! Obviously, the Mandaean scriptures being secret means that the average Mandaean has no idea what they say anyway. And it certainly doesn't affect what they do and believe, although one has to allow that some of them will not tell the full story, as it were. It's certainly a very, very different approach to scripture than that of Christians and Muslims. But at the same time it's important to recognise they are monotheists. They aren't idol worshippers.

These things matter, even in the contemporary Middle East. So they have a book, but more importantly they don't belong to the tradition Muhammad was attacking in the creation of Islam.

APS: When you mention secrecy, that seems to be a factor in many of these religions. In the modern day, the laity or the common people often have little knowledge of the religion, apart from some basic practices, but there is still an esoteric elite that does have an advanced knowledge.

GR: It's still a popular model, yes.

APS: With the displacement of the Mandaeans, for example, as refugees, and the difficulty for the Mandaeans of holding river baptisms—I remember there was a Mandaean priest in Sweden who had trouble acquiring myrtle branches—what do you think the chances are of the survival of that model as these peoples get dispersed due to all the military conflicts and persecution and other disruptions?

GR: I think they'll have to adapt. Both Christianity and Judaism adapted when they were displaced. And if you look at the difference between Jews and Samaritans today, you can see that the Jews have abandoned the Temple so the priest plays a much lesser role in religion than, it's essentially a marginal sacral role. Apart from the Kabbalah tradition, which is quite secretive, the Jewish religion is very public. It had admitted converts before the destruction of the Temple, certainly. There were great changes which enables Judaism to survive, and Christianity even more so. By becoming evangelical, in a way, and becoming quite adaptable to living in different places.

Something like that will have to happen to some of these religions. When you look at the Druze community, it still is cohesive. But you've really got the priests, as it were, bearing on their shoulders the whole weight of their religion. I don't think that can easily last when the communities are dispersed, when the sheikh doesn't any longer live down the road, but the sheikh lives 100 mile away in Los Angeles, or something.

A Yazidi

Then it becomes a very different relationship and I think it will inevitably have to adapt. Furthermore, dealing with intermarriage is a very different thing in Britain and America than it is in Beirut, or the Middle East in general.

APS: Marrying only within the group is a practice that has kept the groups cohesive, in these various different cases, but also prevents it adapting to western conditions. In the Mandaean community there's a strong debate about whether they should accept converts. The Samaritans are an extraordinary group because the name is familiar to every Christian, or more or less everyone in the western world, and beyond, but there are only 750 of them now. I had never realised until I read your book that the population went down as low as 146.

GR: It's tremendously close to extinction, and then they pulled back from the brink.

APS: You mentioned a Samaritan man who, when he was asked what would happen if a Samaritan woman intended to marry out of the community he said that she would have her throat cut in the night like a sheep.

GR: This wasn't I asking but rather there was a documentary made by an Israeli film-maker, in which that question was asked. It is rather a shocking moment. It has happened to Samaritan women who marry Jewish men, and they are cut off, ostracised completely. No violence has actually ever been used, but I think he was not making a threat he would carry out, but they definitely do ostracise people.

APS: Another factor with these ancient minority religions, especially when they're moving to the west, is that some of the social conditions have been fairly static. For example, women have a particular place within the community that's often very limited. Although, for example Jorunn Buckley showed from the manuscript tradition that there were female scribes and perhaps priests earlier in the Mandaean tradition.

GR: Well, I think it's very, very interesting. There are two things: if you look back to the early middle ages, back to the ninth/eighth century and before, women played a larger role in Islam. And if you look back very far to the fifth century BC there was an admiral in the Persian navy who was a woman. So there is a slightly different historical tradition which is very, very different on the status of women than we've seen in the Middle East for the last few centuries. And maybe the fact that there were female scribes illustrates that the former social conditions were more amenable in the past. You may have noticed that Nadja, who features in chapter 1, is very intrigued by that and she's heard about this, and it inspires her, in a way, to a sort of feminist take on Mandaeanism. But it's still very tough. Particularly what's tough is when you're a woman and you marry out. There's no chance of re-admittance, whereas if you're a man and you marry out, you've got a slightly better chance. That's quite tough, I think. Other things like the exclusion of menstruating women is quite common in these groups as well. The Samaritans and the Mandaeans both practise it. In Judaism it exists as well. That's definitely a middle-eastern tradition. But the marriage rule is something that's affecting people more seriously.

APS: These communities are so small and, in the most part, so beleaguered, it's easy to feel sympathetic with them. But the Alawites are unusual in having a substantial amount of power in Syria, because of al-Assad.

GR: Yes, very unusual, yes. Not all of them, and to some extent at the expense of their own faith, of their own distinctive religion and practices, so that inevitably they have really had to make themselves more orthodox in order to get Iranian support. And that's been a feature of the last 30, 40 years, and there's a few references in the book in the book to what the Alawites think is their suppression by their government. Nonetheless, I think that being from a persecuted minority, or an excluded minority, doesn't mean that you're morally any better than anybody else, it just means that you're more vulnerable. I don't wish to excuse anything done by Alawites, but they do face problems. I think one thing that's very important in any future Syria in which Assad's removed, let's say, I think it's very important to address the longstanding social issues that excluded Alawites and made them feel such resentment. But I don't have any further comment on the politics of it. I find them interesting religiously. I'm afraid they weren't very friendly, so I didn't really get a deep understanding on a personal

An Alawite Falconer

level what's it like to be an Alawite. But I think, reading about their beliefs, and catching hold of one or two, and from published material, they're tremendously interesting.

APS: Did you ever come across Walter Birks' book The Treasure of Montségur? He has a quite unlikely theory that the Cathars go back to the Alawites, but he spent some time in British intelligence in Syria.

GR: Well, I shall have a read of that.

APS: Which were your favourites out of all these groups? Which made the greatest impression on you?

GR: The Druze are such an intact community. If you go into the Druze area you're in an area of hundreds of thousands of people who live in a sort of exclusive enclave now. Nearly always did, actually, but the Christians who lived there have mostly left. That's a very different experience from catching one or two Mandaeans on the streets of Baghdad, or wherever, because it's a much more intact social environment. So, to me, that left a visual impression that was very powerful. And I enjoyed talking to them about Greek philosophy too.

APS: Which rituals or practices that you were able to take part in, or observe, most impressed you?

GR: Gosh, that's a good question as well. It's not quite your theme, but the Coptic Good Friday and Easter liturgy are tremendously powerful. Not only because they're so long, but also the use of music in those services, the tonal incantations of the ancient temple priest, gives you a sense of connection with the past. Of course, the Copts' own very powerful devotion is inspirational.

APS: And it was in Coptic?

GR: Yes, of course a lot of Coptic is Greek, many of the words are of very ancient origin, Egyptian. So you have hymns like "Pek Ekthronos" where the first word is Egyptian and "ethronos" is Greek. I haven't studied ancient Egyptian, but it's thrilling to find it still alive in that way.

APS: Did you manage to visit, I think in Cairo, the huge new underground church that the Copts have built?

GR: Yes, I did go to that. It fits 10,000 people.

APS: And many of them are involved in rubbish collecting, aren't they?

GR: That's right, it's an extraordinary part of the city. All of the doors had crosses on.

APS: Well, thank you very much, Gerard. I really enjoyed the book and it was a wonderful interview too.

GR: I'm glad you liked it. Thank you so much.

A Druze Baking a Traditional Dish

Alex Rivera

The Gods of Imagination
Alchemy, Magic, and the Quintessence

Introduction

The imagination is often conceived as merely a mental faculty of the observer or simply limited to the capacity of one's brain activity to conceive of specific images, concepts, ideas, fancies and wish-fulfillments. Writers and artists alike are called "imaginative" because of their success at capturing their audience's imagination and having their consciousness live in a fictional world that seems real to the observer. This immersion in a fictional world is also said to require a "willing suspension of disbelief."

The imagination was thought in powerful, numinous terms in various sources. These sources include Plato's Dialogues, *Corpus Hermeticum*, the Nag Hammadi Codices, the *Greek Magical Papyri*, the *Emerald Tablets of Hermes*, the *Zohar*, and mythological and legendary narratives associated with Bible and alchemical legends. This paper will explore all of these diverse streams of thought that all point to the same *ideal* source of the eternal imagination. This paper is not, however, an attempt to trivialize the concept of divinity or the soul as being only a figment of the mind in man.

The Hermetic Imagination

The Platonic philosophers wrestled with defining what the significance of the imagination meant. For Plato, the imagination was ranked the lowest on his scale of the soul's faculties, resigning it to perceiving only shadows and reflections of the eternal ideas in the realm of appearances. Plato held a negative view of imagination in the fine arts or any kind of material reflection of eternal ideas when he says, "Let us seek the true beauty, not asking whether a particular face is fair, for all such things appear to be in a flux."[1] Indeed, just as the lower soul seeks material objects of vision, so the ideal of contemplation of the higher is the "colorless, intangible essence, visible only to mind who is the pilot of the soul."[2] It is only through the power of philosophy and reason that can correctly transform and interpret the unideal phantasy. In *The Republic*, Book VII, 518c, where it explains the famous allegory of the cave, Plato likens "true knowledge" of being cultivated by the soul as like "inserting vision into blind eyes."

Moving from the classical Greek era and into the Greco-Roman world, the concepts associated with the imagination change. One can also see the Platonic understanding of the imagination shift when reads the *Corpus Hermeticum*, which is made up of eighteen treatises while composed by multiple authors from opposing Hermetic sects. In the Renaissance, they were eventually translated from the Greek originals (brought over to Florence by a monk in 1460) to Latin by Marsilio Ficino on the order of Cosimodo de'

---

1 439d.
2 Phaedrus 247c.

Medici. Because of this, an explosion of interest was set off in Hermetic philosophy and in the allied fields of theosophy, astrology, alchemy and magic. One can say that the *Corpus Hermeticum* was responsible for the Italian Renaissance.

The *Corpus Hermeticum* should not be read as a coherent manual of Hermetic beliefs. Hermetism was a religio-philosophical movement, and different Hermetists believed different things although they shared common ideas. The *Corpus Hermeticum* contradicts itself repeatedly, because it is a collection of texts from people with quite different metaphysical doctrines who all claimed heritage to Hermes. The texts are generally divided into two groups of optimist/monist and dualist/pessimist; however, even the texts within each group tend to disagree with one another. Roughly half of the *Corpus Hermeticum* is anticosmic. For example, the *Corpus Hermeticum* states that the universe is completely evil—so evil, in fact, that it is impossible for God to dwell within it.

> Mind conceives every mental product: both the good, when mind receives seeds from god, as well as the contrary kind, when the seeds come from some demonic being. [Unless it is illuminated by god,] no part of the cosmos is without a demon that steals into the mind to sow the seed of its own energy, and what has been sown the mind conceives – adulteries, murders, assaults on one's father, acts of sacrilege and irreverence, suicides by hanging or falling from a cliff, and all other such works of demons.[3]

This passage underscores a radically dualist disposition of the author. However, it is not impossible for mankind to gain the divine knowledge of God as the Cosmos, yet is still contained in the Mind of God. The imagination is thus rendered as a divine activity, where the initiate is instructed to envision himself as God so that he may obtain an intimate understanding of God:

> And when you yourself can do all this, cannot God do it? You must understand then that it is in this way that God contains within himself the Kosmos, and himself, and all that is; it is as thoughts which God thinks, that all things are contained in Him. If then you do not make yourself equal to God, you cannot apprehend God; for like is known by like. Leap clear of all that is corporeal, and make yourself grow to a like expanse with that greatness which is beyond all measure; rise above all time, and become eternal; then you will apprehend God.
>
> Think that for you too nothing is impossible; deem that you too are immortal, and that you are able to grasp all things in your thought, to know every craft and every science; find your home in the haunts of every living creature; make yourself higher than all heights, and lower than all depths; being together in yourself all opposites of quality, heat and cold, dryness and fluidity; think that you are everywhere at once, on land, at sea, in heaven; think that you are not yet begotten, that you are in the womb, that you are young, that you are old, that you have died, that you are in the world beyond the grave; grasp in your thought all this at once, all times and places, all substances and qualities and magnitudes together; then you can apprehend God.[4]

However, some scholars see this clash between the dualism and monism found in the *Hermetica* as being a sequence of initiation stages in the soul and spirit of the Hermetic

---

3 *Corpus Hermeticum* IX:3. Copenhaver, p. 27.

4 *Corpus Hermeticum*, XI. 17b-21a, pp. 211-29

initiate: "From a theurgic perspective, dualism and acosmicism mark a preliminary stage of the initiate's experience followed by a monist or non-dualist embrace of the entire cosmos, one that marks the culmination of rebirth and immortalization."[5] To provide some further background information, necessary to understand Hermetism, the lore of Hermes will be explored in some detail. As mentioned earlier, the syncretic god Hermes Trismegistus was a union between Hermes with Thoth. Hermes' title of "Thrice-greatest" comes from his Egyptian predecessor, whose epithet "great" was repeated twice or three times by way of superlative. As the moon reflects the light of the sun, so Thoth derives his authority as a scribe and "secretary" of the sun god Ra. In Greek mythology, Hermes is one of twelve gods known as the Olympians. He is the messenger of the gods—the only god who is authorized to visit Heaven, Earth and the Underworld. Hermes represents Mercury, a planet that is associated with information and communication. In the later Hellenistic era, various writers considered Hermes Trismegistus to have been a historical personage, a king, prophet, philosopher and physician (much like Thoth) as well as the author of many widely disseminated writings like the *Corpus Hermeticum* and the *Emerald Tablets* (*Tabula Smaragdina*).

According to Saint Augustine, Hermes was also said to be a contemporary of Moses and at other times preceding from the Israelite Lawgiver.[6] In a long-winded debate between Saint Augustine and the Manichean Bishop Faustus of Milevis, Faustus reportedly suggested, "If, as is said, any prophecies of Christ are to be found in the Sibyl, (1) or in Hermes, (2) called Trismegistus, or Orpheus, or any heathen poet, they might aid the faith of those who, like us, are converts from heathenism to Christianity."[7]

These teachings were said to be written in the holy language of hieroglyphs on the "Pillars of Hermes." Philosophers such as Pythagoras and Plato were also said to have derived their wisdom from these hieroglyphs found on steles.[8] According to Plato in *Philebus* 18b, Socrates tells the story of a "god or godlike man" being "Theuth" (Thoth) observed that sound was infinite and was the first to "notice that the vowel sounds in that infinity were not one, but many…" This indicates that Thoth was also a god associated with being a "spokesman" (a Logos) or an embodiment of reason and inventor of knowledge, much like Hermes.[9]

Spiritual Alchemy and the Stones of Imagination

According to the famous scholar and Theosophist, G.R.S. Mead, Apollonius of Tyana claimed that imagination was a faculty of creative thought: a faculty of God mirrored in man. The passage warrants full citation:

> Imagination, says Apollonius, is one of the most potent faculties, for it enables us to reach nearer to realities. It is generally supposed that Greek sculpture was merely a glorification of physical beauty, in itself quite unspiritual. It was an idealization of form and features, limbs and muscles, an empty glorification of the physical with nothing of course really corresponding to it in the nature of things. But Apollonius declared it brings us nearer to the real, as Pythagoras and Plato declared before him, and as all the wiser teach.
>
> He meant this literally, not vaguely and

---

5 Gregory Shaw. "Taking the Shape of the Gods: A Theurgic Reading of Hermetic Rebirth." (*Aries*, Volume 15, Issue 1, 2015) pp. 136–169.

6 St. Augustine. *The City of God*. Book VIII. 39.

7 *Contra Faustus*. XIII.1.

8 Iamblichus. *De mysteriis*. 1.2.

9 Clement of Alexandria. *Stromata*. VI. 4.

fantastically. He asserted that the types and ideas of things are the only realities. He meant that between the imperfection of the earth and the highest divine type of all things, were grades of increasing perfection. He meant that within each man was a form of perfection, though of course not yet absolutely perfect. That the angel in man, his dæmon, was of God-like beauty, the summation of all the finest features he had ever worn in his many lives on earth. The Gods, too, belonged to the world of types, of models, of perfections, the heaven-world. The Greek sculptors had succeeded in getting in contact with this world, and the faculty they used was imagination.[10]

For Apollonius, the imagination is a method for "pre-planning" something to happen or manifest. It is through this faculty, which our thoughts of intention can meet and even mingle and co-create with powers that are outside of man's consciousness. Apollonius' teachings on the imagination correspond to what is found in the *Emerald Tablets of Hermes*, which relates the alchemical secrets of creation itself. The connection exists because in Arabic Hermetic literature, it connects Apollonius with Hermes. Apollonius is called "Balínús" in Arabic and is depicted as the discoverer and representative of Hermes' teachings. In the Arabic teacher Bahá'u'lláh's *Lawh-i-Hikmat* (*Tablet of Wisdom*), he states, "It was this man of wisdom [Balínús] who became informed of the mysteries of creation and discerned the subtleties which lie enshrined in the Hermetic writings."[11]

The earliest surviving translation of the *Emerald Tablet* is in an Arabic book known as the *Book of Balinas the Wise on Causes*, written around 650 C.E. This is just one of the many legends surrounding the tablet. Dennis William Hauch describes this tablet. "Most stories describe the Tablet as a green-colored stone with raised, bas-relief lettering in the Phoenician alphabet."[12] Here is the *Emerald Tablets of Hermes* as follows:

It is true without lie, certain and most true.
What is Below is like that which is Above. And that which is Above, like that which is Below, serve to bring the wonder of the Universe into existence. And as all things originate from One thing, from the Idea of One Mind: so do all created things originate from this One thing through adaptation. Its father is the Sun, its mother the Moon. The Wind carried it in its belly, its nurse is the Earth. It is the father of all existing things in the entire Universe. Its inherent virtue is perfected when it is changed into Earth.

Separate the Earth from the Fire, the Subtle from the Gross, repeatedly with great skillfulness. It rises from Earth to Heaven, and falls back down again to Earth, thereby con of both the Above and the Below. Thus will you obtain the glory of the entire Universe. Every darkness will leave you. This is the greatest strength of all, because it conquers every subtle thing and penetrates every solid thing. In this way, was the universe created. From this proceeds wonders, of which herewith is an example. Therefore, I am called the three-

10 G.R.S. Mead, *Apollonius of Tyana*, Section XV - From His Sayings and Sermons. Accessed December 21, 2014. http://www.gnosis.org/library/grs-mead/apollonius/apolloniusmead15.htm

11 Bahá'u'lláh, Tablets of Bahá'u'lláh revealed after the Kitáb-i-Aqdas (Haifa: Bahá'í World Centre, 1978) p. 148.

12 Dr. Gottlieb Latz. Translated by Dennis William Hauch. *The Secret of the Emerald Tablet*. (Athanor Book: 2005), 15.

times glorified Hermes, because I possess all three parts of true understanding of the whole Universe. What I have had to say about the operation of the Sun is completed.

The famous axiom of "What is Below is like that which is Above" sounds very close to what is described in the *Gospel of Philip* (Codex II), which records Jesus Christ performing initiation rites that sound much like that one of the Hermetic mystery schools of Alexandria, Egypt: "The Lord did everything in a mystery, a baptism and a chrism and a eucharist and a redemption and a bridal chamber. [...] he said, "I came to make the things below like the things above, and the things outside like those inside. I came to unite them in the place." The correspondence between the microcosm and the macrocosm, the inside and the outside of the totality of creation[13], is made explicit. This is reflective yet somehow different than Platonic thought: that the manifest world is merely a shadow of a greater truth, an ideal that can never be found in our daily reality.

Everything in creation, accordingly has its root in the transcendent, or the "One Thing." The Emerald Tablet itself teaches in veiled language how to produce the alchemical Elixir of Life or "Quintessence," the "Fifth Element," that which is born from the "One Thing." The father of this final product is the sun and the mother being the moon, which "defeats all subtle things and permeates all solids." The sun symbolizes the fire; the moon, water; wind, air; and the earth, obviously, the Earth. The first three elements also correspond to sulphur, salt and mercury.[14]

The Sun gives its life-giving rays throughout the solar system in a cyclical manner while providing its solar seeds into the Earth so that they may be "perfected." All of these come from the One as adaptations, splitting off into specialized roles. The first three principal aspects of the One gather together to form the Earth.

---

13 Throughout Gnostic literature, the "aeons" are considered a part of the "inside", as well as the spirit while the material or the outer body exterior is just that- outside.

14 Daniel Mylius. "Opus Medico Chymicum"

The three principal elements are separated out from the fourth element and purified and then recombined to form a new type of Earth, being the Fifth Element or the "Cosmic Quintessence." That is the key to understanding all alchemy. The "Hermetic art" of alchemy itself as a mirror for psychological or spiritual transformation has a long tradition, going back at least to the time of Zosimos and way before that.

"Separate the Earth from the Fire, the Subtle from the Gross, repeatedly with great skillfulness." This corresponds to the alchemical axiom of the Latin "Solve et Coagula," meaning dissolve and coagulate or reconstitute. Any alchemical operation will involve these two fundamental steps. This process involves purging the influence of the lower and solidifying the influence of the higher and crystallizing it as a permanent substance on Earth. This process dissolves all of the impurities of matter and darkness until all that is left is the "true image" or the true expression of the "One Thing." In this instance, we can see how Plato was using ancient, Hermetic-like ideas when he wrote in *Timaeus* 28a6, about how the divine Craftsman (the "Demiurge"), imitated the unchanging, eternal model above and imposes a mathematical order on the pre-existent primal chaos to generate the cosmos we know. The Demiurge, in this instance, can be seen as a cosmic alchemist or initiator who dissolves and perfects the chaotic realm into multiple structures and shapes based on the Eternal Forms above.

The alchemist raises the subtle into Heaven, from the below to the above, and allows it to descend again by dissolving one's "wish" then coagulating it again after it has been above. The alchemist allows that creative imagination to descend into the Earth and bring with it the perfected substance. By the power of the "One Thing," it becomes so. In the *Corpus Hermeticum*, Poimandres the Man-Shepard (1), we find this idea of ascending into the higher spheres, where the material body is dissolved into light and ascends:

To this Poimandres said: "First, in releasing the material body you give the body itself over to alteration, and the form that you used to have vanishes. To the demon you give over your temperament, now inactive. The body's senses rise up and flow back to their particular sources, becoming separate parts and mingling again with the energies. And feeling and longing go on toward irrational nature. Thence the human being rushes up through the cosmic framework...[15]

To repeat what the *Emerald Tablets of Hermes* tells us, "The unique is of all the strengths the strongest strength. It defeats all subtle things and permeates all solids. In this way, the cosmic was created." An alchemist might argue that this "strength" or force is that of the Philosopher's Stone, the Pearl of the Great Price, the Divine Hermaphrodite, the Astral Fire[16], the Elixir of Life, being the "perfected" (Greek: *teleios*).[17] These objects and symbols represent something that has completed the work of the alchemical process, called the Great Work (*Magnum Opus*). The final product can be called materialized spirit and spiritualized matter or what Carl Jung called the "coniunctio oppositorum."[18] It is the solid, unchanging realization of the above, which stands firm and "unshakable." The spiritual is ironically represented as a physical object; the alchemical offspring or manifestation of the divine itself. The Philosopher's Stone has completed the journey, which encases both

---

[15] 1.24-25.

[16] "The great transcendentally perfect Stone of the Wise is none other than a pure, concentrated and congealed heavenly fire." Peter Steiner. Von der Universal-Materie [The Universal Matter].

[17] In the Greek Mystery Religions, the word "teleios" was also a technical term used for Initiates. (Cf. Baur. *A Greek-English Lexicon of the New Testament*, p. 809a.)

[18] David Henderson. *The Coincidence of the Opposites. Studies In Spirituality 20*, 101-113.

worlds of "perfected" matter and spirit in its alloy.

One can emulate this process and apply it by becoming "co-creators" of manifestation through the imagination since man is created in the "image of God" and is able to define reality as Adam named the animals in the Garden of Eden.[19] The occult author Tracy Twyman makes a poignant observation about this point: "If man is made in 'God's image,' it seems to me that part of our role is to act as his eyes, and his imagination, collapsing the trajectories of probability curves as we observe and thus define the reality around us. In other words, I think we are integral to the process of creation, and that is the crushing responsibility that we must bear. That is one way in which we hold aloft the Heavens on our shoulders."[20] This is the "Hermetic" Law of Attraction in a nutshell.

In its most basic understanding, alchemy is a process where base metals are transformed into gold. This process of transmutation is the basis from which alchemy operates. We most commonly interpret this transmutation of gold into lead literally, and alchemy is understood to be the foundation from which the natural sciences of today originate. Alchemists were even said to look for "course matter" in the form of urine and manure! Modern chemistry, for instance, owes much of its development to this "Hermetic art." However, most alchemists weren't just interested in the exoteric nature of alchemy but were also concerned with the refinement and transformation of the spiritual self as Zosimos advocated.

Hendrik Bogdan describes transmutative process as an initiation, "Just as the alchemists aimed at turning lead into gold through a process that included stages of *nigredo*, *albedo*, and *rubedo*, this process can be viewed as a spiritual one." He continues, "the experience of transmutation is of great importance, since the idea of initiation is partly connected to it. The initiate is often viewed as going through a process of transmutation as he passes through the various rites of initiation."[21] The very word "initiate" stems from the Latin *initiatus* and *initium*, meaning "to begin, originate" and "a beginning, an entrance" respectively.[22] Related words are *initiative*, "that which begins," and *initial*, stemming from *inire*: "to go into, enter upon."[23]

For the alchemist, the human being was seen as a microcosmic reflection of the macrocosmic God, at least on a spiritual level. Alchemy was aimed toward transforming the self and stripping away the unnecessary while refining the virtuous aspects that one comes into a harmonious relationship with God and nature. On the surface level, the alchemist was concerned with proto-chemistry and as Elizabeth Langhorne writes, "...on another, in accord with old belief in the spiritual significance of matter, the effort at transformation was directed not just toward the material without, but toward the soul, within. As lead is transmuted into gold, so the soul can be purified, dissolved, and crystallized anew, to reveal spirit."[24]

The first step in this initiatory path is the stripping away of the unnecessary and reaching the first matter, or *Prima Materia*. Doing this requires the initial stage of dissolving the impure metal into this original form. "According to alchemical theory, there can be no regeneration without corruption, no life without death."[25] This dissolution of the impure metal is what

---

19 Genesis 1:27. Genesis 2:20.

20 *Clock Shavings*. (Dragon Key Press, 2014), 410-411.

21 Henrick Bogdan, *Western Esotericism and Rituals of Initiation*. (Albany: State University of New York Press, 2007), 11.

22 *Etymology Online*, s.v. "Initiation,"

23 Ibid., s.v. "Initial,"

24 John Graham and Jackson: "The Magus and the Alchemist." *American Art*, Vol. 12, No. 3 (Autumn, 1998), pp. 46-67.

25 Bogdan, p. 113.

is known in alchemy as putrefaction. It is the first phase of alchemy, known as *Nigredo* or "blackness," to which this preliminary step is associated. Carl Jung points out in his alchemical analyses, "The *Nigredo* signifies the *mortifactio, putrefactio, solutio, separatio, divisio*, etc., a state of dissolution and decomposition that precedes the synthesis."[26] Indeed, there is a psychological significance to Nigredo.

Dennis William Hauck notes about this process, "Putrefaction is the absolute suppression of ego, an indispensable requirement for moving into higher dimensions of consciousness. Putrefaction is often perceived as a dark depression in which the former ruling principle of the personality must die to make room for a higher identity."[27] Indeed, this alchemical process can also apply to what St. John of the Cross called the "Dark Night of the Soul." The work of alchemical initiation involves the descent of the soul to Hades or Hell, which represents spiritual darkness and the physical blackening of the metals. It is comparable to how Zosimos in his so-called Visions, which presents violent dreams of a priest sacrificing the coarseness of his flesh (as well as flayed, dismembered and boiled alive within the "divine waters," representing the dissolution of metal) upon an altar so that Zosimos can become pure spirit. This higher identity is symbolically similar to that of the Philosopher's Stone, the "Lightning" Stone or the "Foundation Stone" of creation.[28]

---

26 C. G. Jung, *Mysterium Coniunctionis: An Inquiry into the separation and Synthesis of Psychic Opposites in Alchemy*, trans. R. F. C. Hull, 2nd ed., (Princeton: Princeton University Press, 1970), 507.

27 Dennis William Hauck, *The Emerald Tablet: Alchemy for Personal Transformation*, (New York: Penguin Group Publishing, 1999), 114.

28 Please see this article for more information on the "Lightning Stone". http://www.labyrinthdesigners.org/alchemic-authors-1598-1832/elias-ashmole-and-the-prophetic-red-stone/

The legend of the foundation stone of alchemy is one that is especially pronounced in Jewish Midrash. In *2 Enoch* 28:2-4, it states that the Lord placed some enigmatic stones in the abyss during the process of creation. "Then from the waters I hardened big stones, and the clouds of the depths I commanded to dry themselves. And I did not name what fell to the lowest places. Gathering the ocean into one place, I bound it with a yoke. I gave to the sea an eternal boundary, which will not be broken through by the waters. The solid structure I fixed and established it above the waters."

This description matches with Genesis 6-8 when it states, "And God said, 'Let there be a vault between the waters to separate water from water.' So God made the vault and separated the water under the vault from the water above it. And it was so. God called the vault 'sky.' And there was evening, and there was morning—the second day." In this case, the "vault" can be likened to that of the foundation stone of creation, which links yet separates Heaven and Earth. In later Jewish mysticisms, particularly in the Kabbalistic Zohar, this immortal stone of creation (as well as the four elements of the Emerald Tablets) is related once again:

"Whereupon were the foundations thereof fastened?" (Job 38:6). He said: 'When God created the world, He established it on seven pillars, but upon what those pillars rest no one may know, since it is a recondite and inscrutable mystery. The world did not come into being until God took a certain stone, which is called the "foundation stone", and cast it into the abyss so that it held fast there, and from it the world was planted. This is the central point of the universe, and on this point stands the holy of holies. This is the stone referred to in the verses, "Who laid the corner-stone thereof" (Job 38:6), "the stone of testing, the precious corner-stone" (Isaiah 28:16), and "the stone that the builders despise became the head of the corner" (Psalm 128:22).

This stone is compounded of fire, water, and air, and rests on the abyss. Sometimes water flows from it and fills the deep. This stone is set as a sign in the centre of the world. It is referred to in the words, "And Jacob took a stone and set it as a pillar" (Genesis 31:45). Not that he took this stone, which was created from the beginning, but he established it above and below, by making there a "house of God". This stone has on it seven eyes, as it is written, "On one stone seven eyes" (Zecharia 3:9), and it is called "foundation stone", for one thing because the world was planted from it, and for another because God set it as a source of blessing to the world."[29]

In the New Testament, specifically in Matthew 16:18, it says that Jesus Christ gave his divine authority to Simon Bar-Jona, in which he renamed "Peter" (rock) as a metaphorical reference to this Foundation Stone to build his church on earth. All of this is later reflected in the "New Zion" or "New Jerusalem" as described by The Revelation of St. John the Divine, as descending from Heaven at the end of the Apocalypse. Tracy R. Twyman writes about this divine cubic stone:

> In dimensions, it is a perfect cube, and shines like a precious stone, just like the cube stone of the Philosophers. This is part of an alchemical process in which God created Heaven and Earth anew, and expels all impurities from creation back into chaos. It is the death of the old universe, and the birth of a new one, with the heavenly city as the foundation stone, and the throne of God. As in alchemy, it is even likened to a wedding.[30]

She also writes: "What is happening here is a redefinition of reality. Everything that is to be saved is placed inside of the cube, with God. Everything on the outside is to be cast off, into chaos. Those inside are the ones with their names written in the Book of Life. If your name is not there, it is like you never existed."[31] She also compares this divine cube to that of Noah's Ark and the Deluge and even with Cain's city of Enoch, built in the land of Nod. She likens this city as "...Cain's attempt to copy the design of the New Jerusalem with an infernal reflection down below." Finally, she speculates that at the End Times, the Earth, Heaven and Hell will merge together or "commingle in a timeless moment. Perhaps the black and white cubes will merge."[32]

This is comparable to the "Marriage of Heaven and Hell" William Blake once wrote about and even to the "Chemical Wedding" of Christian Rosenkreutz from Rosicrucian lore. Biblical and Hermetic alchemy is a science that is highly relevant to the imagination. Whoever possesses the stone or what Revelations 2:17 calls the "hidden manna" or the "white stone with a new name written on it" has in their possession not only the secrets of immortality but the secrets of creation itself.

The Gnostic Imagination

In Sethian Gnosticism, we also find references to the divine imagination. In the *Apocryphon of John*, it quotes a lengthy section from the lost Book of Zoroaster, which explains how the astral rulers or "powers" create each part of the material body of Adam and list their appropriate correspondences for the purposes of healing. The text tells us, "And the one over the imagina-

---

29 Zohar I:231a.

30 *Clock Shavings*. (Dragon Key Press, 2014), 268.

31 Ibid. p. 271.

32 Ibid. p. 282.

tion, Oummaa."³³ The *Apocryphon of John* itself is brimming with alchemical symbolism.³⁴ The Catholic heresiologist, Irenaeus of Lyons, paraphrases the doctrines of the Valentinian Christians by stating the Demiurge *imagined* the fallen cosmos into existence:

> They go on to say that the Demiurge imagined that he created all these things of himself, while he in reality made them in conjunction with the productive power of Achamoth. He formed the heavens, yet was ignorant of the heavens; he fashioned man, yet knew not man; he brought to light the earth, yet had no acquaintance with the earth; and, in like manner. They declare that he was ignorant of the forms of all that he made, and knew not even of the existence of his own mother, but imagined that he himself was all things.³⁵

Irenaeus describes the Gnostics themselves as "discoverers" and "inventors" of "imaginary fiction" but meant it more as an insult: "These men, following those distinctions, have styled, what he calls ideas, and exemplar, the images of those things which are above; while, through a mere change of name, they boast themselves as being discoverers and contrivers of this kind of imaginary fiction."³⁶ The "divine image" concept is a common one in Gnosis. The "Upper Aeons" are analogous to the Platonic ideal forms, archetypes or simply "types"³⁷. In creating images in these "Upper Aeons," there must be a process of reflection. This imaginal reflection or contemplation is synonymous with the idea of aeonic emanation. This is exactly what occurs in the *Apocryphon of John*:

> For we do not understand these ineffable matters, and none of us knows those [immeasurable] things except for the one who appeared from the Father. This is the one who [spoke to us alone]. For [It is] the one who gazes at Itself [alone] in Its light that surrounds [It], which is the spring of the living water. And It provides for [all] the aeons. And in every way It gazes upon Its image, seeing it in the spring of the Spirit, willing in Its light-water which is in the spring of the pure light[-water which] surrounds It.³⁸

Eugnostos the Blessed repeats this same concept of the ineffable contemplating itself through reflection: "Seeing himself within himself in a mirror, he appeared resembling himself." This process is mirrored (like a fractal) in the *Gospel of Philip* when it says, "Truth did not come into the world naked, but it came in types and images. The world did not receive truth in any other way. There is a rebirth and an image of rebirth. It is certainly necessary to be born again through the image. Which one? Resurrection. The image must rise again through the image. The bridal chamber and the image must enter through the image into the truth: this is the restoration." Recall earlier, that in the *Emerald Tablets of Hermes*, the subtle (spirit) "rises from Earth to Heaven, and falls back down again to Earth." This alchemical process is reflected in the *Gospel of Philip*.

The concept of being immersed or "baptized" in the divine waters of wisdom is also relevant, since it transmutes the body and soul into divine or spiritualized flesh as becoming, "one of them", being the "glories" or the angels, as mentioned

---

33 17.

34 Charron, Régine. The "*Apocryphon of John*" (NHC II, 1) and the Graeco-Egyptian Alchemical Literature. *Vigiliae Christianae*, Vol. 59, No. 4 (Nov., 2005), pp. 438-456.

35 Against Heresies. VII. 3.

36 Ibid. XIV. 3.

37 Types is derivative of the Latin "Typos", meaning "image" or "form".

38 5.

by *Zostrianos* (1.14-17). Alchemically speaking, the metaphor of baptism in water and fire is often used to describe the purifying process of removing the dead, dark metallic body into a luminous and incorruptible gold. In the *Clementine Recognitions*, the Samaritan magician, Simon Magus asks the Apostle Peter in their lengthy debate about engaging in imaginative activity in order to perceive the "ineffable power" beyond the national creator god of the Jews (the Demiurge). Peter routinely denies that such a higher or Supreme God exists beyond "God, our creator":

> Apply your mind to those things which I am going to say, and cause it, walking in peaceable paths, to attain to those things which I shall demonstrate. Listen now, therefore. Did you never in thought reach forth your mind into regions or islands situated far away, and remain so fixed in them, that you could not even see the people that were before you, or know where yourself were sitting, by reason of the delightfulness of those things on which you were gazing?[39]

Peter answers with an affirmative. Simon goes on to explain about his line of questioning:

> In this way now reach forth your sense into heaven, yea above the heaven, and behold that there must be some place beyond the world, or outside the world, in which there is neither heaven nor earth, and where no shadow of these things produces darkness; and consequently, since there are neither bodies in it, nor darkness occasioned by bodies, there must of necessity be immense light; and consider of what sort that light must be, which is never succeeded by darkness. For if the light of this sunfills this whole world, how great do you suppose that bodiless and infinite light to be? So great, doubtless, that this light of the sun would seem to be darkness and not light, in comparison.[40]

Recall earlier that in the *Corpus Hermiticum*, it says that if the reader does not imagine that they are "equal to God, you cannot comprehend God; for like is known by like." Simon's encouraging of Peter to extend his senses beyond the five senses mirrors the *Hermetica*. Simon Magus himself is regarded in scripture as a sinner for his "lawlessness," a lawlessness that resembles the "divine hero" archetype, which will be discussed in the next section.[41] The Gnostic and Hermetic discourse on the imagination is obviously quite different than their Platonic predecessors in how they relate to their magical and theurgical practices in both the affirmative and (mostly) the positive. Even the concept of doceticism can relate to the imagination. While there are certain varieties of doceticism[42], it is essentially the view that Jesus was, in nature, supremely divine, eliminating his humanity and substituting it for a seemingly real one.

The term docetism (Greek, *dokein* "to seem" or "to appear") presents the idea that Christ's incarnation, hence his sufferings, were unreal, phantasmal (hence *phantasia*), appearing only to be human. Christ's true nature was uniquely

---

39 Ante-Nicene Fathers, Vol. 8, Chapter LXI.

40 Ibid.

41 "Ante-Nicene Fathers, Vol VII: Constitutions of the Holy Apostles: Sec. IV.—Of the Law." Ante-Nicene Fathers, Vol VII: Constitutions of the Holy Apostles: Sec. IV.—Of the Law. N.p., n.d. http://www.sacred-texts.com/chr/ecf/007/0070456.htm

42 Doceticism. The Lives and Times of the Popes. Accessed December 27, 2014. http://www.cristoraul.com/ENGLISH/History-of-the-Popes/Dictionary-of-Christian-Biography-and-Literature/DOCETISM.html

divine in substance and by his powers and works associated with his divinity was able to change his shape accordingly. The Greek rendering of Docetae is often translated to mean "appear" or "semblance." According to Strong's Concordance, *dokeo* or *dokein* actually translates to having or form an opinion or judgment, to think, and even to imagine.[43] *Dokein* may even have some commonality with the Greek *hairesis*—meaning literally "choice" or "selection"—which has an interesting secular as well as biblical history. In other words, the

The Magical Hero's Imagination and Conclusion

In terms of Hermetic alchemy, the imagination was thought of as being a refined Quintessence or the Mercurial "Universal Agent," which is perceived by spiritual eyes, by discovering the mystery of things beyond their outward appearance. In Dennis William Hauck's article, he likens the alchemical imagination as a

imagination can be seen as a docetic heresy. There will not be an in-depth overview of this subject in this paper, but it is worth pointing this etymology out.[44][45]

reflective, meditative process. He cites the Swiss Renaissance alchemist and physician Paracelsus and writes:

> 'Therefore should you also know,' said Paracelsus, 'that this perfect Imagination coming from the Astral, issues from the Soul' and 'leads life thus deciphered back to its spiritual reality, and it then takes the name of meditation.' What Paracelsus meant was that the True Imagination re-envisions the divine source of anything and accesses it in meditation. This hidden reality is always present, but the eyes of ordinary men and women do not see it. Only the mind's eye of the purified

---

43 http://biblehub.com/greek/1380.htm Accessed December 23, 2014.

44 Limojon de Saint Didier illustrating a dialogue between Eudoxus and Pirophilus developing in a spiraling ribbon or phylactery: "Fili ex irahe a radio umbram suam" "Oh Son, from the beam extract its shadow".

45 Right and left illustrations of magicians taken from The *Greek Magical Papyri in Translation*. p. 60.

consciousness and the force of the True Imagination can perceive the divine vision of which the alchemists spoke."[46]

We can see similar ideas expressed in the *Greek Magical Papyri*. It presents the Father's Prayer Ritual, under the "Third Utterance," which mandates the practitioner make unintelligible, barbarous words and mantras (*nomina barbara*) and then proceeds to explain, "Thereon open thy eyes; and thou shalt see the Doors thrown open, and the Cosmos of the Gods that is within the Doors; so that for joy and rapture of the sight thy Spirit runs to meet it, and soars up. Therefore, hold thyself steady, and, gazing steadily into thyself, draw breath from the Divine."[47]

The *Greek Magical Papyri* itself is a compilation of various magical techniques and spells. These techniques were, of course, associated with ritual magic—the term "ritual" as its root word in the Latin ritualis, meaning "correct performance."[48] Written in Old Coptic, these spells and initiatory rites were used for cultivating immortality of the soul to love spells, curses and healing rites. The deities used in these spells are taken from a variety of sources, including Greek, Egyptian, Jewish, Gnostic and Christian.

Valerie J Flint, author of *The Rise of Magic in Early Medieval Europe* defines magic as "the exercise of preternatural control over nature by human beings with the assistance of forces more powerful than themselves."[49]

This is a basic definition that accounts for various methods of performing magic, which includes (but is not exclusive to) divination, incantations, astrology and even the Eucharist. Franz Bordon defines magic in terms of the imagination: "Any deliberate cause, may be such as a wish, a thought or any imagination created in this sphere together with the dynamic concentration of willpower, unshaken faith and fullest conviction is bound to be realized with the help of the elements…"[50] Stephen Skinner is careful to differentiate between two kinds of magic: "theurgy" and the "goetia":

> The goes (γόης), the practitioner of goetia (γοητεία), on the other hand, attempts to bring daimones/demons onto the physical plane and to manifest them, or their effects. The relationship of the practitioners of theurgia to practitioners of the goetia is that both attempt to invoke/evoke a spiritual creature (be it god, daimon, angel or demon). The teletai (τελεταί) priest does it for the benefit of the client's immortal soul while the goes does it to benefit the client's material desires.[51]

The aim of theurgy is to make the soul immortal or divine. In a sense, theurgy has a strong link to the imagination. The theurgist aims toward perfecting their "craft" or "performance" in order to basically change the internal reality, which corresponds directly with the external; the outer; and the manifest. A magician can also

---

46 "Searching for the Cosmic Quintessence: How Alchemists Meditated in the Middle Ages and Renaissance," *The Rose+Croix Journal* 10 (2014). 6.

47 V. 3:4.

48 Molendijk, Arie L., Peter Pels, and Barbara Boudewijnse. "British Roots of the Concept of Ritual." *Religion in the making: the emergence of the sciences of religion*. Leiden: Brill, 1998. 277-297. Print.

49 Valerie I. J. Flint *The Rise of Magic in Early Medieval Europe*. Princeton, N.J.: Princeton University Press, 1991. Print.

50 Tim Scott. "Who Was Franz Bardon?" Accessed December 28, 2014. http://www.armory.com/~mortoj/magick/newfiles/bardon.html

51 *Techniques of Graeco Egyptian Magic*. Golden Hoard Press. (2014) p.10.

be defined in one sense as a "hero." In Greek, "*heros*" meant a "demi-god," used in many ways at different times as a figure who gains divinity after a violent death or a mortal who is the offspring of a god and a mortal. A "daimon" was also considered to be the same as a demi-god because such beings were intermediate forces between the gods and the mortal realm in Greek myth and Platonic philosophy. The "hero" is very similar to the idea of the "perfected" stone of philosophy, being the offspring of mortal and immortal elements.

According to Iamblichus, the hero is a supernatural agent among the superior classes of beings that bridge the gap between the various kinds of gods and mankind, which also consists of archangels, angels, daimons and pure souls.[52] This is all comparable to how Eros, an intermediary daimon, is referred to as a magician by Plato. "His father's side, for its part, makes him a schemer after the beautiful and good, courageous, impetuous, and intense, a clever hunter, always weaving new devices, both passionate for wisdom and resourceful in looking for it, philosophizing through all his life, a clever magician, sorcerer, and sophist."[53]

As detailed by E.M. Butler in *The Myth of the Magus*, Simon Magus also follows the trends of other "heroes" and demigods in his claim that he was the "Great Power of God" and was involved in magical contests and debates with Peter the Evangelist and subsequent failure to outperform his Christian opponent.[54] This also factors in with Justin Martyr's claim of there being a statue dedicated to Simon Magus and the confusion of him being associated with the Sabine-Roman god, Semo Sancus.[55] After Simon Magus experiences the power of the Holy Ghost in action, he determines he wants to incorporate it as part of his repertoire of magic but is repudiated by Peter. E.M. Butler comments on this matter: "Reputed to be the founder of Gnosticism, he was mythologized into the first arch-heretic, guilty therefore of the spiritual sin against the Holy Ghost for which there is no forgiveness."[56] This legendary account of Simon Magus suggests very much about not only his personal take on magic but how Simon even desired to "be accounted a supreme power, greater than even the God who created the world."[57]

This very bold statement can yet again inform us of the attitude of a magician and the power wielded. Clearly being a slanderous text, this would suggest that Simon was blasphemous for having believed in this. Naturally, Simon is depicted as the embodiment of heresy while being struck down, supposedly by God, at the request of Peter when flying like the over-ambitious Icarus or like how Prometheus stole fire from Zeus and the Olympian gods. This is the downfall of the Magus like the fall of Lucifer. Simon suffers a heretic's fate as he falls to the ground while breaking his "leg in three places. Then every man cast stones at him and went away home, and thenceforth believed Peter."[58] Indeed, Simon also suffers the consequences of using magic for self-gain and "impiety against Him is, in the matter of religion, to die saying there is another God, whether superior or inferior, or in any way saying that there is one besides Him who really is."[59]

The warning of "daring" to imagine that "that there is another God besides the creator," is what gets Simon into big trouble with Peter.

---

52 *De mysteriis*. I.10.34, 36.

53 *Symposium*. 203c5-204a1.

54 E. M. Butler. *The Myth of the Magus*. Canto ed. Cambridge: Cambridge University Press, 1993. Print. ch. 4

55 1 *Apology* 26. Also, please see my article on this subject: http://theaeoneye.com/2014/10/21/the-simon-sancus-conondrum/

56 Ibid. Pg. 74.

57 *The Clementine Homilies*, II, 23, Pseudo Clementine Literature, Ante-Nicene Fathers, v.

58 *Acts of Peter*. XXXII.

59 Ibid. III. VII.

Simon's rejection of the Judeo-Christian God mirrors the later Gnostics' transgressive attitude towards this God (the Demiurge) as well, as laid out by their enemies such as Irenaeus as well as Plotinus.[60] These Gnostics were also depicted as "sorcerers" and "magicians" much like how Simon is in the Patristics and even Jesus in the Gospels in his display of miracles and exorcisms of demons, by the power of the Holy Spirit. These Gnostic magicians developed their own visionary ascension techniques which correspond to the "divine imagination."

> The link between the divine and human is realized no longer in *ex opere operato* ritual actions, but in an inward focus on maintaining the link between the individual's interior conscience and a God who is even more invisible and incomprehensible than when the temple was still standing, a focus whose outward counterpart became directed to the heavenly temple depicted by Ezekiel as the true palace of the invisible God. Thus earthly liturgical practice becomes displaced by the verbal performance of a heavenly liturgy whose holiness and transcendence leads the participant into increasingly silent acts of visionary imagination and the mystical contemplation of God and his attributes. Thus we seem to have a general line of development from ritual action through verbal liturgy and prayer that culminates in silent contemplation.[61]

In many ways, the Gnostic theurgic ascent is very similar to how Antoine Faivre defined the *vis imaginativa* (imaginative faculty) as "a particular aspect of this wider field that is the creative imagination, [which] is often rooted in a concept of divinity and of humanity as conceived as imagining powers."[62] It goes without saying that many other mystics, alchemists and saints were also heavily acquainted with this "active imaginative" practice as Carl Jung called it. Starting in ancient Hermetism, many throughout history have made their own unique contributions and innovations to this mindful and creative practice.

These practices weren't just for materializing the most ideal lifestyle but were mostly concerned with utilizing the powers of the imagination for the cosmic ascent. For many alchemists, the imagination was also key to gaining the "subtle," "astral," "angelic" or "resurrection" body as testified in the Old Testament, Enochian literature and the New Testament. William Blake would call this kind of body in The Laocoön, "The Eternal Body of Man is The IMAGINATION [sic]." Accordingly, the aim is to enlarge the self and accumulate spiritual power when one is alive to transcend the "punishments of matter" as the *Corpus Hermeticum* puts it.

Instead of renouncing the self, one may magnify it. While the Platonic philosophers saw the imagination as either a lowly faculty of the soul or an intermediate force between the mortal flesh and the divine, the later Gnostics, Hermetists and alchemists thought of the imagination as the divine spirit itself. Through the process of spiritual alchemy that Zosimos advocated, the initiate is given the "gnosis," transmitted during initiation, as a start to a pathway and graduation in stages towards the

---

60 Cf. Irenaeus. *Against Heresies*. 1.16.3. Plotinus. *Enneads* 2.9.4.

61 John D. Turner From Baptismal Vision to Mystical Union With the One: The Case of the Sethian Gnostics. *Practicing Gnosis*. (Brill: Nag Hammadi and Manichaean Studies: 2014), 85.

62 Antoine Faivre, "Vis Imaginativa: A Study of Some Aspects of the Magical Imagination and its Mythical Foundations," in *Theosophy, Imagination, Tradition: Studies in Western Esotericism*, trans. Christine Rhone (Albany: State University of New York Press, 2002), 125.

transformation and radical liberation of the transmuted spirit of gold separated from the lead of cosmic matter and into a permanent synthesis.[63]

The body and soul, originally impure and made from mortal, demiurgic matter of chaos, is transmuted into divine and eternal matter by the Spirit like the indestructible Vajra of Eastern lore. This spiritual matter remains inseparable and indissoluble for the whole of eternity. This is what Jesus Christ meant when he claimed in John 16:33: "But take heart! I have overcome the world." In John 20:1-18, when we are told that Jesus' apostles went to look for the body of Christ in the tomb and did not find it, they are clearly saying that his body was transmuted into spiritual Quintessence in perfect union.

63 Elaine Pagels. The Gnostic Gospels. (Vintage: Reissued Edition, 1989), 37-38.

The Secret Book of John

retold and illuminated by Richard A. Dengel

Jesus said: Recognize what is in your sight and that which is hidden will become manifest

Jesus said: Split wood and I am there. Lift a stone and you will find me there.

Richard A. Dengel

Fragments From The Secret Book of John
An illuminated re-telling

INTRODUCTION.

In *The Secret Book of John*, an illuminated re-telling, the author endeavors to expand and illustrate the text of the Gnostic "gospel" of the same name. English versions of the Secret Book are widely accessible, directly translated from Egyptian (Coptic) and can be found in such sources as The Nag Hammadi Library or Bentley Layton's The Gnostic Scriptures. So why bother with yet another rendition? The decision to illuminate (illustrate) the text ignited a rethinking about the tract's format. Why not create an improvisation grounded in the themes of the prototype? Why not elaborate the ideas of the Secret Book into something else, not dissimilar to it, but not like it either? What follows are a couple pages of that rendition (not yet completed). The pages are not consecutive (there are gaps in this presentation) unless otherwise stated.

Do not expect an exact rendering of the story. Considered alone, *The Secret Book of John* can be baffling. The author has, in many cases altered the text, sometimes changing chronologies and names for the sake of simplicity. Obviously, then, the author invokes a shameless use of poetic license. Writing in the second century, the orthodox Church father Irenaeus accused the Gnostics of a similar faithlessness. "…every one of them," he grumbled, "generates something new every day, according to his ability; for no one is considered initiated among them unless he develops some enormous fictions…"

This draft considers the good father's objection and applauds its challenge. In that spirit the story, adapted from the The Secret Book of John, unfolds…

PAGE 1, THE TITLE PAGE.

The epigraphs are adapted from the *Gospel of Thomas* (GT) in The Nag Hammadi Library. "Recognize what is in your sight…" is from Saying 5. "Split wood…" is from Saying 77. The illustration, based upon a late Byzantine amulet, is after a drawing on the cover of Hans Jonas' *The Gnostic Religion*, paperback edition published in 1963.

PAGES 2-4, THE VISIONS OF JOHN BEGIN.

The following three pages, ("John Despair Not," "Hymn to the First Father," and "Hymn to Barbelo," progress in the order rendered. This sequence occurs just after John has fled the taunting of a Pharisee named Arimanus. As he wanders the wilderness a vision of his resurrected Lord overcomes him. These pages are the first revelations of John as Christ begins to unfold the secret history of the universe.

Page 2: "John, John, despair not. Don't you know me? I am the Father, I am the Mother, I am the Son. I am the One who Death does not corrupt. Hearken to the secrets of the Perfect Man!"

John fell to his knees crying: "Reveal to me this Perfect Man!"

As his Lord spoke, the Aeon's rolled out before him. Salvation's History pricked and glimmered the air. Here are the Mysteries Jesus told him:

PAGE 3:
HYMN TO THE FIRST FATHER

One:
Sing O Muse of the Prime Abyss,
of the Before Man, Androgynous.
Tune your voice to Sprit's Archetype,
to the rolling depth of Moveless Light.

Two:
He without boundary
No-Thing contains
He without catalog No-Thing names
He without evidence No-Thing reveals
He without moment No-Thing seals

Three:
His Knowledge suspends all knowing things,
His Life braids life a helixed string.
His Cup pours out the Aeon's fire
A bubbling spring flaming God-desire.

Four:
The Father, Prototype of Thought
With Idea swelled and with it brought
A Shining Womb, Love's first retort:
Barbelo, Holy Mind's Consort.

Hymn to the First Father

1. Sing O Muse of the Prime Abyss
of the Before Man, Androgynous
Tune your voice to Spirit's Archetype,
to the rolling depth of Moveless Light

2. He without boundary
No-thing contains
He without catalog
No-thing names
He without evidence
No-thing reveals
He without moment
No-thing seals

3. His knowledge suspends all knowing things
His Life braids life a helixed string
His Cup pours out the Aeon's fire
A bubbling spring flaming God-desire.

4. The Father Prototype of Thought,
with Idea swelled and with it brought
A Shining Womb
Love's first retort:
Barbélo, Holy Mind's Consort

Page 4:
Hymn to Barbelo

One:
She sees him first who pre-exits
non-being 3 in pure One-Ness

Two:
Sole inkling of the Primal Name
from Light to Light She came

Three:
She came from Thought to single Thought
perception same as He who sought.

Four:
To those who blink She is a lamp.
To those who stare, a mirror's stamp

Five:
To those who knock She is a door.
To those who seek, Arcanum's core.

Six:
And so She glows, the First of One
just as we pale, like Moon to Sun.

Notes for page 4:

An alternate spelling of Barbelo is Barbero. The origin of Barbelo's name is obscure, perhaps invented ad hoc by the writer of SBJ. Bentley Layton speculates that the name recalls the Egyptian words for "emission," or "projectile," hence rendering a word meaning "the great emission." (*The Gnostic Scriptures*, page 15.)

Hymn to Barbelo

1. She sees Him first who pre-exists non-being in pure One-ness

2. Sole inkling of the Primal Name from Light to Light She came

3. She came from Thought to single Thought Perception same as He who Sought

4. To those who blink She is a Lamp To those who stare, a mirror's stamp

5. To those who knock She is a door To those who seek, Arcanum's Core

6. And so She glows the First of One just as we pale Like Moon to Sun

Epinoia

Page 5, Pleroma.

There then begins the history of the Pleroma, or fullness of the Aeons. At this point, the story sometimes becomes confusing, as names change according to the translation or are duplicated within the translation itself. At any rate, after emanating a Pentad of Aeons, an autonomous spark arises which becomes Christ (sometimes rendered as Chrestos, or Kindly One (see Kurt Rudolph's interpretation of SBJ in his book Gnosis, page 77.) From Christ, the first father elicits 4 lights, forming the Pleroma's core:

Pleroma

From the child-God the Father derived 4 lights, each an indwelling to 3 powers.

The 1st luminary was Understanding name Harmozel. In that Angel were the Aeons Grace, Truth, and Form.

The 2nd luminary: Kindness-Oroiael. In that Angel were the Aeons Insight, Perception, and Memory.

The 3rd luminary: Sensibility-Davethai, who abided Love, Empathy, and Idea.

The 4th luminary: Thoughtfulness-Eleleth who abided Perfection, Peace, and Sophia-Wisdom.

Their emanations accomplished, the MotherFather invested the child with lordship over the Pleroma, the Perfect Fullness of Aeons.

Page 6, Passion.

Now the story takes a unexpected turn. Sophia-Wisdom, the last and "youngest" of the Aeons, attempts to conjure an image of the Father. Her passion has a tragic consequence for both her and the entire Pleroma:

Passion

How does one render the longing of Sophia-Wisdom? Upon her throne, at the Pleroma's extremity, she awakened to her deficiency. The Father was but a recollect, a shadow paling across the Aeons. She wept:

I sleep upon a fire,

sleep…

How should I think to you?

While cold dreams scorch my day,

how should I talk of you?

I reach for you as a light

that burns farther off than you.

More likely am I to be warmed by its

ice and glow

than by any sound from you.

And so…

shall I pray for warmth

or for a brow to solve me?

But if my psalm was heard,

what then?

Would not the reckoning that is my bed

would it not unmake me?

Into herself Sophia went, determined to conjure the Father. The perception gestated, a waxing distortion of the 1. And when she gave birth it was to a hideous squirmy thing with a serpent's body and a lion's head. Its eyes, though blind as smoke, blinked with gleaming thunder. Her passion now emptied, she covered her shame in a luminous cloud and called him Yaltabaoth.

Notes for Passion:

Here is one of the more problematic passages in SBJ. In the Nag Hammadi translation we read: "…Sophia…thought a thought from within herself and the thought of the invisible Spirit and Foreknowledge. She willed a likeness to appear from within herself without the will of the Spirit—it had not approved—and without her partner and without his consideration…And an imperfect product appeared from her, and it was different from her patterns because she created it without her partner." Understanding that Aeons are androgynous, just who was her partner? Her consort's identification remains unclear, while her motivation is likewise ambiguous. Some (Karen L. King for example in The Secret Revelation of John) have posited that Sophia attempted to be like the Supreme 1 by bringing forth likenesses (emanations) from within herself. From her arrogance, sprang the myth's antagonist, Yaltabaoth.

The author takes a different track. Her deficiency arises not from willful arrogance, but from unwilled ignorance. Her alienation from the Father provokes her imagination into an imperfect image of her Source. In this case her consort is not some unnamed male half, but the Father himself. And yes, I know this may sound a bit too Freudian for some…

A word about Yaltabaoth: Stevan Davies in his excellent retelling of this myth argues that the name Yaltabaoth is of such obscure origin that it best be considered to have no specific meaning (page 62, The Secret Book of John Annotated and Explained). Kurt Rudolph seems closer to the mark however. He maintains that the name is of Semitic origin meaning "begetter of Sabaoth," i.e. the heavenly powers. (Gnosis, page 79)

Passion. How does one render the longing of Sophia-Wisdom? Upon her throne at the Pleroma's extremity she awakened to her deficiency. The Father was but a recollect, a shadow pasing across the Aeons. She wept:

"I sleep upon a fire sleep... How should I think to you? While cold dreams scorch my day, how should I talk of you? I reach for you as a light that burns farther off than you. More likely am I to be warmed by its ice and glow than by any sound from you.

And so... shall I pray for warmth, or for a brow to solve me? But if my psalm were heard? What then? Would not the reckoning that is my bed, would it not unmake me?"

Into herself Sophia went, determined to conjure the Father. The perception gestated, a waxing distortion of the 1. And when she gave birth, it was to a hideous, squirmy thing with a serpent's body and a lion head. Its eyes, though blind as smoke, blinked with gleaming thunder.

Her passion now emptied, she covered her shame in a luminous cloud and called him Yaltabaoth.

Page 7, Descent of Sophia.

The focus of the story now turns from the Pleroma to Yaltabaoth, the first of the Archons, or Rulers. Sophia's passion has broken the Pleroma's singularity as Yaltaboth embarks upon a round of copulations producing seven "children." He is called the Blind God since he is ignorant not only of the First Father, but even of his mother, Sophia. In his arrogance he declares: "I Am the Lord whose name is Jealous, for I am a Jealous God. Apart from me, there is no other!" The demiurge's words rip at the fabric of Sophia's being:

Yaltabaoth's boast, preposterous though it was, ruined Sophia's heart. "What child is this? Can Light resist this darkening brute?"

As water at a drain revolves, so round her son she wept and ran. Only uncounted tears, glinting in a starrish wake, attested to her fall. Towards the moveless Pleroma, shrinking now, a dimming hope, she put one final cry:

O Light of Lights in whom I have faith,

trust me not to Chaos.

Incline your ear and save me from this

> lion-faced power
>> and the off-spring of this god, self-willed.

Forsake me not, O Light,

> but restore me to the height of the Aeons.

Notes for page 7: Oh Light of Lights, in whom I have faith…is after Pistis Sophia, GRS Mead interpretation, Book One, Chapter 35 (The Second Repentance of Sophia), logia 1- 4. The illustration conflates Hieronymus Bosch's, The Ascent to Calvary and The Crucifixion of Saint Julia.

Conclusion.

Of course, the story does not end here. There now follows a comic-opera of creation, as Yaltabaoth, in a futile mimic of the Pleroma, attempts to capture and imprison the light of his mother.

As of this date, the story here-in is yet to be completed. Begun in 2005, the book's progress has been agonizingly slow. The plates are created sequentially, each demanding much research and contemplation. These are hand-painted and lettered, using acrylic paints on canvas paper. Twenty-three plates have been completed. The author estimates that there are about 23 more yet to come. Yikes.

Descent of Sophia

1. Yaltabaoth's boast preposterous though it was, ruined Sophia's heart. "What child is this?... Can light resist this darkening brute?"

2. As water at a drain resolves, so round her son she wept and ran. Only uncounted tears, glinting in a starrish wake, attested to her fall. Towards the moveless Pleroma, shrinking now, a dimming hope, she put one final cry:

3. "O Light of Lights in whom I have faith trust me not to Chaos. Incline your ear and save me from this lion-faced power and the off-spring of this god self-willed. Forsake me not O Light, but restore me to the height of the Aeons."

Jeremy Puma

We Are the Immovable Race

There is no scientific, biological evidence that "race" exists. In spite of the protestations of the bigoted crowds, regardless of the nonsense of "Folkish" heathens or others involved in "alternative spiritualties" who claim that DNA requires that we "breed properly," there are no good reasons to consider individual humans any different than one another on the basis of skin color or geographical provenance or even DNA. Sure, many of these groups or individuals will deny being racist, but at the very least they're most certainly what we might call "racialist," attributing socio-cultural differences to outmoded and prejudicial ways of thinking about humans as "other."

"We're not racist," they'll say, "we just think that it's important to acknowledge the difference between races." That is a racist thing to say. Listen: genetics doesn't work that way. Interested in your ancestry? That's cool, but it doesn't make you any biologically different than anyone else. All of the Theosophical Society inspired 19th Century stuff concerning "Root Races" and "Ancestral Memory" needs to die a wretched death on the roadside of alternative history.

What does this have to do with the pursuit of Gnosis? I'm glad you asked. The ancient Sethian Gnostics considered themselves part of a distinct class of people, known variously as "the Immovable Race," "the Unshakable Race," "the Unwavering Race of perfect [humanity]," etc. According to Sethian myth, this "race" consisted of the descendants of Seth, the third son of Adam and Eve. Neither murderer or murdered, neither servant of the Demiurge or punished by the Demiurge for his transgression, the Gnostics saw, in Seth, representation of a third way of living, the way of gnosis.

The Gnostics who participated in this third way of living may very well have been as tribalist as everyone else during the times they were extant. This was a society in which you identified based on your culture, and the Gnostics were no different. They certainly considered themselves superior to those who weren't involved in their ontology (their understanding of Being). However, as far as we're concerned, the idea of the "Immovable Race" or "Unshakable Race" must be updated to include anyone who participates fully in the Gnostic worldview.

In the context of Gnosis, one has to ask oneself: for whom am I participating in the perpetuation of the human experiment? Is it just for me? If so, why not just spend one's life in pursuit of idle pleasures? Is it for my children or blood relatives? If so, why not ensure the livelihood of yourself and your relatives and let everyone else go to hell (sound familiar)? Or, is it for the continued survival of humanity within an imperfect reality? If it's anything other than the latter, the reasoning is specious.

We must also reject the argument, so common in "alternative spirituality" and countercultural circles, that the great majority of individuals are "sheeple," somehow worthless because of a different way of thinking or religious engagement with Being. The most egregious abuses of capitalist society which have resulted in the current state of affairs aren't the result of the average person, who just wants to get by. Instead, a wealthy and powerful contingent of worshipers of Archonic manifestations has essentially (and perhaps unwittingly) established a kind of existential eugenics, ensuring the survival of themselves and their relations at the expense of the rest of us. There is no "grand Illuminati conspiracy;" greed and power are conspiracy enough. Those you call "sheeple" are in fact your allies, or at the very least your fellow travelers.

The Immovable Race are those of us who choose not to participate in the eugenicist game. Instead, we focus our attention on making our world fair and equitable for everyone but outside of the commoditized dialectics of "You and Me Versus the World." How do we do this? We do this by focusing not on external differences between one another, but on our similarities, our mutual needs, and the fact that we're all going down if this ship sinks.

Here's how to start: identify some people who you consider family. This doesn't necessarily mean those related to you by blood. Think of these people as anyone who you value, and who values you in return. Think of these people as anyone who would attend your funeral because they honestly miss you. Now, start talking about the future. You don't have to plan a commune or start talking sister wives, but start thinking about what kind of skills you have, or are interested in learning. Maybe the status quo continues, but if it doesn't, what happens to us?

More importantly, let those people know how valuable they are to you. If you have good neighbors, let them know you appreciate living nearby. Even if you only see someone special once every few years, make it a point to tell her that you love her. Just a simple, "Thanks for being such a great person!" does the trick. There's no need to reach out to total strangers, but break away from the "enlightened" versus "unwashed masses" dialectic endemic within modern society and alternative spirituality.

THIS is how we begin establishing the Immovable Race. This is the groundwork for building a future in which everyone can participate on an even level. There's no need to protest society via sit-ins, or by blocking traffic; you can still be removed from an office or beaten out of the streets. Instead, become Immovable by becoming Transparent. Protest by cutting away even the tiniest strands binding you to the Black Iron Prison. Every head of lettuce you grow for yourself, every connection you deepen with someone valuable to you, every conversation you have about the survival of the human species is a radical blow against the Archons. This is a foundation of Gnosis.

It's already happening in many places. It's open to everyone. We are the Immovable Race, the Sons and Daughters of Seth, and in this we take our stand: that to the Cosmic we are Transparent.

Elizaveta de Stjernvall

Meetings With Rasputin

This episode in my life took place during the second half of World War I, one year before the fall of the tsarist regime. I was very young when the chance came to be in the company of a truly astonishing person who, still today, is the object of many studies and legends. I speak of Rasputin.

It was 1916. The Emperor and Empress of the Russias had seen Rasputin again at the house of the Grand Duchess Militza Nikolaevna. According to rumour, he was blessed with a miraculous gift to cure the ill.

A simple peasant from distant Siberia, he went from village to village caring for sick children with prayer and supernatural powers. Attracted by mysticism and believing in the power of prayer, Tsar Nicholas II was interested in the personality of Rasputin. Everyone knew that the case of Alexis, the crown prince who suffered from haemophilia, was desperate. Rasputin's hour came when he was summoned to court to try to staunch the bleeding of the Tsarevich's nose. Until then, all medical efforts had failed, but Rasputin simply laid his hands on the nose and the bleeding stopped immediately.

One can understand that from that day the imperial family had no other recourse but to call upon Rasputin whenever it was necessary. Rasputin's appearance at court became more and more frequent. Apparently, the imperial couple could not live without the starets, or holy man.

Since the Tsar's functions were extremely demanding, the Tsarina Alexandra Feodorovna received Rasputin most of the time. The role of the starets changed radically. Numerous courtesans began going directly to him. Thus, the simple monk was transformed into a privileged mediator for the petitioners who sought favours and protection of the Tsar.

The hold Rasputin exercised over the courtesans was re-enforced by his prophetic gifts. He had predicted the fate of Russia, his own death and that of the imperial family. More precisely, he had announced to his protectors, "I will die first, then you shall all follow me."

Further, his strange powers as a hypnotist explained the undeniable success he had the women of the court. Although neither monk nor priest, Rasputin did not hesitate to pass himself off as a starets. Finally, this disturbing person who had become legendary joined my circle of friends.

At this time I lived in Saint Petersburg with my husband, a psychiatrist who spent almost all his time with his practice. I felt terribly alone and dreamed of a child to fill my emptiness. Sensitive to my desire, a patient of my husband's, the wife of the minister Shelkovnikov, invited us to her house to meet Rasputin. She intended to ask him if he could foresee the desired birth of a child.

By mischance I had to leave Saint Petersburg. My husband, however, accepted the invitation and told me later that Rasputin was the star of the evening. The wife of the minister had asked the question which plagued me so much, and Rasputin asked my husband, who has considerably older than I was:

"Is your wife young?"

And, to an affirmative response, he added:

"Bring her to me first, and I will say afterwards what will come about."

The starets had the habit of using the second person singular form for everyone.

A month later, we were invited once more to dinner at the same place. When Rasputin entered the dining room I saw for the first time this enigmatic figure. He was of medium height, a bit on the heavy side, full-haired with a thin beard. He wore a kaftan (a loose Russian tunic) and high boots. His blue-green eyes were especially expressive, particularly when he looked at a young woman. Many attributed to that hypnotic gaze the power of holy men to get what they wanted.

There were ten at the table. My friend placed Rasputin at her right and me at her left. While eating he kept looking at me and talking to me, but he became silent whenever the others stopped talking to listen to what he was saying. I assumed he had chosen me to be his interlocutor because of my youth.

When my friend asked Rasputin if I had a possibility of bearing a child, he answered:

"One, surely."

In effect, that was to be the case.

After dinner, the guests went into the salon. I sat on a couch and Rasputin sat beside me.

"Do you know," he said, "that I have never read a single book to this day?"

This confession did not surprise me. Peasants at that time were almost all illiterate.

One of the guests came up and asked Rasputin rather stupidly if he often went to court. The starets ignored the question by turning away toward me.

I had heard that at times he had received up to fifty persons in a single morning. I asked for what motives so many wanted to see him.

"You amuse me!" he exclaimed, "don't you realize that all those who come to see me have something to ask of me? I try my best to satisfy them whether it is a question of someone placed in high circles or a kitchen girl looking for work."

Aware that the evening was coming to a close, Rasputin became more and more enterprising. He insisted that I go see him as soon as possible. He wanted a definite answer.

Nonchalantly, he brought his chair close to mine, and suddenly I felt his hand on my thigh. I moved away brusquely with indignation.

"Are you afraid of me, dear?" he asked in a sweet manner.

"Not the least bit", I said, shocked.

"Know that I see and hear perfectly. You have no reason therefore to sit so close to me."

Despite this light banter, Rasputin insisted nicely. He absolutely expected me to visit. My first reaction was "No, and no!"

But I recall that all my friends, male and female alike, envied me the privilege of meeting the "most famous muzhik", and implored me to invite him to my house so they could meet him too. This is what I said to him that, though he need not expect my visit, he would be nonetheless welcome at my house.

"Name the day and hour!"

It was Saturday evening. On the following Wednesday, Rasputin had to go to Siberia.

"If it suits you", he said, "telephone me on Monday. You only have to say that the doctor's wife is calling."

I rose briskly and asked my hostess to take my place by the starets so that I could leave unnoticed. The switch succeeded and I escaped as planned.

On Monday I called Rasputin. I was told that he never comes to the phone, but when I announced "the doctor's wife," I heard his voice right away.

"Set the day and the hour when I should come!"

"Wednesday at 3:00 in the afternoon", I said laconically.

The propitious day was not far off. Ten women and two men, including my husband, were at my house. We sat about a big table in the dining room. Precisely at 3:00, several rings sounded at the front door. The porter brought Rasputin to the salon where I joined him right away. He seemed in good humour and greeted me with gallantry. I suggested we take tea in the dining room. But, as soon as I opened the door, his aspect changed. At the sight of my impatient guests, he uttered in an irritated voice:

"Damn, all these good ladies!"

I was pleased seeing him expose himself before everyone in an angry mood. I invited him to sit down, while my guests devoured him with their looks. Each waited for Rasputin to take the lead in talk, but he uttered only a few words as he examined his cup of tea. He took a slice of lemon with his fingers, whose cleanliness left much to be desired.

That very night the starets was to leave for Siberia.

"Then, are you coming to wish me bon voyage before I leave?"

"What good would that be? No doubt hundreds will come to see you off."

He smiled. "Let it be! For you, I would always have time."

To my surprise he asked:

"Would a photo of me please you?"

I was trapped.

"The photographer has already sold all his photos of me, but you will receive one very soon. Meanwhile I would like to write a few lines for you to remember me by."

All the women cried out as one:

"For me too, for me too!"

My husband went to look for writing paper. Rasputin scribbled on the sheets of papers the women handed him. It was obvious that he was concentrating each time he applied the pen. I did not have time to read what he wrote for each of my friends, but I heard many exclamations of surprise and of joy.

As for the inscription meant for me, it was very brief, saying simply:

"Love surpasses mountains, Grigori." (Grigori Novikh was his real name. He got the nickname Rasputin because of his dissolute morals. Rasputin derives from rasputstvo "debauched, lustful"; rasputnik "libertine"; Rasputin merited his nickname.)

The writing was in all respects like the scribble of illiterate peasants.

At his departure, Rasputin went about before each of my friends. I do not know what he murmured in their ears, but I saw one after the other jerk away with indignation. Despite the brouhaha, Rasputin approached my great aunt who had recently divorced and remarried:

"And so you've made a new nest my beauty", he said. "Are you sure you won't abandon a nest a second time?"

I must note here that he had never seen my grand aunt before. Then he went up to another guest—the young wife of a doctor—and looked intently at her as he said:

"You won't find happiness in leading a double life." In fact, the young woman was sleeping with both her husband and her father-in-law.

Finally, we went with the starets to the front door, and we heard from the servants that two armed police were stationed in front of the house during his visit. Rasputin seems to have been well protected.

One day during the icy winter I bumped into him on the street for the last time. He was going by in his sleigh drawn by two horses. I was coming out of a chapel where I had prayed long for a very young friend in critical condition. Rasputin stopped his team and invited me to get in, saying:

"I'm going home."

I explained that I was going to visit a dying friend, but he interrupted me.

"Don't worry about her. Your friend will recover."

He had already made place for me on his sleigh when I noticed a group of fools staring curiosity at the person with whom I spoke. Troubled, I uttered a quick "goodbye" and left.

Hardly two months later I was shocked to read in the press that Rasputin was dead. The whole city, my dear Saint Petersburg, spoke of it for some time. Writing on the subject continues to this day.

Thomas Vaughan

The Magic Aphorisms of Eugenius

This is the first truth and also the last.

1. Before all things the Point existed; not the indivisible or mathematical, but the diffusive. It was the monad explicitly, the myriad implicitly. It was light, and also night, beginning, and the end of the beginning; all, and nothing; aye and nay.

2. The monad moved in the dyad, and through the triad came out the faces of the second light.

3. There came out simple, uncreated fire, and under the waters it put on the covering of multiple, created fire.

4. It looked back at the source above, and sealed that below with a signature drawn down, a threefold countenance.

5. Unity created the One and the Trinity distinguished it into Three. The Four exists too, the link and middle term of reduction.

6. Of the visible things water first shone forth; she is the wife of fire that lies upon her; and the pregnant mother of figurables.

7. She was porous on the inside and multicoloured in her coverings her belly had heavens rolled into one and stars unseparated.

8. The separating Demiurge divided her into wide tracts; and as the offspring appeared; the Mother disappeared.

9. However, the Mother bore shining sons, that cast their influence into the land of Chai.

10. These beget their mother in the last days; whose fountain sings in the miraculous grove.

11. This is he that storeth away wisdom; be thou that canst, he that bringeth it forth.

12. He is father of everything created; and from the created son by dissolution of the son in life the father is begotten.
Thou hast the highest mystery of the generating cycle: he is the son of the son who was the father of the son.

To God alone the glory.

Andrew Phillip Smith

Into the Bridal Chamber:
Sin: Some Meanderings On Its Role in Gnosticism

There is a popular trend of ascribing to heretical, heterodox, extinct or obscure forms of Christianity an absence of the qualities we have grown to dislike in modern Christianity. It is a strange inversion of the idea of heresy: the heresy-hunting fathers of the early church ascribed to other versions of Christianity all that they thought should be excluded from their faith. Modern people interested in alternative religion (among whom I count myself) often hope that every oppressive element that has become normative in Christianity should be absent from so-called heretical forms.

Chief among these must be the notion of sin, a concept which, quixotically, may be said to cover a multitude of sins. For traditionally religious people sin may at its best be entwined with a sense of right living and right action, or of genuine conscience. For secular liberal modern people the word sinful often conjures up, under the influence of advertising, a particularly succulent forbidden fruit, a particularly rich chocolate or some other luxury, or even a particularly voluptuous bout of lovemaking. For those in between, who are neither free of religious morality nor empowered by it, the concept of sin is often seen as the source of guilt and repression.

Sin is not as central a concept to Gnosticism as it is to Catholic or Protestant Christianity yet it is not absent entirely. Gnosticism has never reached a stage in which it has become a long-established majority religion with the attendant needs of systematizing and solidifying its doctrine and dogma. Indeed, the term itself has come under a great deal of scrutiny as to whether it is academically meaningful. What this means for us is that we cannot assume that there is, or ever was, any single attitude towards sin in Gnosticism. (For the purposes of this article I will assume the following loose definition of gnosticism: anything related to the Sethian Gnostics and Valentinians of the ancient world, and anything in the Nag Hammadi library that doesn't have some obvious other origins.)

The Sethians are named after Seth, the third son of Adam and Eve, who was a central figure in their mythos. Their approach was more radically at odds with conventional Christian or even Jewish interpretation. The Valentinians, in contrast, were named after Valentinus, an influential second-century gnostic Christian. Valentinians were more reconciled with the emerging Catholic Church, often attending the same churches but meeting separately also and applying esoteric interpretation to the Hebrew Bible and gospels, which were read in an increasingly literal way by proto-Catholics.

Sin is not a consistent theme in surviving Gnostic writings, but there are enough references to it scattered around to give us an idea of the range of attitudes towards it.

In Catholic Christianity sin is the consequence of a life without Christ. As Paul sees it in Romans chapter 8, once Christ had come even the Jewish law could only be the law of sin and death. Original sin had not yet arisen in Catholic Christianity. It would take Augustine of Hippo, former adherent of the Gnostic-influenced Manichaean religion, to make original sin so important to Catholicism and some Protestant sects. It was in fact Irenaeus, the church father who has bequeathed to us most of the earliest accounts of Gnostics and other heterodox groups, who can be identified as the first to argue that the descendants of Adam—all of us humans—were and are all in bondage to sin. As much of Irenaeus' work was written in dialogue with, or rather in resistance to, the Gnostics and other heretics, we may be justified in describing original sin as an anti-Gnostic point of view.

The Greek word in the New testament translated as sin is hamartia, which means "missing the mark". The term originally comes from archery, so "missing the target" might be a better translation. This goes through directly as a Greek loanword into Coptic. But hamartia translates various Hebrew words with meanings such as to stray off the path (hata) or to trespass or transgress. In the Coptic language, the late form of Egyptian written in the Greek alphabet with some additional letters, in which most Gnostic writings survive, hamartia is sometimes used as a direct loanword, but NOBE, the native Coptic word for sin, is also used.

Sin is in its more primitive sense was restricted to action. A murder was a sin. As it became more psychologized sin was understood as an intention that had its expression in sinful action. Wishing to commit a murder or even considering it was then a sin. Jesus famously proclaimed in the Sermon on the Mount that if you commit adultery in your heart you have already sinned (Matt 5:27-30.) In the ultimate magnification of the concept, sin acquires ontological significance; sin is part of the nature of human existence itself. Behind the action is the thought, beyond the thought is the cause: the fall of humanity, the original sin itself.

The skeptical may claim this evolution of sin as a development of ever deeper methods for controlling behaviour. Not only is a particular form of behaviour wrong, but, as Orwell's thought police would assent, the inclination to indulge this behaviour is wrong, and has its cause in an cosmic wrongfulness. Not only, the reasoning goes, is it sinful for a man to lie with another man, it is sinful to even desire this, and it is the devil who produces that desire. In this case it is intriguing to see moderately liberal churches moving the accountability for the sin back to a stage that belongs to a more primitive conception of sin. It is not necessarily sinful, they say, to be homosexual or to have same-sex urges: it is but the act itself is sinful and should be avoided. In the Church of England, for instance, priests can be homosexual but, unlike heterosexual Anglican priests, they must be celibate. Here I might interject with a personal reminiscence. I attended a Church in Wales (Anglican) school and my family had fairly recently taken up active attendance at church. The young vicar of Holy Nativity Church in Penarth was one Father Jeffrey John. He was much more approachable and interesting than the previous vicar and included some more stimulating material in his sermons. He left after a fairly brief period to go to Oxford to study Gnosticism. This was probably the first time I had encountered the term and I remember discussing with my mother whether it was related to agnosticism, which it is only by etymology of course. This was probably around 1977 or 1978, soon after the Nag Hammadi library had first been published in English in its entirety. Not only did Father Jeffrey John first make me wonder about Gnosticism, he later ascended through the Anglican hierarchy. He was in line to become a bishop but the Archbishop of Canterbury backed down. Father Jeffrey John was gay and lived with his male partner in a celibate relationship. It was considered divisive for the more conservative elements of the Anglican communion and Father Jeffrey John never did become a bishop. I hope he still reads his Nag Hammadi library.

What then of the Gnostics? Sin is not the result of evil, or of original sin, per se, but of ignorance (a word which in English, i*gno*rance, derives from the same root as Gnosis). The act of knowing is Gnosis. Sin is from ignorance. Whoever has Gnosis of the truth is free and therefore does not sin.

As the Gospel of Philip puts it, "Whoever knows the truth is free. And whoever is free does not sin, for he who sins is the slave of sin."

(Gospel of Philip 93).

This moves the responsibility for sin into a different plane. Sin becomes the result of a lack of Gnosis. If one is ignorant or lacks Gnosis then one will sin. If one has Gnosis one will not sin. So the way to be free of sin is not specifically by curbing one's behaviour or keeping to the letter of the law. It is by having Gnosis. "Seek ye first the kingdom of Heaven and all else will be added unto you."

A similar notion, but expressed with—dare we say—different metaphors, is found in Paul. For Paul it is not the law that redeems from sin, but Christ. Sin may therefore is the result of ignorance or of sleep. If one had gnosis one could not sin.

What does this absence of sin imply? Does it mean that someone with Gnosis cannot commit an action that would be sinful if someone who existed in ignorance committed it? Or that any actions that this person commits are no longer sinful? For instance, would the one who had gnosis rather than ignorance be able to have any kind of sex without impunity? Or to have sex only under the conditions that are religiously approved? Or would the non-ignorant knower, the Gnostic, not have sex at all? Or, in the option that is probably most agreeable to most of us, only have sex in circumstances with which one's conscience is at ease? (There is arguably no example, apart from that of the psychopath, for which the notion of appropriate sex does not involve some degree of social training.) It is tempting to translate this into the language of Gurdjieff. If one is awake and acts from conscience one will not sin.

Basilides, the second century Gnostic teacher from Alexandria who is perhaps best known today for being included by Carl Jung in his "Seven Sermons to the Dead" and by Aleister Crowley in his Gnostic Mass, elaborates on ignorance as the cause of sin. (in a fragment quoted by Clement of Alexandria. See Bentley Layton, *The Gnostic Scriptures* p. 444) "Not all sins are forgiven, but only those committed involuntarily and out of ignorance."

Therefore if someone actually did commit a sinful act knowingly—let's say deliberately murder someone—even though that person had Gnosis, that sin would not be forgiven. Basilides, whether that is his motive or not, provides an answer to the question that naturally arises out of this approach to sin and bugs everyone. What if someone who is enlightened sins? (One cannot say that Gnosis is identical with enlightenment, but the two notions are comparable.) Basilides answers that the sins of someone with Gnosis aren't forgiven, but the sins of someone without Gnosis are. Thus the burden of responsibility is greater for the Gnostic. The ignorant know not what they do, so may be forgiven.

In another passage Basilides goes on to reason out the causes of suffering. Suffering is the result of sin. Even if a person has not acted out sinfully, the intention to do so (to commit murder or adultery) means that sin is within that person. It transpires that Basilides, who believed in reincarnation, considered that suffering in this life can be a result of sins in a previous life. In the rare case that someone who has not sinned experiences suffering—as examples he offers a newborn baby and, in a veiled allusion, Jesus—the experience of the suffering must benefit the innocent one. So is it only human conventions that create sin? Is it merely external human regulations that cause sin? Or rather, human-implemented religious regulations?

Carpocrates, another Gnostic teacher who lives on for us only through the accounts of his enemies, is said to have believed that nothing is evil by nature. According to Carpocrates we must each go through every kind of experience before the soul can be liberated. Although Irenaeus, who quotes this, is disapproving, he never quite joins the dots and it isn't as certain as we might be led to think that the Carpocratians really did commit wicked and naughty deeds in order to escape the wheel of lives.

It is not clear that Carpocrates really was exhorting his followers to spend their multiple lifetimes pillaging, raping, murdering, eating faeces and getting into heavy S&M, and all those other things that come to mind. What is assumed to be a licence to sanction the worst kinds of human behaviour may in its essence be more of an attitude towards experience. Given the right approach even the worst experiences may benefit the soul.

However, these claims made about Gnostics are quite similar to those of certain modern gurus: ordinary morality no longer applies once one is enlightened. In practice this can lead to all sorts of abusive situations. There is a difference between genuine spiritual liberation and getting your rocks off at the expense of others.

Perhaps in the case of the so-called Borborites or Phibionites, we see an example of transgression that has turned into the kind of abusive sex cult that reminds us of the benefits of sin as an exoteric idea. (See http://www.roger-pearse.com/weblog/2013/12/12/summing-up-the-ancient-accounts-of-the-borborites-phibionites/ for a collection of all the ancient accounts of the Borborites.) The Borborites were accused of holding orgies, consuming semen and menses and a meat loaf of ground aborted foetuses mixed with honey and spices. Perhaps it is all ancient slander produced by the heated imagination of heresiologists. As far as they were concerned Gnostics were either libertines or body-hating ascetics.

We may make a distinction between libertinism and antinomianism, with the former including a pleasure principle lacking from the latter. The forms of antinomianism ascribed to Jesus remain entirely within the realms of religious and social restrictions, and relate the flouting of convention for compassionate purposes. Jesus plucked grain on the sabbath (Mk 2:23–28; Matt 12:-8; Lk 6:1–5), kept the company of sinners (which could be understood as sinning in itself) and had the reputation for being a "winebibber and a glutton". In his adoption of the golden rule, "Do unto others as one would have others do unto oneself," he presented a more objective morality.

The Gospel of Thomas only refers twice to sin. (The Gospel of Thomas may or may not be Gnostic in its original form, or even as it has been preserved for us. But we know that it was found with other genuinely Gnostic writings in Codex II of the Nag Hammadi Library and, even if it predated Gnostic Christianity it would have been interpreted by Gnostics in a Gnostic fashion.) Its two references to sin would fit in well with the Gnostic view of sin as a result of ignorance.

14. Jesus said to them, "If you fast, you will bring sin on yourselves, and if you pray you will be condemned, and if you give to the poor you will injure your spirits."

104. They said to Jesus, "Come, let us pray and fast today."

Jesus said, "What sin have I committed, or how have I been defeated? But when the bridegroom comes out of the bridal chamber, then let them fast and let them pray."

Prayer and fasting is something you need to do if you have sinned and thus is equated with sinning. When the bridegroom is in the bridal chamber there is no need to fast and pray because no sin is being committed. For a Gnostic, and particularly a Valentinian, being in the bridal chamber signified Gnosis.

The strange *Thunder Perfect Mind*, in which contradictory first-person claims and counter-claims are made by a female voice, is something of an outlier as regards the Nag Hammadi Library, but thought should be given to the following, "I, I am sinless, and the root of sin derives from me."

Gnosticism offers us a view of sin that often has much in common with that of the apostle Paul but without some of the vehemence that characterises his approach. So much of our knowledge of the Gnostics depends on the accidental survival of historical material. Yet even the result of this historical erosion may be considered fortuitous. Ancient Gnosticism poses questions about attitudes towards sin and morality rather than dictating them from on high. Whether this was intentional or not is moot: the end result is for us to make up our own minds.

William James

Mysticism
From *The Varieties of Religious Experience*

Over and over again in these lectures I have raised points and left them open and unfinished until we should have come to the subject of Mysticism. Some of you, I fear, may have smiled as you noted my reiterated postponements. But now the hour has come when mysticism must be faced in good earnest, and those broken threads wound up together. One may say truly, I think, that personal religious experience has its root and centre in mystical states of consciousness; so for us, who in these lectures are treating personal experience as the exclusive subject of our study, such states of consciousness ought to form the vital chapter from which the other chapters get their light. Whether my treatment of mystical states will shed more light or darkness, I do not know, for my own constitution shuts me out from their enjoyment almost entirely, and I can speak of them only at second hand. But though forced to look upon the subject so externally, I will be as objective and receptive as I can; and I think I shall at least succeed in convincing you of the reality of the states in question, and of the paramount importance of their function.

First of all, then, I ask, What does the expression "mystical states of consciousness" mean? How do we part off mystical states from other states?

The words "mysticism" and "mystical" are often used as terms of mere reproach, to throw at any opinion which we regard as vague and vast and sentimental, and without a base in either facts or logic. For some writers a "mystic" is any person who believes in thought-transference, or spirit- return. Employed in this way the word has little value: there are too many less ambiguous synonyms. So, to keep it useful by restricting it, I will do what I did in the case of the word "religion," and simply propose to you four marks which, when an experience has them, may justify us in calling it mystical for the purpose of the present lectures. In this way we shall save verbal disputation, and the recriminations that generally go therewith.

1. *Ineffability.*—The handiest of the marks by which I classify a state of mind as mystical is negative. The subject of it immediately says that it defies expression, that no adequate report of its contents can be given in words. It follows from this that its quality must be directly experienced; it cannot be imparted or transferred to others. In this peculiarity mystical states are more like states of feeling than like states of intellect. No one can make clear to another who has never had a certain feeling, in what the quality or worth of it consists. One must have musical ears to know the value of a symphony; one must have been in love one's self to understand a lover's state of mind. Lacking the heart or ear, we cannot interpret the musician or the lover justly, and are even likely to consider him weak-minded or absurd. The mystic finds that most of us accord to his experiences an equally incompetent treatment.

2. *Noetic quality.*—Although so similar to states of feeling, mystical states seem to those who experience them to be also states of knowledge. They are states of insight into depths of truth unplumbed by the discursive intellect. They are illuminations, revelations, full of significance and importance, all inarticulate

though they remain; and as a rule they carry with them a curious sense of authority for after-time.

These two characters will entitle any state to be called mystical, in the sense in which I use the word. Two other qualities are less sharply marked, but are usually found. These are:—

3. *Transiency.*—Mystical states cannot be sustained for long. Except in rare instances, half an hour, or at most an hour or two, seems to be the limit beyond which they fade into the light of common day. Often, when faded, their quality can but imperfectly be reproduced in memory; but when they recur it is recognized; and from one recurrence to another it is susceptible of continuous development in what is felt as inner richness and importance.

4. *Passivity.*—Although the oncoming of mystical states may be facilitated by preliminary voluntary operations, as by fixing the attention, or going through certain bodily performances, or in other ways which manuals of mysticism prescribe; yet when the characteristic sort of consciousness once has set in, the mystic feels as if his own will were in abeyance, and indeed sometimes as if he were grasped and held by a superior power. This latter peculiarity connects mystical states with certain definite phenomena of secondary or alternative personality, such as prophetic speech, automatic writing, or the mediumistic trance. When these latter conditions are well pronounced, however, there may be no recollection whatever of the phenomenon, and it may have no significance for the subject's usual inner life, to which, as it were, it makes a mere interruption. Mystical states, strictly so called, are never merely interruptive. Some memory of their content always remains, and a profound sense of their importance. They modify the inner life of the subject between the times of their recurrence. Sharp divisions in this region are, however, difficult to make, and we find all sorts of gradations and mixtures.

These four characteristics are sufficient to mark out a group of states of consciousness peculiar enough to deserve a special name and to call for careful study. Let it then be called the mystical group.

Our next step should be to gain acquaintance with some typical examples. Professional mystics at the height of their development have often elaborately organized experiences and a philosophy based thereupon. But you remember what I said in my first lecture: phenomena are best understood when placed within their series, studied in their germ and in their over-ripe decay, and compared with their exaggerated and degenerated kindred. The range of mystical experience is very wide, much too wide for us to cover in the time at our disposal. Yet the method of serial study is so essential for interpretation that if we really wish to reach conclusions we must use it. I will begin, therefore, with phenomena which claim no special religious significance, and end with those of which the religious pretensions are extreme.

The simplest rudiment of mystical experience would seem to be that deepened sense of the significance of a maxim or formula which occasionally sweeps over one. "I've heard that said all my life," we exclaim, "but I never realized its full meaning until now." "When a fellow-monk," said Luther, "one day repeated the words of the Creed: 'I believe in the forgiveness of sins,' I saw the Scripture in an entirely new light; and straightway I felt as if I were born anew. It was as if I had found the door of paradise thrown wide open." This sense of deeper significance is not confined to rational propositions. Single words, and conjunctions of words, effects of light on land and sea, odors and musical sounds, all bring it when the mind is tuned aright. Most of us can remember the strangely moving power of passages in certain poems read when we were young, irrational doorways as they were through which the mystery of fact, the wildness and the pang of life, stole into our hearts and thrilled them. The words have now perhaps become mere polished surfaces for us; but lyric poetry and music are alive and significant only in proportion as they fetch these vague vistas of a life continuous with our own, beckoning and inviting, yet ever eluding our pursuit. We are alive or dead to the eternal inner message of the arts according as we have kept or lost this mystical susceptibility.

A more pronounced step forward on the mystical ladder is found in an extremely frequent phenomenon, that sudden feeling, namely, which sometimes sweeps over us, of having "been here before," as if at some indefinite past time, in just this place, with just these people, we were already saying just these things. As Tennyson writes:

"Moreover, something is or seems, That touches me with mystic gleams, Like glimpses of forgotten dreams—

"Of something felt, like something here; Of something done, I know not where; Such as no language may declare."

Sir James Crichton-Browne has given the technical name of "dreamy states" to these sudden invasions of vaguely reminiscent consciousness. They bring a sense of mystery and of the metaphysical duality of things, and the feeling of an enlargement of perception which seems imminent but which never completes itself. In Dr. Crichton-Browne's opinion they connect themselves with the perplexed and scared disturbances of self- consciousness which occasionally precede epileptic attacks. I think that this learned alienist takes a rather absurdly alarmist view of an intrinsically insignificant phenomenon. He follows it along the downward ladder, to insanity; our path pursues the upward ladder chiefly. The divergence shows how important it is to neglect no part of a phenomenon's connections, for we make it appear admirable or dreadful according to the context by which we set it off.

Somewhat deeper plunges into mystical consciousness are met with in yet other dreamy states. Such feelings as these which Charles Kingsley describes are surely far from being uncommon, especially in youth:—

"When I walk the fields, I am oppressed now and then with an innate feeling that everything I see has a meaning, if I could but understand it. And this feeling of being surrounded with truths which I cannot grasp amounts to indescribable awe sometimes.... Have you not felt that your real soul was imperceptible to your mental vision, except in a few hallowed moments?"

A much more extreme state of mystical consciousness is described by J. A. Symonds; and probably more persons than we suspect could give parallels to it from their own experience.

"Suddenly," writes Symonds, "at church, or in company, or when I was reading, and always, I think, when my muscles were at rest, I felt the approach of the mood. Irresistibly it took possession of my mind and will, lasted what seemed an eternity, and disappeared in a series of rapid sensations which resembled the awakening from anaesthetic influence. One reason why I disliked this kind of trance was that I could not describe it to myself. I cannot even now find words to render it intelligible. It consisted in a gradual but swiftly progressive obliteration of space, time, sensation, and the multitudinous factors of experience which seem to qualify what we are pleased to call our Self. In proportion as these conditions of ordinary consciousness were subtracted, the sense of an underlying or essential consciousness acquired intensity. At last nothing remained but a pure, absolute, abstract Self. The universe became without form and void of content. But Self persisted, formidable in its vivid keenness, feeling the most poignant doubt about reality, ready, as it seemed, to find existence break as breaks a bubble round about it. And what then? The apprehension of a coming dissolution, the grim conviction that this state was the last state of the conscious Self, the sense that I had followed the last thread of being to the verge of the abyss, and had arrived at demonstration of eternal Maya or illusion, stirred or seemed to stir me up again. The return to ordinary conditions of sentient existence began by my first recovering the power of touch, and then by the gradual though rapid influx of familiar impressions and diurnal interests. At last I felt myself once more a human being; and though the riddle of what is meant by life remained unsolved, I was thankful for this return from the abyss—this deliverance from so awful an initiation into the mysteries of skepticism.

"This trance recurred with diminishing frequency until I reached the age of twenty-eight. It served to impress upon my growing nature the phantasmal unreality of all the circumstances which contribute to a merely phenomenal consciousness. Often have I asked myself with anguish, on waking from that formless state of denuded, keenly sentient being, Which is the unreality?—the trance of fiery, vacant, apprehensive, skeptical Self from which I issue, or these surrounding phenomena and habits which veil that inner Self and build a self of flesh-and-blood conventionality? Again, are men the factors of some dream, the dream-like unsubstantiality of which they comprehend at such eventful moments? What would happen if the final stage of the trance were reached?"

In a recital like this there is certainly something suggestive of pathology. The next step into mystical states carries us into a realm that public opinion and ethical philosophy have long since branded as pathological, though private practice and certain lyric strains of poetry seem still to bear witness to its ideality. I refer to the consciousness produced by intoxicants and anɔ́sthetics, especially by alcohol. The sway of alcohol over mankind is unquestionably due to its power to stimulate the mystical faculties of human nature, usually crushed to earth by the cold facts and dry criticisms of the sober hour. Sobriety diminishes, discriminates, and says no; drunkenness expands, unites, and says yes. It is in fact the great exciter of the *Yes* function in man. It brings its votary from the chill periphery of things to the radiant core. It makes him for the moment one with truth. Not through mere perversity do men run after it. To the poor and the unlettered it stands in the place of symphony concerts and of literature; and it is part of the deeper mystery and tragedy of life that whiffs and gleams of something that we immediately recognize as excellent should be vouchsafed to so many of us only in the fleeting earlier phases of what in its totality is so degrading a poisoning. The drunken consciousness is one bit of the mystic consciousness, and our total opinion of it must find its place in our opinion of that larger whole.

Nitrous oxide and ether, especially nitrous oxide, when sufficiently diluted with air, stimulate the mystical consciousness in an extraordinary degree. Depth beyond depth of truth seems revealed to the inhaler. This truth fades out, however, or escapes, at the moment of coming to; and if any words remain over in which it seemed to clothe itself, they prove to be the veriest nonsense. Nevertheless, the sense of a profound meaning having been there persists; and I know more than one person who is persuaded that in the nitrous oxide trance we have a genuine metaphysical revelation.

Some years ago I myself made some observations on this aspect of nitrous oxide intoxication, and reported them in print. One conclusion was forced upon my mind at that time, and my impression of its truth has ever since remained unshaken. It is that our normal waking consciousness, rational consciousness as we call it, is but one special type of consciousness, whilst all about it, parted from it by the filmiest of screens, there lie potential forms of consciousness entirely different. We may go through life without suspecting their existence; but apply the requisite stimulus, and at a touch they are there in all their completeness, definite types of mentality which probably somewhere have their field of application and adaptation. No account of the universe in its totality can be final which leaves these other forms of consciousness quite disregarded. How to regard them is the question,—for they are so discontinuous with ordinary consciousness. Yet they may determine attitudes though they cannot furnish formulas, and open a region though they fail to give a map. At any rate, they forbid a premature closing of our accounts with reality. Looking back on my own experiences, they all converge towards a kind of insight to which I cannot help ascribing some metaphysical significance. The keynote of it is invariably a reconciliation. It is as if the opposites of the world, whose contradictoriness and conflict make all our difficulties and troubles, were melted into unity. Not only do they, as contrasted species, belong to one and the same genus, but *one of the species*, the nobler and better one, *is itself the genus, and so soaks up and absorbs its opposite into itself*. This is a dark saying, I know, when thus expressed in terms of common logic, but I cannot wholly escape from its authority. I feel as if it must mean something, something like what the Hegelian philosophy means, if one could only lay hold of it more clearly. Those who have ears to hear, let them hear; to me the living sense of its reality only comes in the artificial mystic state of mind.

I just now spoke of friends who believe in the anæsthetic revelation. For them too it is a monistic insight, in which the *other* in its various forms appears absorbed into the One.

"Into this pervading genius," writes one of them, "we pass, forgetting and forgotten, and thenceforth each is all, in God. There is no higher, no deeper, no other, than the life in which we are founded. 'The One remains, the many change and pass;' and each and every one of us *is* the One that remains.... This is the ultimatum.... As sure as being—whence is all our care—so sure is content, beyond duplexity, antithesis, or trouble, where I have triumphed in a solitude that God is not above."

This has the genuine religious mystic ring! I just now quoted J. A. Symonds. He also records a mystical experience with chloroform, as follows:—

"After the choking and stifling had passed away, I seemed at first in a state of utter blankness; then came flashes of intense light, alternating with blackness, and with a keen vision of what was going on in the room around me, but no sensation of touch. I thought that I was near death; when, suddenly, my soul became aware of God, who was manifestly dealing with me, handling me, so to speak, in an intense personal present reality. I felt him streaming in like light upon me.... I cannot describe the ecstasy I felt. Then, as I gradually awoke from the influence of the anæsthetics, the old sense of my relation to the world began to return, the new sense of my relation to God began to fade. I suddenly leapt to my feet on the chair where I was sitting, and shrieked out, 'It is too horrible, it is too horrible, it is too horrible,' meaning that I could not bear this disillusionment. Then I flung myself on the ground, and at last awoke covered with blood, calling to the two surgeons (who were frightened), 'Why did you not kill me? Why would you not let me die?' Only think of it. To have felt for that long dateless ecstasy of vision the very God, in all purity and tenderness and truth and absolute love, and then to find that I had after all had no revelation, but that I had been tricked by the abnormal excitement of my brain.

"Yet, this question remains, Is it possible that the inner sense of reality which succeeded, when my flesh was dead to impressions from without, to the ordinary sense of physical relations, was not a delusion but an actual experience? Is it possible that I, in that moment, felt what some of the saints have said they always felt, the undemonstrable but irrefragable certainty of God?"

With this we make connection with religious mysticism pure and simple. Symonds's question takes us back to those examples which you will remember my quoting in the lecture on the Reality of the Unseen, of sudden realization of the immediate presence of God. The phenomenon in one shape or another is not uncommon.

"I know," writes Mr. Trine, "an officer on our police force who has told me that many times when off duty, and on his way home in the evening, there comes to him such a vivid and vital realization of his oneness with this Infinite Power, and this Spirit of Infinite Peace so takes hold of and so fills him, that it seems as if his feet could hardly keep to the pavement, so buoyant and so exhilarated does he become by reason of this inflowing tide."

Certain aspects of nature seem to have a peculiar power of awakening such mystical moods. Most of the striking cases which I have collected have occurred out of doors. Literature has commemorated this fact in many passages of great beauty—this extract, for example, from Amiel's Journal Intime:—

"Shall I ever again have any of those prodigious reveries which sometimes came to me in former days? One day, in youth, at sunrise, sitting in the ruins of the castle of Faucigny; and again in the mountains, under the noonday sun, above Lavey, lying at the foot of a tree and visited by three butterflies; once more at night upon the shingly shore of the Northern Ocean, my back upon the sand and my vision ranging through the milky way;—such grand and spacious, immortal, cosmogonic reveries, when one reaches to the stars, when one owns the infinite! Moments divine, ecstatic hours; in which our thought flies from world to world, pierces the great enigma, breathes with a respiration broad, tranquil, and deep as the respiration of the ocean, serene and limitless as the blue firmament; ... instants of irresistible intuition in which one feels one's self great as the universe, and calm as a god.... What hours, what memories! The vestiges they leave behind are enough to fill us with belief and enthusiasm, as if they were visits of the Holy Ghost."

Here is a similar record from the memoirs of that interesting German idealist, Malwida von Meysenbug:—

" I was alone upon the seashore as all these thoughts flowed over me, liberating and reconciling; and now again, as once before in distant days in the Alps of Dauphiné, I was impelled to kneel down, this time before the illimitable ocean, symbol of the Infinite. I felt that I prayed as I had never prayed before, and knew now what prayer really is: to return from the solitude of individuation into the consciousness of unity with all that is, to kneel down as one that passes away, and to rise up as one imperishable. Earth, heaven, and sea resounded as in one vast world-encircling harmony. It was as if the chorus of all the great who had ever lived were about me. I felt myself one with them, and it appeared as if I heard their greeting: 'Thou too belongest to the company of those who overcome.' "

The well-known passage from Walt Whitman is a classical expression of this sporadic type of mystical experience.

"I believe in you, my Soul ... Loaf with me on the grass, loose the stop from your throat;... Only the lull I like, the hum of your valved voice. I mind how once we lay, such a transparent summer morning. Swiftly arose and spread around me the peace and knowledge that pass all the argument of the earth, And I know that the hand of God is the promise of my own, And I know that the spirit of God is the brother of my own, And that all the men ever born are also my brothers and the women my sisters and lovers, And that a kelson of the creation is love."

I could easily give more instances, but one will suffice. I take it from the Autobiography of J. Trevor.

"One brilliant Sunday morning, my wife and boys went to the Unitarian Chapel in Macclesfield. I felt it impossible to accompany them—as though to leave the sunshine on the hills, and go down there to the chapel, would be for the time an act of spiritual suicide. And I felt such need for new inspiration and expansion in my life. So, very reluctantly and sadly, I left my wife and boys to go down into the town, while I went further up into the hills with my stick and my dog. In the loveliness of the morning, and the beauty of the hills and valleys, I soon lost my sense of sadness and regret. For nearly an hour I walked along the road to the 'Cat and Fiddle,' and then returned. On the way back, suddenly, without warning, I felt that I was in Heaven—an inward state of peace and joy and assurance indescribably intense, accompanied with a sense of being bathed in a warm glow of light, as though the external condition had brought about the internal effect—a feeling of having passed beyond the body, though the scene around me stood out more clearly and as if nearer to me than before, by reason of the illumination in the midst of which I seemed to be placed. This deep emotion lasted, though with decreasing strength, until I reached home, and for some time after, only gradually passing away."

The writer adds that having had further experiences of a similar sort, he now knows them well.

"The spiritual life," he writes, "justifies itself to those who live it; but what can we say to those who do not understand? This, at least, we can say, that it is a life whose experiences are proved real to their possessor, because they remain with him when brought closest into contact with the objective realities of life. Dreams cannot stand this test. We wake from them to find that they are but dreams. Wanderings of an overwrought brain do not stand this test. These highest experiences that I have had of God's presence have been rare and brief—flashes of consciousness which have compelled me to exclaim with surprise—God is *here*!—or conditions of exaltation and insight, less intense, and only gradually passing away. I have severely questioned the worth of these moments. To no soul have I named them, lest I should be building my life and work on mere phantasies of the brain. But I find that, after every questioning and test, they stand out to-day as the most real experiences of my life, and experiences which have explained and justified and unified all past experiences and all past growth. Indeed, their reality and their far-reaching significance are ever becoming more clear and evident. When they came, I was living the fullest, strongest, sanest, deepest life. I was not seeking them. What I was seeking, with resolute determination, was to live more intensely my own life, as against what I knew would be the adverse judgment of the world. It was in the most real seasons that the Real Presence came, and I was aware that I was immersed in the infinite ocean of God."

Even the least mystical of you must by this time be convinced of the existence of mystical moments as states of consciousness of an entirely specific quality, and of the deep impression which they make on those who have them. A Canadian psychiatrist, Dr. R. M. Bucke, gives to the more distinctly characterized of these phenomena the name of cosmic consciousness. "Cosmic consciousness in its more striking instances is not," Dr. Bucke says, "simply an expansion or extension of the self-conscious mind with which we are all familiar, but the superaddition of a function as distinct from any possessed by the average man as *self-consciousness* is distinct from any function possessed by one of the higher animals."

"The prime characteristic of cosmic consciousness is a consciousness of the cosmos, that is, of the life and order of the universe. Along with the consciousness of the cosmos there occurs an intellectual enlightenment which alone would place the individual on a new plane of existence—would make him almost a member of a new species. To this is added a state of moral exaltation, an indescribable feeling of elevation, elation, and joyousness, and a quickening of the moral sense, which is fully as striking, and more important than is the enhanced intellectual power. With these come what may be called a sense of immortality, a consciousness of eternal life, not a conviction that he shall have this, but the consciousness that he has it already."

It was Dr. Bucke's own experience of a typical onset of cosmic consciousness in his own person which led him to investigate it in others. He has printed his conclusions in a highly interesting volume, from which I take the following account of what occurred to him:—

"I had spent the evening in a great city, with two friends, reading and discussing poetry and philosophy. We parted at midnight. I had a long drive in a hansom to my lodging. My mind, deeply under the influence of the ideas, images, and emotions called up by the reading and talk, was calm and peaceful. I was in a state of quiet, almost passive enjoyment, not actually thinking, but letting ideas, images, and emotions flow of themselves, as it were, through my mind. All at once, without warning of any kind, I found myself wrapped in a flame-colored cloud. For an instant I thought of fire, an immense conflagration somewhere close by in that great city; the next, I knew that the fire was within myself. Directly afterward there came upon me a sense of exultation, of immense joyousness accompanied or immediately followed by an intellectual illumination impossible to describe. Among other things, I did not merely come to believe, but I saw that the universe is not composed of dead matter, but is, on the contrary, a living Presence; I became conscious in myself of eternal life. It was not a conviction that I would have eternal life, but a consciousness that I possessed eternal life then; I saw that all men are immortal; that the cosmic order is such that without any peradventure all things work together for the good of each and all; that the foundation principle of the world, of all the worlds, is what we call love, and that the happiness of each and all is in the long run absolutely certain. The vision lasted a few seconds and was gone; but the memory of it and the sense of the reality of what it taught has remained during the quarter of a century which has since elapsed. I knew that what the vision showed was true. I had attained to a point of view from which I saw that it must be true. That view, that conviction, I may say that consciousness, has never, even during periods of the deepest depression, been lost."

We have now seen enough of this cosmic or mystic consciousness, as it comes sporadically. We must next pass to its methodical cultivation as an element of the religious life. Hindus, Buddhists, Mohammedans, and Christians all have cultivated it methodically.

In India, training in mystical insight has been known from time immemorial under the name of yoga. Yoga means the experimental union of the individual with the divine. It is based on persevering exercise; and the diet, posture, breathing, intellectual concentration, and moral discipline vary slightly in the different systems which teach it. The yogi, or disciple, who has by these means overcome the obscurations of his lower nature sufficiently, enters into the condition termed *samâdhi*, "and comes face to face with facts which no instinct or reason can ever know." He learns—

"That the mind itself has a higher state of existence, beyond reason, a superconscious state, and that when the mind gets to that higher state, then this knowledge beyond reasoning comes.... All the different steps in yoga are intended to bring us scientifically to the superconscious state or samâdhi.... Just as unconscious work is beneath consciousness, so there is another work which is above consciousness, and which, also, is not accompanied with the feeling of egoism.... There is no feeling of *I*, and yet the mind works, desireless, free from restlessness, objectless, bodiless. Then the Truth shines in its full effulgence, and we know ourselves—for Samâdhi lies potential in us all—for what we truly are, free, immortal, omnipotent, loosed from the finite, and its contrasts of good and evil altogether, and identical with the Atman or Universal Soul."

The Vedantists say that one may stumble into superconsciousness sporadically, without the previous discipline, but it is then impure. Their test of its purity, like our test of religion's value, is empirical: its fruits must be good for life. When a man comes out of Samâdhi, they assure us that he remains "enlightened, a sage, a prophet, a saint, his whole character changed, his life changed, illumined."

The Buddhists use the word "samâdhi" as well as the Hindus; but "dhyâna" is their special word for higher states of contemplation. There seem to be four stages recognized in dhyâna. The first stage comes through concentration of the mind upon one point. It excludes desire, but not discernment or judgment: it is still intellectual. In the second stage the intellectual functions drop off, and the satisfied sense of unity remains. In the third stage the satisfaction departs, and indifference begins, along with memory and self-consciousness. In the fourth stage the indifference, memory, and self-consciousness are perfected. [Just what "memory" and "self-consciousness" mean in this connection is doubtful. They cannot be the faculties familiar to us in the lower life.] Higher stages still of contemplation are mentioned—a region where there exists nothing, and where the meditator says: "There exists absolutely nothing," and stops. Then he reaches another region where he says: "There are neither ideas nor absence of ideas," and stops again. Then another region where, "having reached the end of both idea and perception, he stops finally." This would seem to be, not yet Nirvâna, but as close an approach to it as this life affords.

In the Mohammedan world the Sufi sect and various dervish bodies are the possessors of the mystical tradition. The Sufis have existed in Persia from the earliest times, and as their pantheism is so at variance with the hot and rigid monotheism of the Arab mind, it has been suggested that Sufism must have been inoculated into Islam by Hindu influences. We Christians know little of Sufism, for its secrets are disclosed only to those initiated. To give its existence a certain liveliness in your minds, I will quote a Moslem document, and pass away from the subject.

Al-Ghazzali, a Persian philosopher and theologian, who flourished in the eleventh century, and ranks as one of the greatest doctors of the Moslem church, has left us one of the few autobiographies to be found outside of Christian literature. Strange that a species of book so abundant among ourselves should be so little represented elsewhere—the absence of strictly personal confessions is the chief difficulty to the purely literary student who would like to become acquainted with the inwardness of religions other than the Christian.

M. Schmölders has translated a part of Al-Ghazzali's autobiography into French:—

"The Science of the Sufis," says the Moslem author, "aims at detaching the heart from all that is not God, and at giving to it for sole occupation the meditation of the divine being. Theory being more easy for me than practice, I read [certain books] until I understood all that can be learned by study and hearsay. Then I recognized that what pertains most exclusively to their method is just what no study can grasp, but only transport, ecstasy, and the transformation of the soul. How great, for example, is the difference between knowing the definitions of health, of satiety, with their causes and conditions, and being really healthy or filled. How different to know in what drunkenness consists,—as being a state occasioned by a vapor that rises from the stomach,—and *being* drunk effectively. Without doubt, the drunken man knows neither the definition of drunkenness nor what makes it interesting for science. Being drunk, he knows nothing; whilst the physician, although not drunk, knows well in what drunkenness consists, and what are its predisposing conditions. Similarly there is a difference between knowing the nature of abstinence, and *being* abstinent or having one's soul detached from the world.— Thus I had learned what words could teach of Sufism, but what was left could be learned neither by study nor through the ears, but solely by giving one's self up to ecstasy and leading a pious life.

"Reflecting on my situation, I found myself tied down by a multitude of bonds—temptations on every side. Considering my teaching, I found it was impure before God. I saw myself struggling with all my might to achieve glory and to spread my name. [Here follows an account of his six months' hesitation to break away from the conditions of his life at Bagdad, at the end of which he fell ill with a paralysis of the tongue.] Then, feeling my own weakness, and having entirely given up my own will, I repaired to God like a man in distress who has no more resources. He answered, as he answers the wretch who invokes him. My heart no longer felt any difficulty in renouncing glory, wealth, and my children. So I quitted Bagdad, and reserving from my fortune only what was indispensable for my subsistence, I distributed the rest. I went to Syria, where I remained about two years, with no other occupation than living in retreat and solitude, conquering my desires, combating my passions, training myself to purify my soul, to make my character perfect, to prepare my heart for meditating on God—all according to the methods of the Sufis, as I had read of them.

"This retreat only increased my desire to live

in solitude, and to complete the purification of my heart and fit it for meditation. But the vicissitudes of the times, the affairs of the family, the need of subsistence, changed in some respects my primitive resolve, and interfered with my plans for a purely solitary life. I had never yet found myself completely in ecstasy, save in a few single hours; nevertheless, I kept the hope of attaining this state. Every time that the accidents led me astray, I sought to return; and in this situation I spent ten years. During this solitary state things were revealed to me which it is impossible either to describe or to point out. I recognized for certain that the Sufis are assuredly walking in the path of God. Both in their acts and in their inaction, whether internal or external, they are illumined by the light which proceeds from the prophetic source. The first condition for a Sufi is to purge his heart entirely of all that is not God. The next key of the contemplative life consists in the humble prayers which escape from the fervent soul, and in the meditations on God in which the heart is swallowed up entirely. But in reality this is only the beginning of the Sufi life, the end of Sufism being total absorption in God. The intuitions and all that precede are, so to speak, only the threshold for those who enter. From the beginning, revelations take place in so flagrant a shape that the Sufis see before them, whilst wide awake, the angels and the souls of the prophets. They hear their voices and obtain their favors. Then the transport rises from the perception of forms and figures to a degree which escapes all expression, and which no man may seek to give an account of without his words involving sin.

"Whoever has had no experience of the transport knows of the true nature of prophetism nothing but the name. He may meanwhile be sure of its existence, both by experience and by what he hears the Sufis say. As there are men endowed only with the sensitive faculty who reject what is offered them in the way of objects of the pure understanding, so there are intellectual men who reject and avoid the things perceived by the prophetic faculty. A blind man can understand nothing of colors save what he has learned by narration and hearsay. Yet God has brought prophetism near to men in giving them all a state analogous to it in its principal characters. This state is sleep. If you were to tell a man who was himself without experience of such a phenomenon that there are people who at times swoon away so as to resemble dead men, and who [in dreams] yet perceive things that are hidden, he would deny it [and give his reasons]. Nevertheless, his arguments would be refuted by actual experience. Wherefore, just as the understanding is a stage of human life in which an eye opens to discern various intellectual objects uncomprehended by sensation; just so in the prophetic the sight is illumined by a light which uncovers hidden things and objects which the intellect fails to reach. The chief properties of prophetism are perceptible only during the transport, by those who embrace the Sufi life. The prophet is endowed with qualities to which you possess nothing analogous, and which consequently you cannot possibly understand. How should you know their true nature, since one knows only what one can comprehend? But the transport which one attains by the method of the Sufis is like an immediate perception, as if one touched the objects with one's hand."

This incommunicableness of the transport is the keynote of all mysticism. Mystical truth exists for the individual who has the transport, but for no one else. In this, as I have said, it resembles the knowledge given to us in sensations more than that given by conceptual thought. Thought, with its remoteness and abstractness, has often enough in the history of philosophy been contrasted unfavorably with sensation. It is a commonplace of metaphysics that God's knowledge cannot be discursive but must be intuitive, that is, must be constructed more after the pattern of what in ourselves is called immediate feeling, than after that of proposition and judgment. But *our* immediate feelings have no content but what the five senses supply; and we have seen and shall see again that mystics may emphatically deny that the senses play any part in the very highest type of knowledge which their transports yield.

In the Christian church there have always been mystics. Although many of them have been viewed with suspicion, some have gained favor in the eyes of the authorities. The experiences of these have been treated as precedents, and a codified system of mystical theology has been based upon them, in which everything legitimate finds its place. The basis of the system is "orison" or meditation, the methodical elevation of the soul towards God. Through the practice of orison the higher levels of mystical experience may be attained. It is odd that Protestantism, especially evangelical Protestantism, should seemingly have abandoned everything methodical in this line. Apart from what prayer may lead to, Protestant mystical experience appears to have been almost exclusively sporadic. It has been left to our mind-curers to reintroduce methodical meditation into our religious life.

The first thing to be aimed at in orison is the mind's detachment from outer sensations, for these interfere with its concentration upon ideal things. Such manuals as Saint Ignatius's Spiritual Exercises recommend the disciple to expel sensation by a graduated series of efforts to imagine holy scenes. The acme of this kind of discipline would be a semi- hallucinatory mono-ideism—an imaginary figure of Christ, for example, coming fully to occupy the mind. Sensorial images of this sort, whether literal or symbolic, play an enormous part in mysticism. But in certain cases imagery may fall away entirely, and in the very highest raptures it tends to do so. The state of consciousness becomes then insusceptible of any verbal description. Mystical teachers are unanimous as to this. Saint John of the Cross, for instance, one of the best of them, thus describes the condition called the "union of love," which, he says, is reached by "dark contemplation." In this the Deity compenetrates the soul, but in such a hidden way that the soul—

"finds no terms, no means, no comparison whereby to render the sublimity of the wisdom and the delicacy of the spiritual feeling with which she is filled.... We receive this mystical knowledge of God clothed in none of the kinds of images, in none of the sensible representations, which our mind makes use of in other circumstances. Accordingly in this knowledge, since the senses and the imagination are not employed, we get neither form nor impression, nor can we give any account or furnish any likeness, although the mysterious and sweet-tasting wisdom comes home so clearly to the inmost parts of our soul. Fancy a man seeing a certain kind of thing for the first time in his life. He can understand it, use and enjoy it, but he cannot apply a name to it, nor communicate any idea of it, even though all the while it be a mere thing of sense. How much greater will be his powerlessness when it goes beyond the senses! This is the peculiarity of the divine language. The more infused, intimate, spiritual, and supersensible it is, the more does it exceed the senses, both inner and outer, and impose silence upon them.... The soul then feels as if placed in a vast and profound solitude, to which no created thing has access, in an immense and boundless desert, desert the more delicious the more solitary it is. There, in this abyss of wisdom, the soul grows by what it drinks in from the well-springs of the comprehension of love, ... and recognizes, however sublime and learned may be the terms we employ, how utterly vile, insignificant, and improper they are, when we seek to discourse of divine things by their means."

I cannot pretend to detail to you the sundry stages of the Christian mystical life. Our time would not suffice, for one thing; and moreover, I confess that the subdivisions and names which we find in the Catholic books seem to me to represent nothing objectively distinct. So many men, so many minds: I imagine that these experiences can be as infinitely varied as are the idiosyncrasies of individuals.

The cognitive aspects of them, their value in the way of revelation, is what we are directly concerned with, and it is easy to show by citation how strong an impression they leave of being revelations of new depths of truth. Saint Teresa is the expert of experts in describing such conditions, so I will turn immediately to what she says of one of the highest of them, the "orison of union."

"In the orison of union," says Saint Teresa, "the soul is fully awake as regards God, but wholly asleep as regards things of this world and in respect of herself. During the short time the union lasts, she is as it were deprived of every feeling, and even if she would, she could not think of any single thing. Thus she needs to employ no artifice in order to arrest the use of her understanding: it remains so stricken with inactivity that she neither knows what she loves, nor in what manner she loves, nor what she wills. In short, she is utterly dead to the things of the world and lives solely in God.... I do not even know whether in this state she has enough life left to breathe. It seems to me she has not; or at least that if she does breathe, she is unaware of it. Her intellect would fain understand something of what is going on within her, but it has so little force now that it can act in no way whatsoever. So a person who falls into a deep faint appears as if dead....

"Thus does God, when he raises a soul to union with himself, suspend the natural action of all her faculties. She neither sees, hears, nor understands, so long as she is united with God. But this time is always short, and it seems even shorter than it is. God establishes himself in the interior of this soul in such a way, that when she returns to herself, it is wholly impossible for her to doubt that she has been in God, and God in her. This truth remains so strongly impressed on her that, even though many years should pass without the condition returning, she can neither forget the favor she received, nor doubt of its reality. If you, nevertheless, ask how it is possible that the soul can see and understand that she has been in God, since during the union she has neither sight nor understanding, I reply that she does not see it then, but that she sees it clearly later, after she has returned to herself, not by any vision, but by a certitude which abides with her and which God alone can give her. I knew a person who was ignorant of the truth that God's mode of being in everything must be either by presence, by power, or by essence, but who, after having received the grace of which I am speaking, believed this truth in the most unshakable manner. So much so that, having consulted a half-learned man who was as ignorant on this point as she had been before she was enlightened, when he replied that God is in us only by 'grace,' she disbelieved his reply, so sure she was of the true answer; and when she came to ask wiser doctors, they confirmed her in her belief, which much consoled her....

"But how, you will repeat, *can* one have such certainty in respect to what one does not see? This question, I am powerless to answer. These are secrets of God's omnipotence which it does not appertain to me to penetrate. All that I know is that I tell the truth; and I shall never believe that any soul who does not possess this certainty has ever been really united to God."

The kinds of truth communicable in mystical ways, whether these be sensible or supersensible, are various. Some of them relate to this world,—visions of the future, the reading of hearts, the sudden understanding of texts, the knowledge of distant events, for example; but the most important revelations are theological or metaphysical.

"Saint Ignatius confessed one day to Father Laynez that a single hour of meditation at Manresa had taught him more truths about heavenly things than all the teachings of all the doctors put together could have taught him.... One day in orison, on the steps of the choir of the Dominican church, he saw in a distinct manner the plan of divine wisdom in the creation of the world. On another occasion, during a procession, his spirit was ravished in God, and it was given him to contemplate, in a form and images fitted to the weak understanding of a dweller on the earth, the deep mystery of the holy Trinity. This last vision flooded his heart with such sweetness, that the mere memory of it in after times made him shed abundant tears."

Similarly with Saint Teresa. "One day, being in orison," she writes, "it was granted me to perceive in one instant how all things are seen and contained in God. I did not perceive them in their proper form, and nevertheless the view I had of them was of a sovereign clearness, and has remained vividly impressed upon my soul. It is one of the most signal of all the graces which the Lord has granted me.... The view was so subtle and delicate that the understanding cannot grasp it."

She goes on to tell how it was as if the Deity were an enormous and sovereignly limpid diamond, in which all our actions were contained in such a way that their full sinfulness appeared evident as never before. On another day, she relates, while she was reciting the Athanasian Creed,—

"Our Lord made me comprehend in what way it is that one God can be in three Persons. He made me see it so clearly that I remained as extremely surprised as I was comforted, ... and now, when I think of the holy Trinity, or hear It spoken of, I understand how the three adorable Persons form only one God and I experience an unspeakable happiness."

On still another occasion, it was given to Saint Teresa to see and understand in what wise the Mother of God had been assumed into her place in Heaven.

The deliciousness of some of these states seems to be beyond anything known in ordinary consciousness. It evidently involves organic sensibilities, for it is spoken of as something too extreme to be borne, and as verging on bodily pain. But it is too subtle and piercing a delight for ordinary words to denote. God's touches, the wounds of his spear, references to ebriety and to nuptial union have to figure in the phraseology by which it is shadowed forth. Intellect and senses both swoon away in these highest states of ecstasy. "If our understanding comprehends," says Saint Teresa, "it is in a mode which remains unknown to it, and it can understand nothing of what it comprehends. For my own part, I do not believe that it does comprehend, because, as I said, it does not understand itself to do so. I confess that it is all a mystery in which I am lost." In the condition called *raptus* or ravishment by theologians, breathing and circulation are so depressed that it is a question among the doctors whether the soul be or be not temporarily disseveread from the body. One must read Saint Teresa's descriptions and the very exact distinctions which she makes, to persuade one's self that one is dealing, not with imaginary experiences, but with phenomena which, however rare, follow perfectly definite psychological types.

To the medical mind these ecstasies signify nothing but suggested and imitated hypnoid states, on an intellectual basis of superstition, and a corporeal one of degeneration and hysteria. Undoubtedly these pathological conditions have existed in many and possibly in all the cases, but that fact tells us nothing about the value for knowledge of the consciousness which they induce. To pass a spiritual judgment upon these states, we must not content ourselves with superficial medical talk, but inquire into their fruits for life.

Their fruits appear to have been various. Stupefaction, for one thing, seems not to have been altogether absent as a result. You may remember the helplessness in the kitchen and schoolroom of poor Margaret Mary Alacoque. Many other ecstatics would have perished but for the care taken of them by admiring followers. The "other-worldliness" encouraged by the mystical consciousness makes this over-abstraction from practical life peculiarly liable to befall mystics in whom the character is naturally passive and the intellect feeble; but in natively strong minds and characters we find quite opposite results. The great Spanish mystics, who carried the habit of ecstasy as far as it has often been carried, appear for the most part to have shown indomitable spirit and energy, and all the more so for the trances in which they indulged.

Saint Ignatius was a mystic, but his mysticism made him assuredly one of the most powerfully practical human engines that ever lived. Saint John of the Cross, writing of the intuitions and "touches" by which God reaches the substance of the soul, tells us that—

"They enrich it marvelously. A single one of them may be sufficient to abolish at a stroke certain imperfections of which the soul during its whole life had vainly tried to rid itself, and to leave it adorned with virtues and loaded with supernatural gifts. A single one of these intoxicating consolations may reward it for all the labors undergone in its life—even were they numberless. Invested with an invincible courage, filled with an impassioned desire to suffer for its God, the soul then is seized with a strange torment—that of not being allowed to suffer enough."

Saint Teresa is as emphatic, and much more detailed. You may perhaps remember a passage I quoted from her in my first lecture. There are many similar pages in her autobiography. Where in literature is a more evidently veracious account of the formation of a new centre of spiritual energy, than is given in her description of the effects of certain ecstasies which in departing leave the soul upon a higher level of emotional excitement?

"Often, infirm and wrought upon with dreadful pains before the ecstasy, the soul emerges from it full of health and admirably disposed for action ... as if God had willed that the body itself, already obedient to the soul's desires, should share in the soul's happiness.... The soul after such a favor is animated with a degree of courage so great that if at that moment its body should be torn to pieces for the cause of God, it would feel nothing but the liveliest comfort. Then it is that promises and heroic resolutions spring up in profusion in us, soaring desires, horror of the world, and the clear perception of our proper nothingness.... What empire is comparable to that of a soul who, from this sublime summit to which God has raised her, sees all the things of earth beneath her feet, and is captivated by no one of them? How ashamed she is of her former attachments! How amazed at her blindness! What lively pity she feels for those whom she recognizes still shrouded in the darkness!... She groans at having ever been sensitive to points of honor, at the illusion that made her ever see as honor what the world calls by that name. Now she sees in this name nothing more than an immense lie of which the world remains a victim. She discovers, in the new light from above, that in genuine honor there is nothing spurious, that to be faithful to this honor is to give our respect to what deserves to be respected really, and to consider as nothing, or as less than nothing, whatsoever perishes and is not agreeable to God.... She laughs when she sees grave persons, persons of orison, caring for points of honor for which she now feels profoundest contempt. It is suitable to the dignity of their rank to act thus, they pretend, and it makes them more useful to others. But she knows that in despising the dignity of their rank for the pure love of God they would do more good in a single day than they would effect in ten years by preserving it.... She laughs at herself that there should ever have been a time in her life when she made any case of money, when she ever desired it.... Oh! if human beings might only agree together to regard it as so much useless mud, what harmony would then reign in the world! With what friendship we would all treat each other if our interest in honor and in money could but disappear from earth! For my own part, I feel as if it would be a remedy for all our ills."

Mystical conditions may, therefore, render the soul more energetic in the lines which their inspiration favors. But this could be reckoned an advantage only in case the inspiration were a true one. If the inspiration were erroneous, the energy would be all the more mistaken and misbegotten. So we stand once more before that problem of truth which confronted us at the end of the lectures on saintliness. You will remember that we turned to mysticism precisely to get some light on truth. Do mystical states establish the truth of those theological affections in which the saintly life has its root?

In spite of their repudiation of articulate self-description, mystical states in general assert a pretty distinct theoretic drift. It is possible to give the outcome of the majority of them in terms that point in definite philosophical directions. One of these directions is optimism, and the other is monism. We pass into mystical states from out of ordinary consciousness as from a less into a more, as from a smallness into a vastness, and at the same time as from an unrest to a rest. We feel them as reconciling, unifying states. They appeal to the yes-function more than to the no-function in us. In them the unlimited absorbs the limits and peacefully closes the account. Their very denial of every adjective you may propose as applicable to the ultimate truth,—He, the Self, the Atman, is to be described by "No! no!" only, say the Upanishads,—though it seems on the surface to be a no-function, is a denial made on behalf of a deeper yes. Whoso calls the Absolute anything in particular, or says that it is *this*, seems implicitly to shut it off from being *that*—it is as if he lessened it. So we deny the "this," negating the negation which it seems to us to imply, in the interests of the higher affirmative attitude by which we are possessed. The fountain-head of Christian mysticism is Dionysius the Areopagite. He describes the absolute truth by negatives exclusively.

"The cause of all things is neither soul nor intellect; nor has it imagination, opinion, or reason, or intelligence; nor is it reason or intelligence; nor is it spoken or thought. It is neither number, nor order, nor magnitude, nor littleness, nor equality, nor inequality, nor similarity, nor dissimilarity. It neither stands, nor moves, nor rests.... It is neither essence, nor eternity, nor time. Even intellectual contact does not belong to it. It is neither science nor truth. It is not even royalty or wisdom; not one; not unity; not divinity or goodness; nor even spirit as we know it," etc., a*d libitum*.

But these qualifications are denied by Dionysius, not because the truth falls short of them, but because it so infinitely excels them. It is above them. It is *super*-lucent, *super*-splendent, *super*-essential, *super*-sublime, *super* everything that can be named. Like Hegel in his logic, mystics journey towards the positive pole of truth only by the "Methode der Absoluten Negativität."

Thus come the paradoxical expressions that so abound in mystical writings. As when Eckhart tells of the still desert of the Godhead, "where never was seen difference, neither Father, Son, nor Holy Ghost, where there is no one at home, yet where the spark of the soul is more at peace than in itself." As when Boehme writes of the Primal Love, that "it may fitly be compared to Nothing, for it is deeper than any Thing, and is as nothing with respect to all things, forasmuch as it is not comprehensible by any of them. And because it is nothing respectively, it is therefore free from all things, and is that only good, which a man cannot express or utter what it is, there being nothing to which it may be compared, to express it by." Or as when Angelus Silesius sings:—

"Gott ist ein lauter Nichts, ihn rührt kein Nun noch Hier; Je mehr du nach ihm greiffst, je mehr entwind er dir."

To this dialectical use, by the intellect, of negation as a mode of passage towards a higher kind of affirmation, there is correlated the subtlest of moral counterparts in the sphere of the personal will. Since denial of the finite self and its wants, since asceticism of some sort, is found in religious experience to be the only doorway to the larger and more blessed life, this moral mystery intertwines and combines with the intellectual mystery in all mystical writings.

"Love," continues Behmen, is Nothing, for "when thou art gone forth wholly from the Creature and from that which is visible, and art become Nothing to all that is Nature and Creature, then thou art in that eternal One, which is God himself, and then thou shalt feel within thee the highest virtue of Love.... The treasure of treasures for the soul is where she goeth out of the Somewhat into that Nothing out of which all things may be made. The soul here saith, *I have nothing*, for I am utterly stripped and naked; *I can do nothing*, for I have no manner of power, but am as water poured out; *I am nothing*, for all that I am is no more than an image of Being, and only God is to me I AM; and so, sitting down in my own Nothingness, I give glory to the eternal Being, and *will nothing* of myself, that so God may will all in me, being unto me my God and all things."

In Paul's language, I live, yet not I, but Christ liveth in me. Only when I become as nothing can God enter in and no difference between his life and mine remain outstanding.

This overcoming of all the usual barriers between the individual and the Absolute is the great mystic achievement. In mystic states we both become one with the Absolute and we become aware of our oneness. This is the everlasting and triumphant mystical tradition, hardly altered by differences of clime or creed. In Hinduism, in Neoplatonism, in Sufism, in Christian mysticism, in Whitmanism, we find the same recurring note, so that there is about mystical utterances an eternal unanimity which ought to make a critic stop and think, and which brings it about that the mystical classics have, as has been said, neither birthday nor native land. Perpetually telling of the unity of man with God, their speech antedates languages, and they do not grow old.

"That art Thou!" say the Upanishads, and the Vedantists add: "Not a part, not a mode of That, but identically That, that absolute Spirit of the World." "As pure water poured into pure water remains the same, thus, O Gautama, is the Self of a thinker who knows. Water in water, fire in fire, ether in ether, no one can distinguish them; likewise a man whose mind has entered into the Self." " 'Every man,' says the Sufi Gulshan-Râz, 'whose heart is no longer shaken by any doubt, knows with certainty that there is no being save only One.... In his divine majesty the *me*, the *we*, the *thou*, are not found, for in the One there can be no distinction. Every being who is annulled and entirely separated from himself, hears resound outside of him this voice and this echo: *I am God*: he has an eternal way of existing, and is no longer subject to death.' " In the vision of God, says Plotinus, "what sees is not our reason, but something prior and superior to our reason.... He who thus sees does not properly see, does not distinguish or imagine two things. He changes, he ceases to be himself, preserves nothing of himself. Absorbed in God, he makes but one with him, like a centre of a circle coinciding with another centre." "Here," writes Suso, "the spirit dies, and yet is all alive in the marvels of the Godhead ... and is lost in the stillness of the glorious dazzling obscurity and of the naked simple unity. It is in this modeless *where* that the highest bliss is to be found." "Ich bin so gross als Gott," sings Angelus Silesius again, "Er ist als ich so klein; Er kann nicht über mich, ich unter ihm nicht sein."

In mystical literature such self-contradictory phrases as "dazzling obscurity," "whispering silence," "teeming desert," are continually met with. They prove that not conceptual speech, but music rather, is the element through which we are best spoken to by mystical truth. Many mystical scriptures are indeed little more than musical compositions.

"He who would hear the voice of Nada, 'the Soundless Sound,' and comprehend it, he has to learn the nature of Dhâranâ.... When to himself his form appears unreal, as do on waking all the forms he sees in dreams; when he has ceased to hear the many, he may discern the ONE—the inner sound which kills the outer.... For then the soul will hear, and will remember. And then to the inner ear will speak THE VOICE OF THE SILENCE.... And now thy *Self* is lost in SELF, *thyself* unto THYSELF, merged in that SELF from which thou first didst radiate.... Behold! thou hast become the Light, thou hast become the Sound, thou art thy Master and thy God. Thou art THYSELF the object of thy search: the VOICE unbroken, that resounds throughout eternities, exempt from change, from sin exempt, the seven sounds in one, the VOICE OF THE SILENCE. *Om tat Sat*."

These words, if they do not awaken laughter as you receive them, probably stir chords within you which music and language touch in common. Music gives us ontological messages which non-musical criticism is unable to contradict, though it may laugh at our foolishness in minding them. There is a verge of the mind which these things haunt; and whispers therefrom mingle with the operations of our understanding, even as the waters of the infinite ocean send their waves to break among the pebbles that lie upon our shores.

"Here begins the sea that ends not till the world's end. Where we stand, Could we know the next high sea-mark set beyond these waves that gleam, We should know what never man hath known, nor eye of man hath scanned.... Ah, but here man's heart leaps, yearning towards the gloom with venturous glee, From the shore that hath no shore beyond it, set in all the sea."

That doctrine, for example, that eternity is timeless, that our "immortality," if we live in the eternal, is not so much future as already now and here, which we find so often expressed to-day in certain philosophic circles, finds its support in a "hear, hear!" or an "amen," which floats up from that mysteriously deeper level. We recognize the passwords to the mystical region as we hear them, but we cannot use them ourselves; it alone has the keeping of "the password primeval."

I have now sketched with extreme brevity and insufficiency, but as fairly as I am able in the time allowed, the general traits of the mystic range of consciousness. *It is on the whole pantheistic and optimistic, or at least the opposite of pessimistic. It is anti-naturalistic, and harmonizes best with twice-bornness and so-called other-worldly states of mind.*

My next task is to inquire whether we can invoke it as authoritative. Does it furnish any *warrant for the truth* of the twice-bornness and supernaturality and pantheism which it favors? I must give my answer to this question as concisely as I can.

In brief my answer is this,—and I will divide it into three parts:—

(1) Mystical states, when well developed, usually are, and have the right to be, absolutely authoritative over the individuals to whom they come.

(2) No authority emanates from them which should make it a duty for those who stand outside of them to accept their revelations uncritically.

(3) They break down the authority of the non-mystical or rationalistic consciousness, based upon the understanding and the senses alone. They show it to be only one kind of consciousness. They open out the possibility of other orders of truth, in which, so far as anything in us vitally responds to them, we may freely continue to have faith.

I will take up these points one by one.

1.

As a matter of psychological fact, mystical states of a well-pronounced and emphatic sort *are* usually authoritative over those who have them. They have been "there," and know. It is vain for rationalism to grumble about this. If the mystical truth that comes to a man proves to be a force that he can live by, what mandate have we of the majority to order him to live in another way? We can throw him into a prison or a madhouse, but we cannot change his mind—we commonly attach it only the more stubbornly to its beliefs. It mocks our utmost efforts, as a matter of fact, and in point of logic it absolutely escapes our jurisdiction. Our own more "rational" beliefs are based on evidence exactly similar in nature to that which mystics quote for theirs. Our senses, namely, have assured us of certain states of fact; but mystical experiences are as direct perceptions of fact for those who have them as any sensations ever were for us. The records show that even though the five senses be in abeyance in them, they are absolutely sensational in their epistemological quality, if I may be pardoned the barbarous expression,—that is, they are face to face presentations of what seems immediately to exist.

The mystic is, in short, *invulnerable*, and must be left, whether we relish it or not, in undisturbed enjoyment of his creed. Faith, says Tolstoy, is that by which men live. And faith-state and mystic state are practically convertible terms.

2.

But I now proceed to add that mystics have no right to claim that we ought to accept the deliverance of their peculiar experiences, if we are ourselves outsiders and feel no private call thereto. The utmost they can ever ask of us in this life is to admit that they establish a presumption. They form a consensus and have an unequivocal outcome; and it would be odd, mystics might say, if such a unanimous type of experience should prove to be altogether wrong. At bottom, however, this would only be an appeal to numbers, like the appeal of rationalism the other way; and the appeal to numbers has no logical force. If we acknowledge it, it is for "suggestive," not for logical reasons: we follow the majority because to do so suits our life.

But even this presumption from the unanimity of mystics is far from being strong. In characterizing mystic states as pantheistic, optimistic, etc., I am afraid I over-simplified the truth. I did so for expository reasons, and to keep the closer to the classic mystical tradition. The classic religious mysticism, it now must be confessed, is only a "privileged case." It is an *extract*, kept true to type by the selection of the fittest specimens and their preservation in "schools." It is carved out from a much larger mass; and if we take the larger mass as seriously as religious mysticism has historically taken itself, we find that the supposed unanimity largely disappears. To begin with, even religious mysticism itself, the kind that accumulates traditions and makes schools, is much less unanimous than I have allowed. It has been both ascetic and antinomianly self-indulgent within the Christian church. It is dualistic in Sankhya, and monistic in Vedanta philosophy. I called it pantheistic; but the great Spanish mystics are anything but pantheists. They are with few exceptions non-metaphysical minds, for whom "the category of personality" is absolute. The "union" of man with God is for them much more like an occasional miracle than like an original identity. How different again, apart from the happiness common to all, is the mysticism of Walt Whitman, Edward Carpenter, Richard Jefferies, and other naturalistic pantheists, from the more distinctively Christian sort. The fact is that the mystical feeling of enlargement, union, and emancipation has no specific intellectual content whatever of its own. It is capable of forming matrimonial alliances with material furnished by the most diverse philosophies and theologies, provided only they can find a place in their framework for its peculiar emotional mood. We have no right, therefore, to invoke its prestige as distinctively in favor of any special belief, such as that in absolute idealism, or in the absolute monistic identity, or in the absolute goodness, of the world. It is only relatively in favor of all these things—it passes out of common human consciousness in the direction in which they lie.

So much for religious mysticism proper. But more remains to be told, for religious mysticism is only one half of mysticism. The other half has no accumulated traditions except those which the text-books on insanity supply. Open any one of these, and you will find abundant cases in which "mystical ideas" are cited as characteristic symptoms of enfeebled or deluded states of mind. In delusional insanity, paranoia, as they sometimes call it, we may have a *diabolical* mysticism, a sort of religious mysticism turned upside down. The same sense of ineffable importance in the smallest events, the same texts and words coming with new meanings, the same voices and visions and leadings and missions, the same controlling by extraneous powers; only this time the emotion is pessimistic: instead of consolations we have desolations; the meanings are dreadful; and the powers are enemies to life. It is evident that from the point of view of their psychological mechanism, the classic mysticism and these lower mysticisms spring from the same mental level, from that great subliminal or transmarginal region of which science is beginning to admit the existence, but of which so little is really known. That region contains every kind of matter: "seraph and snake" abide there side by side. To come from thence is no infallible credential. What comes must be sifted and tested, and run the gauntlet of confrontation with the total context of experience, just like what comes from the outer world of sense. Its value must be ascertained by empirical methods, so long as we are not mystics ourselves.

Once more, then, I repeat that non-mystics are under no obligation to acknowledge in mystical states a superior authority conferred on them by their intrinsic nature.

3.

Yet, I repeat once more, the existence of mystical states absolutely overthrows the pretension of non-mystical states to be the sole and ultimate dictators of what we may believe. As a rule, mystical states merely add a supersensuous meaning to the ordinary outward data of consciousness. They are excitements like the emotions of love or ambition, gifts to our spirit by means of which facts already objectively before us fall into a new expressiveness and make a new connection with our active life. They do not contradict these facts as such, or deny anything that our senses have immediately seized. It is the rationalistic critic rather who plays the part of denier in the controversy, and his denials have no strength, for there never can be a state of facts to which new meaning may not truthfully be added, provided the mind ascend to a more enveloping point of view. It must always remain an open question whether mystical states may not possibly be such superior points of view, windows through which the mind looks out upon a more extensive and inclusive world. The difference of the views seen from the different mystical windows need not prevent us from entertaining this supposition. The wider world would in that case prove to have a mixed constitution like that of this world, that is all. It would have its celestial and its infernal regions, its tempting and its saving moments, its valid experiences and its counterfeit ones, just as our world has them; but it would be a wider world all the same. We should have to use its experiences by selecting and subordinating and substituting just as is our custom in this ordinary naturalistic world; we should be liable to error just as we are now; yet the counting in of that wider world of meanings, and the serious dealing with it, might, in spite of all the perplexity, be indispensable stages in our approach to the final fullness of the truth.

In this shape, I think, we have to leave the subject. Mystical states indeed wield no authority due simply to their being mystical states. But the higher ones among them point in directions to which the religious sentiments even of non-mystical men incline. They tell of the supremacy of the ideal, of vastness, of union, of safety, and of rest. They offer us *hypotheses*, hypotheses which we may voluntarily ignore, but which as thinkers we cannot possibly upset. The supernaturalism and optimism to which they would persuade us may, interpreted in one way or another, be after all the truest of insights into the meaning of this life.

"Oh, the little more, and how much it is; and the little less, and what worlds away!" It may be that possibility and permission of this sort are all that the religious consciousness requires to live on. In my last lecture I shall have to try to persuade you that this is the case. Meanwhile, however, I am sure that for many of my readers this diet is too slender. If supernaturalism and inner union with the divine are true, you think, then not so much permission, as compulsion to believe, ought to be found. Philosophy has always professed to prove religious truth by coercive argument; and the construction of philosophies of this kind has always been one favorite function of the religious life, if we use this term in the large historic sense. But religious philosophy is an enormous subject, and in my next lecture I can only give that brief glance at it which my limits will allow.

"Mysticism" is comprised of
lectures XVI and XVII of
The Varieties of Religious Experience by Henry James.
Footnotes have not been included.

Book Reviews

The Book of Celtic Magic: Transformative Teachings from the Cauldron of Awen
384pp

The Journey into Spirit: A Pagan's Perspective on Death, Dying, and Bereavement
336pp

Kristoffer Hughes

Llewellyn

Kristoffer Hughes is unusual. His two books on Celtic neo-pagan tradition are unusual in that he is a Welshman from Anglesey who speaks Welsh as a first language, thus giving him an important native perspective on Celtic traditions. His book on death is also informed by an unusual viewpoint, that of an autopsy technologist, a pathologist working in mortuaries (UK term) or morgues (US term).

The Book of Celtic Magic could as easily have been called "The Book of Welsh Magic", though the latter title would undoubtedly have stunted its commercial appeal. Most of it draws on his own Welsh tradition. I liked the way that he acknowledges the Celtic inheritance as primarily cultural (rather than ethnic), describing it as Celtica. This functions both to acknowledge the ongoing scholarly reassessment of Celticity, recognising that the tradition is primarily a revived one (though even that goes back three centuries or so now) and in making it available to people who, it must be emphasised, haven't grow up in a Celtic country. What is a Celtic country? My definition is that it is a country where a Celtic language is spoken or has been spoken in comparatively recent times. By the preceding definition Canada (Nova Scotia has a Gaelic-speaking community) and Argentina (a Welsh-speaking community in Patagonia) would count as Celtic countries, I suppose.

There are sections on using the Welsh gods, many of whom are figures from the Mabinogi and associated poetry and tales that are now kings, magicians, witches and the like, but were probably originally gods. Tree and plant based lore receives a good treatment. Ogham divination receives the single extended nod to Irish tradition, although ogham stones (in irish) are in Wales too.

Poetry is an essential aspect of Celtic culture and Hughes has composed several poems for use in rituals. There are places in the Mabinogi where poems are recited in a magical context, so this is entirely appropriate and authentic. Those particular poems are *englynion* (singular *englyn*), compact verses of three or four lines which are still an essential part of the living tradition of poetry in the Welsh language. Hughes' englynion are all in English, which is fine as this is an English language book. I have to say that they are for the most part doggerel, but even so doggerel itself has a an important place in the magical tradition. I have to say that I didn't quite like him using the term englyn for them. The englyn forms are in strict metre and is very complex and disciplined, and extremely difficult to render into English. Hughes' verses are the equivalent of *penillion*, rough and informal rhyming poems that are part of the folk tradition in Wales. It's a quibble on my behalf, but it does misrepresent the term a little. Overall *The Book of Celtic Magic* is a useful window into genuinely Welsh and Celtic magi and pagan tradition that is accessible to anyone anywhere in the world.

The Journey Into Spirit is a very different book. Written from a modern pagan perspective it utilises neo-pagan concepts occasionally but is in most ways a more direct meditation on death and dying. Hughes is no stranger either to death or the dead. The most affecting parts of the book are the sections in which he writes on his vocation as a pathologist. He sees himself to some extent as a modern psychopomp. The morgue, with its stainless steel surfaces, its medical hygiene, and its heavily regulated legal status is in the experience of Kristoffer Hughes still a liminal zone. His perspective is oddly moving, both human and of the gods.

Yet it is not only in cutting up cadavers that Hughes experiences death. A number of untimely deaths of friends and family have clearly affected him profoundly. He was also called in to perform autopsies on the victims of the 7/7 terrorist attack in London.

Hughes writes clearly, with an occasional poetic turn of phrase and some humour. Nothing in his books prepared me for his performance at a pagan conference, Spirit of Brighid, in my home town at which I gave a talk on Gnosticism. On stage he is campness itself. With a mouth like a sailor (fishnet-stockinged beneath the bell bottoms), it is easy to believe that he is a drag queen in his spare time. His talk was funny, impassioned and dramatic.

I was glad I had already given my talk and didn't have to follow him.

I particularly enjoyed his critique of the popular monotheistic idea of the survival of the personality after death. "I'm a druid, a drag queen and a pathologist. Imagine what it's like in my head! I don't want that to survive for eternity!" In his talk he seemed closer to not believing in any kind of survival after death than in the book, although this may just have been the way that it all came together on the day. His message was to "do epic shit" while we can. In these books Kristoffer has done a little of his epic shit.

Rediscover the Magick of the Gods and Goddesses: Revealing the Mysteries of Theurgy

Jean-Louis De Biasi

306pp

Llewellyn

Book titles can very often be misleading. The tendency is not necessarily to come up with a title that encapsulates the essence of the book but to attract buyers. *Rediscover the Magick of the Gods and Goddesses: Revealing the Mysteries of Theurgy* is not a misleading title yet it somehow fails to truly describe the contents. From the title and a cursory flick through I had assumed this to be a general overview of pagan pantheons and guidelines on their use. It is the much more specific than that. The final word in the title, "theurgy" is the key, but it is also useful to know that this is the product of a specific esoteric group, the Aurum Solis. Jean-Louis de Biasi, the author, is the Grand Master of this order.

I found some of the book's orientation to the promotion of a particular order a little irritating. In truth this isn't excessive, but I would much prefer something that is of general use to the practitioner rather than tied to such a particular scheme.

De Biasi's first language is French and the English can be a little awkward at times. Nevertheless, the author does a good job of describing the western tradition of theurgy. Rooted in Hermeticism and Neoplatonism, his theurgy is a golden chain the links of which extend through the centuries in various forms.

He does contrast theurgy with goetia, high magic with low. While there is certainly something to be said for this distinction, and for the importance of transcendent elements in any spiritual or magical practice, he is rather dismissive of other traditions. Sure, low magic can be over-materialistic but high magic can be abstract and over-cerebral. On the other hand, de Biasi also disregards non-pagan traditions entirely. His focus is western but he has no interest in Christianity and even kabbalah is dismissed as inadequate. I can't completely agree with this dismissal, but I did find it refreshing to see the Roman Emperor Julian the Apostate, who restored a revived paganism as the official religion of the Roman Empire, lauded so much. To be honest I'm pretty tired of Christianity myself these days.

The gods and goddesses of the title are from the Egyptian and Greco-Roman pantheons. Each chapter has questions and exercises at the end, and rituals and invocations are interspersed throughout the book. On the whole this book is unusual in its focus, both in its emphasis on pagan neoplatonism and hermetism, and in representing a modern Hermetic order that doesn't take its cues from the Golden Dawn or Thelema.

Jesus the Sufi: The Lost Dimension of Christianity
Max Gorman
Crucible Publishers, 2007. £8.99

Sufism is Islamic mysticism, particularly Sunni Muslim mysticism. This is a popular and historically plausible definition of Sufism. It is also one that Max Gorman is eager to circumvent. Many of the great Sufi teachers, though brought up as Muslims, eschewed religious definition. Gorman quotes the great Rumi, whose funeral was attended by mourners of all religions, as saying,

I am no Christian, no Jew, no Magian, no Musulman

Not of the East, not of the West.

Not of the land, not of the sea

My place placeless, my trace traceless.

Thus Sufism is rather the spiritual inner tradition that has existed in all ages and, though it often manifests within a religious context, is independent of any particular religion. One might object that until a few centuries after Islam began no one ever referred to themselves as a Sufi, and might dispute whether the "Egyptians, Persians and Greeks" who preceded the Sufis would have recognised the resemblance. Certainly "Sufi" isn't the term I would prefer. There is, I believe, a tradition of referring to Sufis as "Knowers" or Gnostics. Yet I'm not sure I would use "Gnostic" for the inner teachings of the ages either. In referring to people of other ancient traditions as Sufis and using Sufism as your model there is the risk of not seeing important differences between traditions. Yet one can also see connections that might not otherwise have been visible.

In any case, that is Max Gorman's approach in *Jesus the Sufi*. Jesus has of course always been seen by Muslims as a prophet and precursor to Muhammad. I myself have been fascinated by the Muslim tradition of sayings and stories of Jesus. This Jesus is a teacher and the tales told about him are very much in the mould of Sufi teaching stories. This was definitely a creative tradition. As Jesus was not central to Islam, Muslims obviously felt free to invent new stories about Jesus in a way in which it was not possible for them to do with Muhammad nor, beyond the early centuries, Christians to do with Jesus.

Yet some of the sayings particularly belong to older traditions preserved perhaps via Islam's contact with Syrian Christianity or via other channels. Robert M. Price has suggested that behind the otherwise unknown sayings of Jesus quoted by Al Ghazali there may be a lost manuscript collection of sayings of Jesus.

In his discussion of a Sufi understanding of Jesus Max Gorman includes a wide range of Jesus traditions. One quirk, which many might regard as nitpicking, is his inclusion of a saying of Jesus found in a papyrus fragment at Oxyrhynchus that ends "And the kingdom of Heaven is within you and whosoever knoweth himself shall find it. And having found it ye shall know yourselves that ye are the sons and heirs of the Father, the Almighty, and shall know yourselves that ye are in God and God in you. And ye are the city of God" (p.37)

This is actually an early—and inaccurate— reconstruction of one of the Gospel of Thomas fragments. It is an intriguing saying that conjures up all sorts of possibilities in the way that we view ourselves. Yet Jesus never said it. It is simply a tentative reconstruction that turned out to be wrong. Although Max Gorman does not cite his source, I recall that reconstruction as being from M.R. James' *The Apocryphal New Testament* (OUP, 1955 p.27). Rev J.G.R. Ousley's Aramaic gospel (*The Gospel of the Holy Twelve*, quoted on p. 92) is flat out inauthentic.

Much of our knowledge of ancient Christianity was based on similar scholarly difficulties and it is likely that our knowledge of these things will continue to be contingent or, often, simply inaccurate. Of course, most scholars would allow that there are plenty of sayings preserved in the gospels of the New testament that were never spoken by Jesus. Those of a conservative bent may simply declare themselves unconvinced by the reasoning. Far fewer people, if presented with the evidence, would assert that Ousley's gospel or the Oxyrhynchus reconstruction, really were spoken by Jesus. I continue to be fascinated by this awkward interplay between notions of authentic spiritual tradition that are communicated and renewed down the ages and a more postmodern approach that acknowledges that we are humans interacting with material objects that survive from the past. I suspect that Max, who mentions in his brief biographical note that he has little sympathy for our times, would detest any mention of postmodernism. Yet I find it almost encouraging that late forgeries or spurious reconstructions can actually be spiritually meaningful and add to the tradition of Jesus sayings. I included a few of these in my book on the agrapha, *The Lost Sayings of Jesus: Annotated & Explained*.

I should add that I feel awkward making such pedantic points but the issue of Sufism as the central hub of esotericism, and being the way in which Jesus should be understood, which is implied by the book, is a sticky one for me, as much as I love the Sufis. Yet, as Jesus said according to the ninth century Maaruf Karkhi, "Remember cotton when it is put over your eyes."

Gorman in fact quotes from a wide range of sources aside from Sufi and early Christian sources. including Thomas Merton, Gurdjieff, and various poets. With a little manouvering the book could have approached its subject from another perspectives. The author seems to have a connection with the work of Idries Shah, the most influential English-language populariser of Sufism.

Though I find aspects of the scholarship and the esoteric approach old-fashioned there is much insight to be gained into Jesus in the short chapters of this book. I particularly appreciated his discussion of the parables, many of which are of course unfamiliar. I also found the examination of the meaning of the four elements intriguing.

It is recommended to anyone who wants a different approach to the mystical Jesus, or rather to the esoteric Jesus, or to . . . alright, to the Sufi Jesus.

Andrew Phillip Smith

A Coptic Handbook of Ritual Power (Macquarie Papyri)
160pp (with DVD)
Malcolm Choat (Editor), Iain Gardner (Editor),
Brepols Publishers

This handbook of "ritual power", a term which seems to have become an academically acceptable euphemism for magic, comes in an expensive academic edition which limits its availability for most readers. It is the sort of book that would have to be sought out at a good academic library. It's true that the subject matter only appeals to a minority but for anyone interested in Gnosticism or ancient magic it's very eye opening. This is an ancient magical text that shows clear connections to Sethian Gnosticism.

Inside are photographs of each page of the very beautiful codex, transcriptions of the Coptic and an English translation in more than one format with full scholarly apparatus including a lexicon. The detailed commentary is more concerned with comparative material and notes on the Coptic than on any overarching interpretation. The text itself shows that magical practice goes hand in hand with Gnosticism, something that I was long resistant to myself, but now find very fascinating. The transcription was checked by musician, apocalyptic Coptologist and supporter of The Gnostic, David Tibet. Included with the large format trade paperback is a DVD which contains high resolution photographs of the manuscript.

This book will be of interest both to those who do in-depth research into Gnosticism and those who investigate ancient magic. It is well-produced and thorough but both the cost and the subject matter will limit its interest. It is also one of the few academic works on Gnosticism that references Choronzon, Thelema and John Dee. (p.12 note 35 if you are interested.)

Chaos Craft
Julian Vayne and Steve Dee
257pp

Chaos Craft began as a series of blog posts by Julian Vayne and Steve Dee on the Blog of Baphomet. Divested of its hyperlinks, blog rolls, archives sidebar, and url it makes a surprisingly satisfying whole. The end product is a book not a mere hard copy of the blog.

The book is structured around the mashup of the eightpointed star of Chaos Magick and the Wiccan/pagan eightfold year, which celebrates the quarter and cross-quarter days of the solstices and equinoxes, and the ancient festivals of Lughnasa/Lammas, Halloween, St Brigid's day/Imbolc and May Day. The eight points of the chaos star were associated by Peter Carroll with the eight colours of magic in a novel by Terry Pratchett (who passed away today, as I write this) and hence each of the festivals of the wheel of the year is associated with a colour and a particular brand of magic. This gives the book its skeleton around which a variety of flesh, sinews and, to strain a metaphor, organs are disposed.

Julian Vayne is a leading light in the UK Chaos Magick scene, Steve Dee less well known. The credits for each article are given at the end and I found it fun sometimes to guess who was the author of a particular piece before I reached the end. I found that Julian's pieces often have a more aesthetic quality to them, are more confident and often written with authority. Steve is gentler and more humane. Julian throws out challenges to the reader while Steve more often questions himself. I enjoyed the contrast between Julian's assertiveness and Steve's gentler, more self-doubting and questioning approach. I know that I'm more like Steve, who incidentally comes from the same part of the world as me.

I've had a rather armchair interest in chaos magic for a few years. There are a great many influences at work in this collection in addition to paganism and Chaos Magick. Steve's Gnosticism and interest in Gurdjieff lift the book up away from the overly relativistic side of Chaos Magick. Gurdjieff, Gnosticsm and magic is a combination not too far away from my own set of interests.

I have to say that I found the accounts of the eight festivals themselves somewhat less interesting than the rest of the material. The discussions are eclectic in the best Chaos Magic style, bringing in everything from Nina Simone to Yazidi texts, Buddhism, sci-fi, and the eight-pointed kitchen sink.

Is the mix too dispersed? Steve sums up the problem and appeal of eclecticism perfectly,

> As we push our trolley around the spiritual supermarket seeking to fill our Kia-shaped hole, do we stock up on the nutritious sustenance offered by deep reflection on the Upanishads or do we neck a pile of spiritual sugar highs that ultimately give us a gnostic hangover? (p.24)

As a matter of fact I don't feel that either of the authors are wallowing around aimlessly in a relatavistic slop. This book suggests that there is a lot more to Chaos Magick than the good old sigil and a wank.

The Manichaean Codices of Medinet Madi

James M. Robinson

James Clarke & Co.311pp

The discoveries of both the Nag Hammadi library in 1945 and the Dead Sea Scrolls in 1947 are well known. Less familiar even to those interested in Gnosticism is discovery of seven Manichaean papyrus codices at Medinet Madi in Egypt in 1947. The codices followed the usual tortuous path of acquisition by antiquities dealers before they ended up in respectable collections, notably those of Carl Schmidt in Berlin and the library of Sir Chester Beatty in Dublin. The story was complicated by developments in the Second World War. The chaos particularly towards the end of war resulted in part of the collection being put on a train bound for Leningrad and then lost. The surviving manuscripts were eventually housed in the Berlin Museum and the Cheater Beatty Library in Dublin.

A few years ago I attended a tour at the Chester Beatty by the curator. He recounted the story about the loss of papyrus codices on the train to Leningrad. He also showed a badly decomposed codex known as the "sod of turf". It looked like a chunk of organic matter. It had been so damaged it was considered impossible to restore it. Its name came from its resemblance to "turf", the squares of peat cut from the peat bogs of Ireland and still used as fuel today.

The story of the Medinet Madi Codices is a fascinating one. James M. Robinson was intimately involved in popularising the Nag Hammadi Codices and helping them through to publication. This book, however, is not aimed at a general audience. As Robinson explains, much of it is raw research material for scholars giving extensive detail on the known history of the codices themselves subsequent to their discovery in 1929.
As colourful as some of the details of this history are, this is a book for the dedicated scholar and expert in Manichaeism.

Living Theurgy
Jeffrey S Kupperman
Avalonia
282pp

Neoplatonism isn't sexy. In contrast to Gnosticism we don't see movie reviewers discussing the Neoplatonic themes of the latest sci-fi blockbuster. We don't see Japanese anime plundering the writing of Plotinus for ideas for their latest cartoon epic. Nor do we find newspapers speculating over the significance of the latest discovery of a Neoplatonic papyrus fragment. New age stores do not have shelves devoted to Neoplatonism. You cannot find Neoplatonist churches on the Internet. As far as I know there isn't even a modern cult that claims to be Neoplatonist. Ancient Neoplatonists weren't even accused of holding orgies or eating sperm.

It is not that Neoplatonism is Gnosticism's ugly sister. Perhaps she may be beautiful, more beautiful, even too beautiful. She just gives the impression of being too poised, to elegant, too stiff, too difficult to have a conversation with.

Jeffrey Kupperman's achievement in Living Theurgy is to reveal a Neoplatonism one really would want a relationship with. Kupperman is an academic as well as a Gnostic and occultist. The depth of his learning is considerable and is evidenced on every page. Kupperman sums up his perspective thus,

> *Living Theurgy* is an amalgam of sorts. You will find it filled with scholarship. I am a professional scholar as well as a writer. However, unlike many scholarly treatises, I do not approach the subject as one filled with some kind of "anthropological atheism" or "methodological agnosticism". Nor, however, is it coming from a "method of compassion." All of these represent the viewpoints of scholars standing outside of what the study, attempting to grasp foreign ideas without being grasped in return. The idea of this being at all possible is somewhat difficult. The Western academic system is a product of Platonism, and everything within it engages with Plato in some manner, even if it is through rejection. Without Platonism there is no academy.

Although scholarly, *Living Theurgy* is written from the perspective that the Neoplatonists essentially knew what they are talking about ... I hold that the contemplative and theurgical practices espoused by the Neoplatonists, from Plotinus through Ficino, effectively bring about changes in the practitioner, regardless as to the divine or psychological, or both, causes of these changes.

There is a lot here for Kupperman to explain and he does a grand job of it. Along the way the author introduces exercises based on Neoplatonic principles or on actual passages from writings. Theurgia is a form of magic and so we are introduced to such practices as medicinal astrology, the use of talismans and even to animated statues and ensouled icons. The later section of the book is in effect a Neoplatonic grimoire and is full of practices that dovetail with the philosophical, cosmological, and ethical material in the earlier part of the book.

In short, this is a thorough and accessible introduction to a living Neoplatonism in both theory and practice.

Time, Fate, and Spider Magic

Orryelle Defenestrate-Bascule

Avalonia

362 pages

This is an exceedingly difficult book to categorise. Orryelle (the use of the first name implies no personal familiarity with the author: it is merely easier to type than his full name) is an artist and performer, surely more primarily an artist than a writer. He approaches his/her/hir text like a painter slapping on pigment, smudging it here and there, indulging in neologisms, sdrow desrever and palindromesemordnilap. As an artist Orryelle is extraordinary, slightly reminiscent in places of Austin Osman Spare, not only in style and quality of draftmanship but in inventiveness too. Androgyny and multiple arachnid limbs are particular leitmotifs. Aside from the embedded pictures and full-page drawings there are occasional and delightful marginalia such as clock hands that progressively move forward through a series of pages eventually developing into the eight-pointed star of chaos magic, and an ouroborous that swallows its own tail and then develops into a caduceus and finally an infinity symbol. These are typical of the daft, quirky and charming tone that is part of the book. I found myself reading the book backwards at one point and realised how appropriate it was.

But it has its darkly experimental side too. Orryelle has involved himself in some extreme practices, including body modification and a period of taking oestrogen. This is very much an account of personal magical experimentation and experience, always associated in some way with the arts. The book is (dis)organised into four gates. Chaos magick is prominent, as is the Nordic tradition and goddess devotion, but it is magically multicultural. Orryelle defines himself as a ChaosOrder magician, an appropriate rejection of binary divisions. Time is a theme, spiders are present in all forms through the book, fate a little less so. A thirteen-hour clock is in there somewhere, too.

At over 350 pages there is a lot to digest here, including the arachnean grimoire *The Book of the Spider*. The overall effect is very much of the web that occurs as a motif several times in the text. Themes, ideas, musings, personal experience, and ritual activity criss cross in strands and gossamer lines.

I was very happy to discover that Orryelle was having an exhibition of his work at Gallery X in Dublin, together with Dublin-resident artist Dolorosa Delacruz. In person he is very gentle despite his crusty exterior. His performances (I attended both the opening and closing nights) involved violin played through various effects pedals, including looping and octave shifting. He sang songs of his own devising while playing a chess game with himself using his alchemical chess set. The pawns were charming little glass alchemical vessels while the other pieces were cast in tactile and heavy bronze. The chess pieces had been adapted as alchemically significant symbols such as a red eagle. The rooks were genuinely rooks of the crow family. His paintings are worlds in themselves, combining esoteric and sexual imagery in a way that is never clichéd.

His performances are quirky and powerful, his paintings unique and accomplished. His image-oriented books are extraordinary too. Time, Fate and Spider Magic is quite a bit less accessible yet there is a lot in there for anyone who is interested in the overlap of art and magic, or in individual esoteric experience and experimentation.

The Complete Lenormand Oracle Handbook: Reading the Language and Symbols of the Cards

Caitlin Matthews

416pp

Healing Arts Press

Lenormand is a system of divination based on a pack of cards on which are typically displayed a reduced version of the standard playing card deck and an image derived from the everyday world. Named after the French cartomancer Mlle Marie-Anne Adelaide Lenormand, known as the sybil of the salons, the pack is in fact older than her, though seemingly not much older than around 1800. The Lenormand deck has 36 cards selected from the playing card deck, the 2s, 3s, 4s, and 5s having been discarded. There are spreads available with varying numbers of cards, culminating in the grand in which all 36 cards are laid out. The cards have their own order, numbered 1 to 36, which does not follow the playing card order. Each card has a name, an image, a playing card and possibly a mnemonic verse.

This is not a history of Lenormand nor an attempt at an esoteric understanding of the cards. The main purpose of the book is to teach the reader to use the pack for divination. Caitlin Matthews is systematic and thorough in this aim.

Matthews gives extensive examples of readings derived from real cases, along with exercises and self-tests for which the answers may be found in the back of the book.

I cannot speak for the divinatory power of Legormand, nor of these ease with which it might be learned as an oracle. Matthews gives extensive examples of readings derived from real cases, along with exercises and self-tests for which the answers may be found in the back of the book.

But the overall effect is of finding oneself in an alternate universe of the Tarot. Instead of the Tarot cards The Magician, The Hermits, The Lovers, The Wheel of Fortune. We have Stork, Scythe, Garden, Anchor, Clover, Ring, Coffin, and so on. I am no adept at the Tarot myself, but I can sympathise with Caitlin Matthews who early on in the book describes how she had become somewhat tired of the developing sophistication of the Tarot, with dozens of new glossy and photoshopped packs appearing every year. In *The Complete Lenormand Oracle Handbook*, Caitlin Matthews has opened up an entirely new world of card reading and symbolism. It is like meeting the Tarot again for the first time, new and fresh and strange.

The Book of Primal Signs: The High Magic of Symbols

Nigel Pennick

256pp

Destiny Books

Any book that has in its early pages Coelbren Y Beirdd, the bardic alphabet most likely devised by the eighteenth century Welsh antiquarian Iolo Morganwg, is fine by me. Nigel Pennick introduces it in his opening discussion of runes and the alphabet in general, which seem to have had a single origin in Canaan, as sign and symbol.

Pennick shows how symbols do not have intrinsic meanings. In the 1960s he and some friends of his attempted, unsuccessfully, to reclaim the use of the swastika for the non-Nazi pagan movement. Although it is commonly recognised now that the swastika was used for millennia before it was appropriated by the Nazis, it is still more or less impossible to use it without evoking Nazi associations. This book is thick with research and it is fascinating to discover a British World War I Christmas card with a lucky swastika on it, or that there was a Swastika Laundry just down the road from me in Dublin until 1989.

Although the meaning of any particular symbol is extraordinarily flexible and self-contradictory, the persistence of geometrical symbols is remarkable.

Just about every page has one or more photographs of historical objects that demonstrate the use of symbols varying from strictly geometrical shapes such as the pentagram and hexagram and various combinations of crosses and circles to common symbolic beasts to odd yet persistent ornamental designs like the fleur-de-lys, the pineapple, or plaits and knots, to the obscurely named pothook, trefot, skirl and hexflower. The author is a pagan but the book is suitable for anyone interested in the history of signs and symbols, and the subtitle "The high Magic of Symbols" is somewhat misleading. Yet there is plenty of material from the traditions of folklore and esotericism.

The book covers a wide range of fairly modern material too, from the signs adopted in the most obscure aspects of twentieth-century British culture to the origin of the peace sign and the anarchist circled-A.

A fiery preface mourns the decline of traditional crafts and traditional ornamentation n the west and their replacement by commercial trademarks.

Its organisation by symbol lends it to use as a reference book but it is also a fascinating ramble through the thickets of imagery.

Alchemy and Astral Projection
Ken Henson
Four Candles Press
100pp

Alchemy and astral projection, while both part of the western esoteric tradition, are not usually encountered in combination. Ken Henson's approach is not however a wacky New Age conceit of the sort that produces a new idea by picking two arbitrary existing ideas and mixing them. (Soccer mindfulness, Taoist crystal magic, monastic Christian Tantra, reincarnation for entrepreneurs, the Tarot of anything). Rather Henson has identified seeming references to astral projection in a careful study of alchemical materials. References to astral projection seem to pepper alchemy through the ages. Key to this is a quotation by Paracelsus, "During sleep the sidereal man may by the power of the imagination be sent out of the physical form, at a distance to act for some purpose."

According to Henson Paracelsus addresses spirit travel several times. A good part of the book outlines the mystical thread in alchemy and relates it to other Hermetic or Neoplatonic currents. The second part of the book looks at the use of the alchemical processes through which the alchemist can gain access to the Macrocosm or Astral Plane. Describing the seven alchemical processes (the author acknowledges that there are all sorts of differences in number, name and order) Henson lists attributes, symbols and broad categories of techniques to allow the practitioner to experience atral travel and development. I haven't seen anything quite like this before and enjoyed the spirit of experimentation that fits very well into the esoteric alchemical tradition without making too grand a claim for itself. A third section examines the categories of entities that might be experienced.

The book is beautifully presented, with several full colour illustrations by Ken Henson which range from the gorgeous to the charming. The book has an interesting origin. Henson had visited the Lloyd Library in 2005 as a result of his interest in the work of John Uri Lloyd, author of the hollow earth novel Etidorhpa (Aphrodite spelled backwards) and was able to view some of the original art that illustrated the book. I had never heard either of John Uri Lloyd nor of Etidorhpa before. First published in 1895 it sounds like the kind of weird fiction with esoteric undertones that should have a cult following. Ken Henson's work appears on the cover of this issue of The Gnostic and his strange and marvellous black mirror self-portraits are dotted around inside.

Henson, having lectured at the Lloyd Library, found himself in the lucky position of being funded by a Curtis G. Lloyd Research Fellowship, the terms of which were for him to read alchemy books from the library's collection, write and illustrate the book, give a lecture and hold an exhibition. It all seems a million years away from the usual commercial anxieties that define modern life for creative people. And that is the effect that the book conveys, in the best way possible.

Biographies

Sarane Alexandrian (1927-2009) was a member of the surrealist group in Paris in the years directly after World War II. He is the author of more than 60 books, including novels, a memoir, and studies of occultism, eroticism, and art. He died in Paris in 2009.

Miguel Conner isn't in this issue. It's the only issue he hasn't been in! He was in issue 1 and issue 2 and issue 3 and issue 4, and even issue 5! But he isn't in issue 6. How can that be? What's going on? He and the editor are still friends, so why the absence? Send him some money via Patreon and he'll tell you.

Tobias Churton is Britain's leading scholar of Western Esotericism, a world authority on Gnosticism, Hermeticism, and Rosicrucianism. An Honorary Fellow of Exeter University, where he is faculty lecturer in Rosicrucianism and Freemasonry, he holds a master's degree in Theology from Brasenose College, Oxford, and is the author of many books, including *Gnostic Philosophy*, *The Invisible History of the Rosicrucians*, and *Aleister Crowley: The Beast in Berlin*. He lives in England.

Arthur Craddock looks like a haddock.

Rev. Bill Darlison is a retired Unitarian Minister. He was minister to the Dublin Unitarian congregation from 1996-2010, and from 2013-14 he was President of the General Assembly of Unitarian and Free Christian Churches in Britain and Ireland. His book *The Gospel and the Zodiac: The Secret Truth about Jesus* (Duckworth, 2007) attempts to show that the Gospel of Mark is structured on the zodiac and so is not a historical document. His blog is Roads for Travelling Souls, and his email address is billdarlison@hotmail.com

Stevan Davies is Professor of Religious Studies at Misericordia University. He has studied the non-canonical gospels and acts for over thirty years. Among his books are *The Gospel of Thomas and Christian Wisdom* (Bardic Press) *The Gospel of Thomas: Annotated and Explained*, *The Secret Book of John: Annotated and Explained* (both SkyLight Paths) and T*he Revolt of the Widows: The Social World of the Apocryphal Acts* (Bardic Press, 2012). He has also published *New Testament Fundamentals* and *Jesus the Healer: Possession, Trance and the Origins of Christianity*, republished by Bardic Press. His website (www.misericordia.edu/users/davies/thomas/thomas.htm) is a leading Internet resource on the Gospel of Thomas.

Steve Dee currently lives in Devon in the UK with his family and assorted pets. He has been involved with magical practice for the past 20 years and while he is not good with labels, "Chaos Magician", "Gnostic explorer" or "Nightside Unitarian" probably come close to capturing what he does. He is the co-author of *Chaos Craft* with Julian Vayne and also co-wrote "Vampyre Alchemy" that appears in the collection *Gods and Monsters* edited by Michael Kelly. In his spare time he likes surfing and playing loud music that in middle age now requires the wearing of ear plugs.

Richard Dengel's avocation is as an artist, writer, and game designer living in Havertown, PA. He has designed his own set of Tarot cards loosely based upon the Secret Book of John. The pages enclosed in this issue evolved directly from those cards. Called the Gnostic Tarot, they have seen limited publication in *The Encyclopedia of Tarot*, Vols III and IV (US Games Systems, Inc). Richard has been studying Gnosis and Gnosticism for over 30 years. For him, this "heresy" is never-ending source of hope and inspiration, provoking not only art and poetry, but short-stories as well. During the day he is a software architect and project manager at the Wharton School, University of Pennsylvania (USA).

Elizaveta de Stjernvall was an early pupil and associate of G.I. Gurdjieff. Nicolas de Stjernvall, her son by Gurdjieff, is the author of *My Dear Father Gurdjieff*, also published by Bardic Press, from which volume this is taken.

Andrea Frank. Internationally award winning documentary filmmaker, ceramic artist and chef Dree Andrea van Mechelen from Amsterdam, currently residing in New York City, writes and illustrates using the pseudonym Andrea Frank.

Andrea is convinced that in 2012 the World as we know it indeed came to an End. For a decade now, she has stated that December 21st marked the day that so called 'normal' people would enter the Maya-state. Whereas those considered 'on the spectrum', including herself, would find a way to be-come balanced and 'normal'.

A Jacky of all trades, Master of none, Andrea herself is slowly building her own bridges in the land of mental instability, where she believes all Gnostics currently reside, to lay the ground work for the expected coming into balance for all humans.

Andrea works with children and young adults who are labelled 'mentally challenged'. She is of the opinion that they are the first generation of Tachyon consciousness embodied on Planet Earth; the frequency of unconditional love. Empaths, often in chaos, unaware that they are. Pioneers who, together with the Gnostics, will bring the understanding that, in order to manifest our full potential, there is no need to ascend. Completing the descend into heathy physical matter is the way 'God', ourselves intended it. Heaven on earth is real, if and when you are willing to co-create it; to embody the frequency, the timeline, that is empathy.

Andrea is currently writing a series of books about the journey of the Modern Gnostic in the Era of Tachyon consciousness, including a practical guide *The Tachyon Self-Remembers– a tool box*. Please visit her at www.dreeinthebigcity.com and www.tachyonconsciousness.org for information.

Z'ev ben Shimon Halevi is the author of several books on the Toledano Tradition of Kabbalah, a teacher of the discipline, with a worldwide following, and a founder member of the Kabbalah Society.

Ken Henson. A Curtis G. Lloyd Fellow at the Lloyd Library and Museum, Ken Henson is the author and illustrator of *Alchemy and Astral Projection: Ecstatic Trance in the Hermetic Tradition* (2014). He also recently collaborated with the Philosophical Research Society to restore and reissue Manly P. Hall and John Augustus Knapp's Revised New Art Tarot. Ken's art has been widely exhibited and his writings have been published in periodicals such as *Abraxas Journal* and *Clavis Journal*. He has his MFA in Painting from the University of Cincinnati, and is an Associate Professor and the Head of Illustration at the Art Academy of Cincinnati in Ohio.

William James(1842-1910) was a pioneering psychologist and philosopher. The elder brother of novelist Henry James, his most famous work is *The Varieties of Religious Experience*. He treated religion and spirituality, including mystical and devotional experience, as a significant part of human life. He was also the coiner of the term "stream of consciousness".

Jeffrey S. Kupperman has studied hermetics, Kabbalah and the Western Mystery Tradition for the last fifteen years. He has degrees in psychology, graphic designs and religious studies, where his emphasis was in Western mythology as well as mystical and occult practices. He is the publisher and designer of the *Journal of the Western Mystery Tradition*.

Gary Lachman is the author of several books on the link between consciousness, culture, and alternative thought. His books include *Turn Off Your Mind: The Mystic Sixties and the Dark Side of the Age of Aquarius*; *A Secret History of Consciousness*; *In Search of P.D. Ouspensky*; *A Dark Muse*; *Rudolf Steiner: An Introduction to His Life and Thought*; *Politics and the Occult: The Left, the Right, and the Radically Unseen*, and *The Quest for Hermes Trismegistus*. As Gary Valentine he was a founding member of the rock group Blondie.

Sean Martin is a writer based in Edinburgh. Among his books are *The Gnostics: The First Christian Heretics* (Oldcastle Books, 2nd edition, 2010), and *Andrei Tarkovsky* (Kamera Books, 2011). Among many current projects is a documentary about David Lindsay, which he hopes to complete at some point between now and the end of time.

Jeremy Puma is the author of *This Way, How to Think Like a Gnostic*, and *A Gnostic Prayerbook*. He currently co-edits and contributes to *Invironment*, an online magazine discussing the intersection of the Inner and the Outer. (http://www.medium.com/invironment)
Jeremy resides in Seattle, Washington.

Gerard Russell is a former United Nations and British diplomat. During his time with the British foreign service, which took him to Cairo, Jerusalem, Baghdad, Jeddah and Kabul, he was described as "the formost expert on the Islamic world in his generation." He is fluent in both Arabic and Farsi. He is the author of *Heirs to Forgotten Kingdoms* (Simon and Schuster, 2014)

Andrew Phillip Smith is the editor of *The Gnostic*. Or perhaps editor emeritus by now. His new books *Lost Teachings of the Cathars* and *Secret History of the Gnostics* will be published by Watkins Publications in November 2015. He is currently working on *John the Baptist and the Last Gnostics*, which traces back the history of the Mandaeans. Work in progress includes biographies of Rodney Collin and Alan Moore, a book on the Gospel of Thomas, *From Seth to Mani*, a volume on ancient Gnostic individuals, and a Gnosticism-based novel with the subtitle "Down and Out in London and Alexandria".

Scott Stanley Smith is a freelance business journalist whose 1,300 articles have appeared in 175 publications, including *Investor's Business Daily, Success, Entrepreneur, Chief Executive, Christian Science Monitor, Los Angeles Magazine*, and *American Airlines' American Way*. He has interviewed such influentials as Bill Gates, Stan Lee, Meg Whitman, James Meredith, Howard Schultz, Barbara Corcoran, General Barry McCaffrey, Richard Branson, Kathy Ireland, Kirk Douglas, and Dean Koontz. He is also the author of *Extraordinary People: Real Life Lessons on What It Takes to Achieve Success*

www.ExtraordinaryPeopleBook.com

As a companion to *God Reconsidered: Searching for Truth in the Battle Between Atheism and Religion*, he created www.GodReconsidered.com to encourage reader participation in the exciting process of discovery.

Food for Thought

The Great Beast is the only object of idolatry, the only ersatz of God, the only imitation of something which is infinitely far from me and which is I myself.

Simone Weil

The Gnostics are arranged in hierarchy, and between the Gnostic who knows his Lord and the Gnostic who knows himself, the Gnostic who knows himself is higher in that hierarchy.

Sheikh Alawi

Religions hate novelty. All the various religious truths have supposedly been with us since the primordial mythic time. From claims that our sect alone follows the original teachings of the Buddha, to claims that all other teachings than ours are innovative blasphemy against Allah's Quran, religions can be seen to presume original perfection from which changes can only be devolution toward error. Accordingly, if in fact one is engaged in changing the original pattern of a religion, one must insist that one's changes are actually the divinely commanded restoration of the original pattern, and that the pattern now in effect is a catastrophic deviation from the ideal original.

Stevan Davies

Once his wife had gone, God became a stressed lone parent, given to fits of uncouth rage and tyrannical demands. Instead of love and compassion, there was fear and trembling, as in the hearts of cowering children who, in the midst of their games, suddenly hear the dread step of their drunken father with his belt in his hand.

Lynn Picknett

Gods seem a bit like sausages, if you want to enjoy them you shouldn't watch people making them.

Peter Carroll

Of the twenty-two civilizations that have appeared in history, nineteen of them collapsed when they reached the moral state the United States is in now.

Arnold Joseph Toynbee

It was not man who made the myths but the myths, or the archetypal substance they reveal, which made man. We shall have to come, I am sure, to think of the archetypal element in myth in terms of the wind that breathed through the harp-strings of individual brains and nerves and fluids, rather as the blood still today pervades and sustains them.

Owen Barfield

Life itself is but the shadow of death, and souls departed but the shadows of the living. All things fall under this name. The sun itself is but the dark simulacrum, and light but the shadow of God.

Thomas Browne,

Within the armor is the butterfly and within the butterfly—is the signal from another star.

Philip K Dick

No real understanding of the Christ can be gained if one relies merely on the Gospel, especially in the form in which it has been handed down. There exists nowhere today a less true understanding of Christ than in the various faiths and confessions.

Rudolf Steiner

The Council of Nicaea celebrated the marriage of church and state, whose child would become the Dark Ages.

James Wasserman

God is a Being of perfect simplicity and truth, both in deed and word, and neither changes in himself nor imposes upon others.

Plato

The divine One is a negation of negations, and a desire of desires. What does 'One' mean? Something to which nothing is to be added. The soul lays hold of the Godhead where it is pure, where there is nothing beside it, nothing else to consider.

Meister Eckhart

For while belief binds, experience liberates.

Max Gorman

A shadow in a dream is man. But when God sheds a brightness, shining life is on earth, and life is sweet as honey.

Pindar

The Buddha never taught that the self 'is not', but only that 'it cannot be apprehended.'

Edward Conze

Soul, when it is allowed an existence at all, sits somewhat vaguely within the machine, never defined. If anything goes wrong with the machine, why, the soul is forgotten instantly.

D.H.Lawrence

With Western man the value of the self sinks to zero. Hence the universal depreciation of the soul in the West. Whoever speaks of the reality of the soul or psyche is accused of 'psychologism.'

C.G.Jung

The Pentecostal experience is not a goal to be reached, nor a place to stand, but a door through which to go into a greater fullness of life in the Spirit. It is an event which becomes a way of life in which often charismatic manifestations have a place.

W. Hollenweger

Men are convinced of your arguments, your sincerity, and the seriousness of your efforts only by your death.

Albert Camus

From now on, then, my child, return to your divine nature.

Teachings of Silvanus

Also Available from Bardic Press

The Gnostic 1 - 5

Voices of Gnosticism
Miguel Conner

Spirit Possession and the Origins of Christianity
Stevan Davies

My Dear Father Gurdjieff
Nikolai de Stjernvall

New Nightingale, New Rose: Poems From the Divan of Hafiz
translated by Richard Le Gallienne

*The Quatrains of Omar Khayyam:
Three Translations of the Rubaiyat*
translated by Edward Fitzgerald, Justin McCarthy and Richard Le Gallienne

Door of the Beloved: Ghazals of Hafiz
translated by Justin McCarthy

The Gospel of Thomas and Christian Wisdom
Stevan Davies

The Four Branches of the Mabinogi
Will Parker

Christ In Islam
James Robson

Songs of Sorrow and Joy
Ashford Brown

Planetary Types: The Science of Celestial Influence
Tony Cartledge

Visit our website at www.bardic-press.com
email us at info@bardic-press.com

THE GNOSTIC